THE
TRANSFORMATION
OF
AUTHORSHIP
IN AMERICA

THE
TRANSFORMATION
OF
AUTHORSHIP
IN AMERICA

Grantland S. Rice

THE UNIVERSITY OF CHICAGO PRESS   *Chicago & London*

PS
25
.R52
1997

GRANTLAND S. RICE teaches literature
at the Ohio State University.

Chapter 5 is a substantially revised and altered version of "Crèvecoeur and the
Politics of Authorship in Republican America," *Early American Literature* 28,
no. 2 (1993): 91–119. Reprinted with permission.

Chapter 6 first appeared as "Brackenridge and the Resistance to Textual
Authority," in *American Literature* 67, no. 2 (June 1995): 257–281.
Reprinted with permission.

The University of Chicago Press, Chicago 60637
The University of Chicago Press, Ltd., London
© 1997 by The University of Chicago
All rights reserved. Published 1997
Printed in the United States of America
06 05 04 03 02 01 00 99 98 97   5 4 3 2 1

ISBN: 0-226-71123-4 (cloth)
ISBN: 0-226-71124-2 (paper)

Library of Congress Cataloging-in-Publication Data

Rice, Grantland S.
    The transformation of authorship in America / Grantland S. Rice.
        p.   cm.
    Includes bibliographical references (p.   ) and index.
    1. American literature—History and criticism—Theory, etc.
2. Politics and literature—United States—History. 3. Literature
and society—United States—History. 4. Authors and publishers—
United States—History. 5. Authors and readers—United States—
History. 6. Authors, American—Economic conditions.
7. Authorship—History. I. Title.
PS25.R52 1997
810.9´358—dc20   96-43890
                                                              CIP

For S. E. Q.

I concluded at length that
the People were the best Judges of my Merit;
for they buy my Works . . .

Benjamin Franklin

The majority has enclosed thought
within a formidible fence.
The writer is free inside that area,
but woe to the man who goes beyond it.
Not that he stands in fear of an auto-da-fé,
but he must face all kinds of
unpleasantness and everyday persecution.

Alexis de Tocqueville from
DEMOCRACY IN AMERICA

I could not have completed this book without the help of a grant from the National Endowment for the Humanities and a Stephen Botein Fellowship from the American Antiquarian Society. An Abram L. Sachar International Fellowship awarded by Brandeis University allowed me to conduct several months of research at the British, Bodleian, and Cambridge University Libraries. Some of the final revisions for this project were undertaken while I was a Security Pacific Fellow at the Huntington Library.

My biggest debt of gratitude goes to Michael T. Gilmore for his trenchant commentary and unflagging encouragement over the years. He has been a brilliant teacher, dedicated mentor, and loyal friend. Anyone familiar with his work cannot fail to see the influence it has had on this study. I am also indebted to Wai Chee Dimock for her incisive intellect and tireless advocacy. In addition, I want to acknowledge the generosity of Sacvan Bercovitch who read and critiqued an early draft of the manuscript and of Philip Gura who offered his advice and support. My account of the relationship between liberalism and libertarianism was sharpened by a dialogue one summer with Stanley Fish, while my understanding of the Enlightenment in general and Habermas in particular have been substantially refined by conversations with Keith Baker and John Bender. As readers for the University of Chicago Press, Mitchell Breitwieser and Emory Elliott provided important critical readings of the project, while Alan Thomas and his editorial staff, particularly senior manuscript editor Lila Weinberg, helped to shape a more compelling argument. Finally, and most important, I am especially grateful to my family for their love and support.

Introduction

This book is an attempt to answer a bowdlerization of Max Weber's famous question in the principle section of *The Protestant Ethic and the Spirit of Capitalism:* "How could an activity, which was at best ethically tolerated, turn into a calling in the sense of Benjamin Franklin?"[1] By this, Weber meant the abrupt volte face of the modern age, when commercial self-interest and material acquisitiveness became honorable after having been anathematized for centuries. My version of Weber's question, however, concerns the activity of authorship rather than that of acquisition. This query, simply put, is how independent public writing, vigorously suppressed in America throughout the seventeenth century and the first decades of the eighteenth century, could become estimable by the time of the early Republic.

I came upon this intellectual problem on the heels of two revelations. First, in the course of research at the British Library, I was startled to discover a large number of seventeenth-century political writings which had been published in London to circumvent the New England theocracy's tight control over the domestic printing trade. The fact that there was an unusually effective regime of censorship in early New England, although well-known to most colonial historians, is not something one finds in the standard critical works of American literary history. And while most literary theorists are familiar with Michel Foucault's famous claim in "What is an Author?" that "texts, books, and discourses really began to have authors . . . to the extent that authors became subject to punishment . . . [and] to the extent that discourses could be transgressive," few Americanists, it would seem, have undertaken the historical spadework to determine how, indeed, this could be so.[2]

The second finding came about as a consequence of my admiration for, but uneasiness with, critic Michael Warner's recent application of Jürgen Habermas's theory of a "structural transformation of the public sphere" to early American culture.[3] Meditating on the widespread glorification of publicity in the colonies in the last half of the eighteenth century, a valorization which encompassed authors, their texts, printers, printing, and reading, Warner argues that the emergence of a bourgeois public sphere in America allowed a new form of political discourse which could be separate from both the state and civil society and could therefore regulate or criticize both. The central feature of this new discourse—what made it an ideal medium for realizing what Habermas argues elsewhere is the *possibility* for pure communicative rationality—was its impersonality.[4] Since writers were evacuated from their communications when they transcribed them into print, an expanding print culture in eighteenth-century America, together with a set of beliefs about the virtue of textuality, what Warner terms in his study "republican print ideology," provided the material and ideological basis for a short-lived participatory public sphere. He concludes that this realm, touted as the *res publica* by republicans, brought into being two contradictory developments: new freedom for individuals to assert their citizenship and new opportunities for average Americans to make effective public use of their reason, and the gradual erosion of such liberty brought about by a perversion of the same principles of rational nonparticularity which allowed the emergence of this discursive domain in the first place.

The source of my skepticism about the idea of an abrupt flowering and decline of an open and viable sphere of sociopolitical discourse in republican America came from several directions. First, it went against instincts inscribed by my training as a historian which have taught me to be wary of claims about sudden historical developments. In the case of *The Structural Transformation of the Public Sphere,* Habermas argues not only that the institutions of a bourgeois public realm developed in the West in barely a century but also that the media of publicity soon after became "colonized," the public sphere eroded, and that private individuals lost their critical relation to both the state and civil society. Is it possible, I wondered, to come up with an alternative analytic model which offered more historical continuity?

My second objection concerned the applicability of the optimism of Habermas's theory of communicative rationality to the American case. Looking through commentary on writing, printing, textuality, and reading in hundreds of seventeenth- and eighteenth-century broadsides, pamphlets, newspapers, and magazines, I have been astounded, again and again, by the anxiousness with which colonists greeted the rise and expansion of an indigenous commercial print culture. Writers fretted over their increasing dependence on technology, worried about the erosion of authorial control, and pondered about the fragility and vicissitudes of literary proprietorship. Journalists and essayists complained about intransigent and self-interested printers; poor, erroneous, and altered typography; and inadequate distribution. Commentators warned audiences about the conceits of "author-less" texts and condemned a species of writing which concealed its designs behind anonymity. And spokesmen cursed an expanding readership too animated in its appetite for the novel and the emotional, and too passive in its susceptibility to the "truths" of texts.

Finally, my third reservation stemmed from an observation of the profound similarities in the rhetoric between early American champions of a republican print sphere and eighteenth-century advocates of a free market. Jürgen Habermas argues that it was the rise of a self-governing commercial exchange society beginning at the end of the seventeenth century which provided the material basis for the emergence of the domain of the bourgeois public sphere (with its literary, philosophical, and political permutations). Habermas, however, only allows several suggestive paragraphs in his study to entertain the possibility that the *res publica* might have been as much an ideological effect as it was a material by-product of nascent laissez-faire capitalism.[5] The idea of a *res publica,* where the communications of individuals, evacuated of such idiosyncrasies and biases as personality, skills, and social standing, competed with other such communications, and where reason carried the day, was strikingly analogous to contemporaneous formulations made by proponents of laissez-faire. Precursors to Adam Smith had argued that a principled society would follow from the predictability and peacefulness of commerce, and that as liberal individuals came to allow their goods to be exchanged under the preconditions of justice, and where items could be valued in their abstract relation with other items, a rational and fair society would emerge. The correspondences between late eighteenth-century arguments propounding the virtues of a free market and late eighteenth-century valorizations of the merits of a public print sphere, what Oliver Wendell Holmes was to coin later as the "marketplace of ideas," suggest that any analysis of communication in early America could not be undertaken apart from its grounding in laissez-faire economic theory.[6]

With these observations in mind, and with the Weberian question they engendered as a destination point on the horizon, I set about articulating the terms of a "transformation of authorship in America." The following is the result of this effort. I argue below that a dramatic shift in not only the material conditions, but also in the very meaning of public writing, produced new literary forms and aesthetic practices by the beginning of the nineteenth century.

Employing some of the methodologies of *l'histoire du livre,* this project questions a tradition of scholarship which has emphasized the liberating characteristics of print culture, especially in relation to the development of the free press and the constitution of a "Fourth Estate" and other institutions Habermas argues derived from a "bourgeois public sphere." Beginning with an account of the efforts of early religious dissenters to circumvent censorship in the colonies by having their criticism printed abroad, the study deconstructs the historiographical binary of censorship and the free press. It suggests instead that while the lapse of censorship and the explosion of print culture in the last half of the eighteenth century may have freed writers from the threat of persecution from church and state, they did so only by transforming printed texts from a practical means for assertive sociopolitical commentary into the more inert medium of property and commodity.

This project is divided into three principle sections. Part One, "The Transformation of Authorship in America," makes the historical argument that there was a dramatic change in the conditions of public writing in New England beginning in the first decades of the eighteenth century. Notwithstanding its engagement with the traditional scholarship of *l'histoire du livre,* the underlying argument of this section makes a subtle but important departure from the most basic assumption held by historians of the book in that it contests the notion that there has ever been such a historically transcendent artifact as "*the* book." Breaking away from an isomorphic account of the printed word given to us by Romanticism which has tended to isolate and homogenize public writing as "productive" or "creative," the four chapters which make up Part One argue that the framing conditions which determined what could be recognized as a book and what description might account for the activity of authorship were challenged, upended, and finally wholly redefined by the rise of economic liberalism in America. In claiming this, I want to emphasize that this study traces the trajectory of a specific mode of public writing developing out of the peculiar intellectual and material conditions of Puritan radicalism in colonial New England. This work does not purport to account for *all* forms of authorial projection in colonial America, which might include anything from broadsides, ballads, and poetry to ephemera, plays, and manuscript culture. Nor does this project suggest that the particular mode of civic criticism outlined here was wholly limited to an Anglo-American or Protestant context. One could certainly find corollaries to the New England dissenters presented here among the Spanish, Dutch, and French colonists, just as one might find among the writings of the embattled Quakers the intimation of a similar sphere of sociopolitical critque. Nevertheless, I justify my focus on Protestant

New England for three important reasons: a particular interpenetration of Puritan political theory and civic republicanism which in some sense legitimated the publication of the dissenting conscience as a condition of a virtuous social order, the tight control the New England theocracy maintained over the press which accentuated the political nature of public writing, and the influence of the amalgam of Puritan and civic-republican ideas on later writers who inherited an ambiguous authorial heritage once public writing came to be reconfigured as the production of literary property.

Within this first section, Chapter One surveys the efforts of a group of dissenting writers to circumvent the Puritan theocracy's rigorous attempt to contain a rapidly expanding print sphere. Suggesting that the New England orthodoxy was well aware of how the geographic and demographic reach of print threatened the cohesiveness and stability of its covenanted communities, this chapter explores the tension between this threat and the philosophical imperative advanced by Puritan reformers that citizens or "visible saints" take an active role in government by publicizing their conciences on matters of the state. Exploiting two extraordinary periods for press freedom in seventeenth-century England, writers like John Child and Thomas Maule exposed their dissenting views to a wider reading public, leveraging political reform from abroad and justifying their actions by invoking Puritan political theories of participatory citizenship. For New England Puritans, this chapter concludes, public writing was a political activity both ideologically and materially. It was viewed as a means by which Protestant reformers could express their citizenship, and it was an activity strictly regulated by the state through the administrative venue of censorship. The meaning of "authorship" in this early context was thus consistent with its premodern etymology, which is to say that it denoted individual agency and intentional or rhetorical activity.

If Chapter One demonstrates how a mixture of civic republicanism and Puritan political theory legitimated the publication of the dissenting conscience at the same time the New England theocracy strove to contain such dissent, Chapter Two sets out to interrogate the extent to which we can take the rhetoric of this philosophical imperative at face value once it became a cachet of the Enlightenment. This critique is important because celebrations of the *res publica* and libertarian principles of a free press were deployed with increasing frequency in the first four decades of the eighteenth century, as colonial governments gradually abandoned a priori for a posteri methods of controlling an expanding commercial print culture. This chapter takes up what traditional libertarian accounts have described as the foundational moment for the liberty of the press in America, the famous John Peter Zenger trial of

1734–1735, and attempts to make two interrelated arguments: first, that the development of a free press was the concomitant of a dramatic transformation in political economics, whereby the coercive restraint of the New England theocracy was gradually replaced by the more subtle control of an internally regulated commercial society; and second, that this shift in control, accompanied by a general redefinition of authorship, posed a series of new obstacles for the ideal of participatory citizenship. In the case of the Zenger trial, this chapter argues that Zenger's gesture toward a supervisory public sphere was a strategic, even cynical front for an extremely limited partisan agenda. Having capitalized their own newspaper and hired Zenger to stir up animosities toward New York Royalist Governor William Cosby, a group of rival politicians then framed an imprisoned Zenger in print as the tyrannized private citizen of a despotic ruler in order to win popular support for their cause. Far from an unambiguous victory for the autonomous, oppositional conscience of classical republicanism, I suggest that the Zenger case demonstrates how eighteeth-century politicians were able to mobilize republican rhetoric in order to secure particular ends. Consequently, the rise of a commercial free press, in some sense underwritten in the middle decades of the eighteenth-century by the persuasive ideological rhetoric of a *res publica* and neoclassical ideals of civic criticism, may have actually threatened to erode the ideal of participatory politics in as much as it promised to secure it by rendering an American reading public a passive audience to the textual representations of skilled political denizens.

Chapter Three turns to the figure many consider the father of American print culture, Benjamin Franklin, to explore more specifically what I am terming a general redefinition of the meaning of authorship. Focusing on the *Autobiography,* the plot of which spans the crucial period between 1706 and the 1780s, I argue that Franklin documents both a residual notion of authorship, where secular writing was generally seen as a subjective aspect of religious, civic, and filial participation, and an emergent ideology, where both writers and books were increasingly figured as objective facets of social utility and cultural production. Aside from providing a "literary" thematization of my historical argument, this chapter questions a long tradition of scholarship which has viewed Franklin as a proleptic purveyor of laissez-faire capitalism. It attempts to resituate the *Autobiography* in an eighteenth-century context, proposing that Franklin was a historical figure caught up within the emerging discourses of the Enlightenment, and for whom the rise of a commercial print sphere intimated the problem of alienation. Noting structural similarities between Franklin's philosophy of print and printed currency and nineteenth-century sociologist Georg Simmel's famous meditation on money, this chapter claims that Franklin stumbled on a parallel problematic between the objectification of texts and what Marx in the nineteenth century and Lukács in the twentieth century were to term in different formulations "reification." It concludes that even such a vociferous proponent of a commercial print culture as Franklin admitted some concern that the redefinition of writing posed a fundamental threat to the integrity of the writer.

In concluding Part One, Chapter Four follows Franklin's death in 1790 with the passing into law of the 1790 Federal Copyright Act. This chapter suggests that far from being a simple and uncontested move to protect the rights of authors, the development of the legal fiction of "literary property" in America signaled a radical cultural attempt to reconfigure what it meant to communicate to a reading public in print, one that did not develop evenly nor result in an easy or clear verdict. Surveying the endless polemics over the idea of literary property, debates which made copyright one of the most controversial issues in antebellum America, this chapter makes two large claims. The first of these is that the legal structure of the 1790 Federal Copyright Act, far from determining a substantive definition of authorship, merely suspended two contradictory notions of authorial activity in its strenuous attempt to accommodate the political activity of public writing to an economic framework. These two ideas were a utilitarian conception which defined authorship as the invention of useful knowledge and sought to guarantee the free circulation of that knowledge, and a Lockean conception which figured authorship as the creation of unique, possessable property and sought to guarantee the ownership of that property to its creator. I suggest that the failure of legal theorists to work through these conflicting juridical models evidences an incomplete rationalization of literary activity in the realm of commercial law, a failure that demonstrates how the communicative, rhetorical, and ultimately political activity of public writing did not translate easily into the predicatable workings of the market. My second claim in this chapter is more subtle and turns to literary evidence in Washington Irving's *The Sketch Book*. I argue that despite the fact that most writers in antebellum America argued frequently and vociferously for the independence afforded by strict copyright protection, authors like Irving were also unsettled by the whole concept of literary property, especially in the way in which it entailed the legal transformation of a public and political activity into one that was private and productive. I conclude by relating this tension between the material and ideological interests of American authors both to the antebellum concern over the "calamities of authors" and to the sociological foundations of the American literary "renaissance."

Part Two, "The Aesthetic Response," explores some of the aesthetic consequences of the transformation suggested by Part One. Looking specifically at two amorphous "works" which thematize their intermediary status somewhere between *belle lettres* and novel-writing, Michel-Guillaume Jean de Crèvecoeur's *Letters from an American Farmer* (1782) and Hugh Henry Brackenridge's *Modern Chivalry* (1792–1815), this section argues that both examples reflect the tension between a residual mode of authorship as civic commentary and an emergent mode of public writing as literary production, an issue subsequent critics have taken up in their discussions of whether or not the narratives can be classified as novels. But I then go one step further to argue that the texts represent two very different strategies of accommodation to the changing conditions of authorship. Whereas Brackenridge attempts to extricate his social criticism from the vicissitudes of a commercial print trade, Crèvecoeur exploits its full potential, finding in the anonymity and ambiguity of a commercialized print discourse both a means to political ascendancy *and* protection from political persecution in an uncertain revolutionary moment.

To even call these titles "works" is something of a misnomer, since both Crèvecoeur and Brackenridge brought these narratives to publication in various volumes over a number of years in different geographic locations. Crèvecoeur expanded and substantively rewrote two radically different versions of the 1782 English edition of *Letters* in French in 1784 and 1787; *Modern Chivalry* was published in at least seven discreet volumes written over a period of twenty-three years and printed by four publishers in three locations. In this section I make the formal argument that both titles occupy an intermediary space between the genre of sociopolitical criticism on the one hand and that of the novel on the other. Furthermore, I assert that it is precisely the shapelessness of these two titles, reflecting two transitional authorial postures located between authorship as political participation and authorship as literary production, which has led post-Romantic critics, in their search for the organic literary work, to confusion and misapprehension, in the case of Crèvecoeur, or depreciation and neglect, in that of Brackenridge.

Chapter Five begins with the assertion that readers and critics have not taken into account Crèvecoeur's self-acknowleged debt to Abbè Raynal, whose philosophical critique of the way in which economic considerations dominated the East and West Indies was one of the five most sought-after forbidden bestsellers in pre-Revolutionary France. Claiming that Crèvecoeur began writing the 1782 English edition of *Letters* as a similar means of shocking sociopolitical criticism, whereby the optimistic microeconomic empiricism of an aspiring American *philosophe* is shown to be false-consciousness by underlying structural economic realities, this chapter explores how the ambiguous fictionality of the narrative enabled Crèvecoeur to subsequently negotiate the rapidly changing political world of the 1780s and 1790s. I suggest that Crèvecoeur's narrativization of the macropolitical arguments of Raynal yielded a remarkably malleable text, one which allowed him to enter into a transatlantic sphere of discourse without making potentially deleterious philosophical or political commitments. Trapped in an uncertain Revolutionary moment with conflicting national identities and affiliations, Crèveceour's authorial posture was a means of survival. I conclude by demonstrating how Crèvecoeur exploited this flexibility to secure a public reputation and subsequent political standing, linking his strategy of authorial evasion to both the development of the novel in America and the emerging technological and sociological features of a commercial print culture.

Chapter Six is in some sense the Janus Face to Chapter Five. It demonstrates how *Modern Chivalry* marks Brackrenridge's vigorous critique of a dangerous spirit of consolidation and homogenization brought about by the rise of a commercial print trade. Brackenridge's concern was with what he saw as a leveling of public writing underwritten by libertarian principles of a free press and the uncritical Republican celebration of texts and textuality. If Crèvecoeur's *Letters* signaled an emerging mode of authorship which valorized the recession of the writer, underwrote textual ambiguity, and championed the development of the literary commodity, *Modern Chivalry* represents the sum of Brackenridge's deliberate strategies to extricate his social criticism from an exploding print culture's insistent logic of objectification and equivalency. Moreover, it reveals Brackenridge's authorial efforts to inculcate in his readership a skeptical disposition toward the emerging morphology of a commercial print realm.

Part Three brings together the historical argument of Part One and the aesthetic claims of Part Two to offer what I hope is an exciting new way of accounting for the sociological origins of the early American seduction plot. I begin by reasserting my claim that the practice of sociopolitical criticism, underwritten by an amalgam of Puritan and civic-republican theories of citizenship and reinforced by the political pamphleteering of the Revolution, constituted a unique intellectual heritage for authorship in America. Unlike most of the countries of Europe, the American colonies, especially those of New England, had no continuous tradition of vocational arts (e.g., playwrights, patronage writers, or romancers) from which the modern American literary artist could emerge. While acknowledging the obvious formal relationship between the development of the early American seduction novel and the long tradition of novel and romance writing in England and on the Continent, Chapter Seven claims that it was this indigenous heritage which made novel-writing an acceptable, even socially rewarding cultural practice for civic-minded Republicans. "The composition of political invectives," early America's most famous novelist Charles Brockden Brown could assert in 1799, "appears to me to have hitherto been the literary harvest of America, and this is the harvest which critics must superintend." Outlining the tension between the imperatives of this genealogy and the demands imposed by a consolidating literary marketplace, Chapter Seven argues that the early American seduction novel emerged, at least in part, as a rhetorical effect, both formally and thematically, of a tradition of civic writing attempting to persist in a commercial print culture. This argument is substantiated by two observations about the particular morphology of early American fiction: a formal posture of authorial evasiveness, and a thematic preoccupation with novels and novel-reading. I argue that by accentuating the illicit potency of their writing, foregrounding the seductive power of narrative fiction at the same time they heralded its virtuous didacticism, early American novelists practiced a form of "literary coquetry," a strategic attempt to maintain the communicative and performative power of writing in a culture which was reconfiguring the printed word as a static literary good.

Finally, a brief Afterword both opens out this argument and brings the project full circle by pointing out Nathaniel Hawthorne's invocation in the *House of Seven Gables* (1851) of the very same Salem dissenter with which I begin this study. I argue that Hawthorne not only brought to the foreground the genealogical link between Protestant political dissent and antebellum authorship by giving the family of his embattled author-figure the name "Maule"; he dramatized this historical continuity, in the transformation of the young daguerreotypist Matthew Maule, from an independent sociopolitical critic to a bourgeois property owner, as the erosion of viable civic activism in the face of institutional enfranchisement and material success. For some of the best-known writers of the American Renaissance who (like Hawthorne) sought meaningful political sinecures throughout their lives, most of whom fretted obsessively about the loss of intellectual independence which accompanied popular artistic success, Hawthorne's story of the dissenter Maule's capitulation to affluence and security must have been one that was painfully illustrative and resonant.

Throughout this study, I maintain that the sudden post-Revolutionary emphasis on the virtue of free expression was really a concomitant to what Joyce Appleby and Albert O. Hirshman, following Isaiah Berlin, have described as the general redefinition of the notion of liberty in republican America.[7] That is, the celebration of a free press reflected the move from a "positive" classical republican and civic humanist notion of liberty as a corporate body's right of self-determination and the individual's right to share in the power of the state by participating in the life of the polis to a Lockean idea of liberty as the "negative" right of self-interested individuals to act and to secure possession of property without undue restraint.[8] Exposing a facet of the idea of an eighteenth-century *res publica* not sufficiently recognized in the formulations of Jürgen Habermas, I assert that popular notions of an anonymous "republic of letters" were often rhetorical analogs to contemporaneous theories of *le deux commerce*—ones which legitimated the orderly production and circulation of private literary goods by rationalizing the evacuation of writers from their texts. Consequently, I install a history coextensive to but not entirely compatible with that of Habermas, who wants to find a redemptive interregnum between the development of a commercial exchange society and the eventual erosion of a bourgeois public print sphere. I support this line of argument by tracing the gradual but continuous replacement of a political understanding of authorship with an exclusively economic one, noting the development of legal justifications which increasingly emphasized the material at the same time they muted the communicative nature of public writing. I then conclude by suggesting how the aesthetic strategies American prose writers deployed to maintain critical agency in the face of objectification and conventionalization precipitated out what we now take to be some of the formal characteristics of early American letters. Not least in importance among these characteristics was a self-reflexive preoccupation, structurally as well as thematically, with authorship, texts, and textuality, a concern which extended well into the nineteenth century.

The unique contribution I ultimately hope to make to the study of American literary history lies in the way in which this project traces the persistence of a long and indigenous tradition of immanent social criticism in America. This is a heritage, I argue, which found its origins in the political beliefs and social practices of seventeenth-century nonseparating congregationalists who came to America as a community of Protestant zealots self-consciously committed to the imperatives of social reform. Popularizers and practitioners of an intellectual tradition more properly associated with the Renaissance, the Massachusetts Bay Puritans, like radical Protestants in England, reasoned along classical lines in demanding a continuous and dynamic confrontation of the informed individual conscience with the moral issues of the state. Historians like Basil Hall, and, more recently, Margo Todd, have even gone so far as to argue that such contestation was the very foundation for Puritanism, essentializing Puritans as a group of reformers from within and defining them as "all those restlessly critical and occasionally rebellious members of the Church of England who desired some modifications in church government and worship, but not . . . those who deliberately removed themselves from that Church."[9]

The philosopher Michael Walzer has argued on philosophical grounds how it is political domination which makes social criticism not only possible but necessary, and how social critics are effective only to the extent to which they remain morally connected to their community. Like Walzer's first foray into the history of sociopolitical dissent, his influential *Revolution of the Saints* (1965), this book begins in the seventeenth-century where I focus on the efforts of "connected" Protestant dissenters to circumvent the New England theocracy's strict control over the printing trade by publishing their sociopolitical criticism abroad in England.[10] I argue that it is because these dissenters wrote under the threat of persecution and, perhaps more important, because they remained members of the Protestant community (unlike antinomians like Ann Hutchinson and radical separatists like Roger Williams who broke away from a civil realm they considered irremediably "dead") that their criticism was potent socially and politically. I then set out to describe the transformation by which this power was threatened by new vicissitudes which accompanied the cultural redefinition of authorship from a political activity to an economic one. In doing so, my work chronicles the patterns of critical argument, increasingly aestheticized in form and content, which evolved historically as writers continued to reassert the importance of social criticism for participatory politics. The story I tell here is thus far from the usual one of the "progress" or "rise" of an American literature, an account which has come from an almost exclusive focus on the continuity of literary forms and the influence of the aesthetic heritage of Romanticism. While I certainly recognize the importance of formal traditions which have framed most of the traditional scholarly work on literature in early America, I think such concerns have been decontextualized historically by the projection back in time of a postromantic focus on literary art and philology. Alternatively, this project is an attempt to sustain a critical dialectic between, on the one hand, a history of formal conventions, and, on the other, a tradition of sociopolitical writing, rooted in the philosophy and practice of Puritan and Classical conceptions of citizenship, which was challenged by the triumph, over the course of the eighteenth century, of economic liberalism.

I should add that the themes developed in this book are not simply antiquarian. This book's focus on the changing conditions of political writing at the very beginnings of the modern association between political and economic liberalism carries, I think, profound implications for interpreting the recent changes in the conditions of authorship in Eastern Europe. The Hungarian poet and political activist Miklós Haraszti, for instance, has argued that dissident writers in the post-Stalinist era of glasnost have exchanged the perils of state censorship for the "velvet prison" of commercial success. While liberal reform has brought an unprecedented freedom of expression to intellectuals and artists, Haraszti notes, it has also threatened to destroy "the basis of authentic artistic activity, not just political *diktat* but the individual's *Weltanschauung* within an all-embracing and unified society." He concludes, eerily, that whereas "traditional censorship presupposes the inherent opposition of creators and censors . . . the new censorship strives to eliminate this antagonism. The artist and the censor—the two faces of official culture—diligently and cheerfully cultivate the gardens of art together."[11]

Recently, the Czech novelist Ivan Klíma has come to similar, if slightly less pessimistic, conclusions. While critical of peers like Haraszti for their "blasphemous disregard for a barely attained and still insecure freedom," Klíma admits that "the material conditions for the flourishing of culture, and thus of literature, are not simple" in post-Communist countries. Noting that sales of his previously banned books have dropped from the hundreds of thousands to several thousand, Klíma acknowledges that the transformation in the Czech Republic has brought about "a declining interest in what might be called dissident or non-conformist culture." He concludes, grudgingly, that the cultural heroes who had "found the courage to express the truth, and in their actions and writings had expressed what ordinary citizens believed but were not brave enough to say aloud," either became political pariahs after the revolution (and were summarily defeated in the 1992 parliamentary elections) or simply lost their readership.[12]

Haraszti and Klíma's laments over the political costs engendered by the remaking of communication into commodity parallel those made by many late eighteenth- and early nineteenth-century American authors who added their voices to the patriotic rhetoric celebrating a democratic "republic of letters" but who were also increasingly anxious about that ideal's commercial foundations. They suggest that what I am calling the "transformation of authorship in America" was not simply an isolated historical phenomenon; rather, it remains an ongoing challenge for countries around the world which, following the West, are turning to increasingly decentralized forms of government. By deliberating on the nature of the structural changes the rise of economic liberalism brings to the practice of social and political criticism, this project ultimately attempts to discover how the public writer, traditionally seen as one of the constitutive elements of a "just society," can remain effective and essential in our age of advanced liberalism.

PART I

THE
TRANSFORMATION
OF
AUTHORSHIP

The World Turned Upside Down: Sociopolitical Criticism in Puritan America

Perry Miller once claimed that our understanding of Puritan political thought had been obscured since the Enlightenment by ideas "generated in the course of a sweeping revolt against everything for which the Puritans stood." In particular, Miller lamented the way in which the political philosophy of Puritanism had been "deplored or condemned as unfortunate remnants of medievalism."[1] Following Miller's subsequent efforts to resurrect the rich intellectual foundations of Puritan social theory, revisionist historians of the 1960s, 1970s, and 1980s sought to restore to Puritan political theory a more radical intellectual heritage, viewing Puritan conceptions of the state as decidedly more activist, progressive, practical, and reformist than previously thought. The English historian Christopher Hill led the way with a series of books which portrayed a rising bourgeoisie finding in Calvinist beliefs a way to challenge and transform a static medieval world, and he was followed by scholars like Michael Walzer who attributed to Puritan beliefs the collapse of that most ubiquitous medieval doctrine, the Great Chain of Being.[2] More recently, as if to demonstrate the revisionary imperative in Puritan historiography itself, historians like Margo Todd have turned in a new direction, linking the radical reformism of Puritanism not to Max Weber and R. H. Tawney's pious bourgeoisie but to two broader intellectual developments sweeping early Modern Europe: neoclassical ideals of civic republicanism and Christian humanism.[3]

Perry Miller would not have been surprised by this most recent recontextualization of Puritan political thinking. Miller had gone so far as to argue that the congregational system of the New England Puritans bore a remarkable 17 affinity to a classical political tradition which employed the republican doctrine of the "one, the few, and the many." Miller claimed that the property-sustained civic personality of the Greek *polis* was transformed in Protestant thinking into the "visible saint" of the Puritan church. These members, Miller noted, were called "citizens," and they elected delegates to the General Court, chose judges, and passed laws. Those not elected to visible sainthood, he argued, termed "inhabitants" by Puritan leaders, were much like the members of the household excluded from the *polis* in Greek thought; they had "equality before the law, property rights, police protection . . . [but] were allowed no voice in government or in the choice of ministers."[4]

Perhaps because of the well-documented exclusion of the "inhabitants" from the affairs of the Puritan State, rendered most clearly in vivid accounts of the antinomian controversies and the persecutions of religious noncomformists, we are not used to thinking of the Puritan theocracy as a form of participatory government. Yet to the politically eligible (those formally elected to "visible sainthood" and committed to their covenanted communities) Puritan political thinkers repeatedly stressed the importance of an independent, civic-minded conscience, and they repeatedly enjoined citizens to take a participatory role in the same ongoing project of social and political reconstitution which had brought them to America. Consequently, as Margo Todd argues for the English context, "social reformism [was] a Puritan distinctive." Puritans reasoned "along classical lines that the common weal was to be achieved . . . by inculcating virtuous behavior in the individual citizen . . . [and they demanded] a continuous, dynamic confrontation of the informed individual conscience with moral issues in a civic government."[5]

Departing from such a revisionary view of Puritan political thought, this chapter sets out to recover a tradition of civic authorship in Protestant New England, a heritage, grounded in the tenets of classical republicanism and Christian humanism, with imperatives that might be summarized by the very first lines of Milton's famous meditation on the virtues and problems of an unlicensed press, the *Areopagitica* (1644): "They who to States and Governours of the Commonwealth direct their speech . . . or wanting such accesse in a private condition, write that which they forsee may advance the public good."[6] Just as the English Puritan John Milton argued for a free press on the basis that a godly social order demanded continual watchfulness and unending civic renewal, the nonseparating congregationalists of the Massachusetts Bay colony valorized, in principle if not in fact, the importance of free political expression. Consequently, they viewed public writing in almost exclusively political terms, and they considered authorship as an often *too* efficacious means for citizens to participate in the political sphere.

To suggest the existence as well as some of the contours of this tradition of authorship, I want to begin with a polemic by a Massachusetts dissenter entitled *Truth Held Forth and Maintained* (1695).[7] The volume, an exegesis of Salem resident Thomas Maule's views on religion, and a condemnation of the Puritan theocracy for its intolerance and disposition toward persecution, is filled with criticism of the provincial authorities. Attacking what he called "the hireling teachers" of the Massachusetts orthodoxy for becoming too secure in their public offices, and scorning Puritan ministers who served "a time in Schools of learning, by which they gather[ed] outward knowledge" when it would be better for them to work with their hands for "outward subsistence," Maule excoriated the Puritans for distancing themselves through sinecure and specialized knowledge from the people they purported to represent.[8] Maule did not stop with problems of an elite and secure caste of Puritan officeholders. He charged the Puritans with cruelties to Native Americans akin to those of the Spaniards, cheating and plying them with rum under the auspices of the Society for the Propagation of the Gospel. And in the most interesting section of the book, Maule attacked what he saw as the Salem Witchcraft Delusion, interpreting the event as the visitation of God's vengeance on New England for its persecution of religious dissenters and its other sins, pointing out how the execution of the supposed witches was abated once a minister and others "accounted eminent" were accused.

The story of Thomas Maule is the story of an early American dissenting writer's successful justification for Thomas Aquinas's secular claim that *"homo est naturaliter politicus, id est, socialis"* ("man is by nature political, that is, social"), and he was perhaps the first to argue successfully for the importance of a viable public print sphere.[9] Unable to get the volume licensed or printed in Boston, where a seventy-five-year-old tradition of rigorous government censorship suppressed independent public writing, Maule had to secure a license from New York, and he was forced to forward the manuscript to Quaker printer William Bradford to see it in circulation.[10] Once it was printed and had attracted the attention of the Massachusetts Bay rulers and clergy, Maule was arrested and brought before the lieutenant governor and the council, his house and bookstores searched, and copies of the text seized. When Maule "owned the Booke to be his and that he wrote it, except errors committed by the Printer," the court indicted him.

The precise reasons for Maule's acquittal are best left to intellectual and legal historians, but several factors are worth noting here. Answering to the charge of printing a book without a license, Maule apparently turned to the fraught issue of colonial sovereignty, replying that although the Massachusetts rulers controlled the press, he had the liberty of a British subject to print the book and the right of a British merchant to sell it like other goods. Maule also demanded and received a trial by a jury "of his equals," a jurisdictional move that was to be fundamental to the success of the 1735 Zenger case. Finally, and perhaps most significantly, Maule's argument to the jury exploited the persistent tension in Puritan political thinking between compulsivity and voluntarism, what Timothy Breen has characterized as an ongoing battle in colonial New England between discretionary and delegated conceptions of civil authority.[11] One of the very first documents printed in Puritan America, the *Freedman's Oath,* issued from Stephen Daye's state-controlled Cambridge press in 1642, reflected this ambiguity.[12] While coercive in the sense that it demanded that subjects of the Massachusetts commonwealth submit to "the wholesome Lawes and Orders" of the government, it also provided that when such subjects were "called to give [their] voyce touching any such matter of this state," they were to judge by their "own conscience" what would best "tend to the public weal of the body, without respect of persons, or favor of any man."[13] While the judge in Maule's case attempted to apply the discretionary understanding, claiming that Maule's book "contained a great deal of blasphemous matter against the Churches and Government . . . tend[ing] to overthrow all good in Church and Commonwealth which God hath planted amongst his people in [the] Province," Maule worked to apply the delegated one, suggesting that if the magistrates impugned on the freedom of one writer of "truths," the civic and religious liberties of other colonists would likewise disappear. He addressed the jury irreverently, but with an intellectual persuasiveness that apparently hit home:

> if your Power by which you act against me, do long continue, he that now enjoys a good Estate, under your Government, in seven years time, after this rate, may not be left worth a Grote; for as you are set to watch over the people, things are at that pass, through your means, *that they have the greater need to watch over you,* otherwise they are like to be undone by the heavy burdens you lay upon them.[14]

Maule's appeal to the jury for the need for such a supervisory public, despite the attendant threat of blasphemy and civil disorder, convinced the court, and in the face of the protests of the judge, Maule was set free.

Given some encouragement by the verdict, Maule composed another piece of political criticism soon afterward, entitled *New England Persecutors Mauled with Their Own Weapons* (1697). While the central aim of the pamphlet was to provide a detailed account of the trial, Maule again sought to provide a

"true account" of the New England orthodoxy's persecution of religious dissenters, offering a humanist "jeremiad" at the same time that conservative Puritan Nehemiahs, recalling the Old Testament leader who saved Jerusalem by
rebuilding a protective wall which citizens had allowed to crumble, attacked
the toleration of dissenting voices as threats to Winthrop's "City on a Hill."[15]
Maule's verses concluded:

> Unto religion these Free-men do pretend
> We may all see that money is their end

> From all Bloody Free-men pray God deliver me
> They are for Hanging all, that one with them not be.

> Balsaam's State is theirs, who for unrighteous gain
> The people do Oppress, themselves for to
> maintain.[16]

Maule did not attack persecution for the injustices it brought on its victims.
Like most religious men of the seventeenth century, Maule undoubtedly believed that the suppression of many dissenting views was a necessary evil in a
voluntaristic and hence fragile commonwealth. Even Milton's spirited call for
a free Protestant press in the *Areopagitica* argued that dissenting views which
threatened the godliness of society had to be vigorously silenced. Rather,
Maule reasoned that persecution allowed leaders to veil their personal interests
in the guise of higher religious ends. And as the previous passage I have cited
suggests, the freedom of public expression in Maule's writing was not justified
along the lines by which we have come to expect. That is, a free press was not
defended as an abstract natural right, prior to government, as it was to be in the
emerging tradition of Anglo-American libertarianism. The freedom of expression posited by Maule, in contrast, was figured as the essential means by
which the true ecclesia of the *civitas dei,* the individual moral conscience, could
supervise the civic authority to which he agreed to submit for the good of the
whole; it was the means by which colonial leaders were encouraged to keep
their public and private interests separate.

Maule's call for a disinterested public writing was thus based on political
rather than religious or moral imperatives, more concerned with the require-
ment that citizens take responsibility for continually reforming their government than it was with either an Augustinian private conscience or the extreme
libertarian ideal of sacrosanct individual rights. Much like thinkers in the
Country opposition in English politics prior to the English Civil War, a group
one historian has claimed formed a unique "alliance" with Puritanism, Maule

aspired to the goal "of public spirit, unmoved by private interest, untainted by court influence and corruption—[a] representative, in short, of the highest good."[17] Perhaps this was the reason Maule was so successful in his battle with the nonseparating Congregationalists of the Massachusetts orthodoxy: he invoked the very same political principles which had brought the Puritans to New England to reform—not remake—what they saw as a corrupted ecclesiastical polity in England.

■ ■ ■

I want to argue below that the efforts of Thomas Maule suggest some of the conditions of a viable civic print culture in seventeenth-century New England. The flowering of this fragile sphere of sociopolitical commentary, in turn, was the result of two factors. First, in their political thinking, nonseparating Congregationalists in New England found a compelling yet frightening correlation between Calvin's conscientious saint who freed himself from the stultified controls of the corporate church and Machiavelli's "masterless" individual cut loose from the corruption of hierarchical and particularistic ties. As a consequence, to distinguish Calvin's restless saint from the self-interested Florentine prince of Renaissance political thinking, the New England clergy stressed the importance of an active civic life. As Michael Walzer has argued in the English context, the oppositional intellectual tradition of Puritanism insisted that "political activity was a creative endeavor in which the saints were privileged as well as obligated to participate . . . [that] saints were responsible for their world . . . and [were] responsible above all for its continual reformation."[18]

As a result, political thinkers in Puritan America, as they had in England, adopted two contradictory conceptions of human agency: a classical assertion that man was *zoon politikon,* by nature a citizen, and conceived of public expression, in a long tradition of republican thought, as a means for "visible saints" to participate in the *civitas Dei;* and a concurrent Calvinist notion that postlapsarian man was asocial, by nature a corrupt creature hating but needing submission, and which conceived of independent expression as a threat to the tranquillity of a voluntaristic Christian commonwealth.[19] These two conceptions, while not necessarily mutually exclusive on intellectual grounds, were not easily negotiated on practical ones, and they reflected the problematic attempt on the part of Puritan intellectuals to constitute what they considered a cohesive, virtuous social order by providing for effective political agency while restraining the disintegrating forces of self-interest and anarchy.[20]

The latter concern led to what I will argue was a second, paradoxical factor in the development of a viable public print culture in Puritan New England: the unusual effectiveness of the New England theocracy's censorship and suppression of unorthodox public expression. The conditions within which public writing in New England emerged were wholly unlike those in Europe. The geographically isolated New England theocracy was far more effective than states were in Europe in controlling access to printing presses, suppressing clandestine publications, and restricting the importation of books. While English booksellers and readers could arrange travel across the channel to the relatively free presses of Amsterdam, and while French booksellers and readers could rely on the vigorous clandestine book trade operating between Paris and the frontier borders, the literate in New England were almost wholly dependent on a native press and occasional imports. As a consequence, public writing in America remained a fraught political phenomenon to be reckoned with by the state long after the efforts to suppress the press had proved ineffectual in England, and long after the Court of High Commission and the Star Chamber turned the regulation of printing over, first to the commercial apparatus of the Stationer's Company, then to the self-regulating copyright requirements articulated in the 1709 Statute of Anne.[21]

I make this historical argument, in part, to put pressure on those of recent scholars who, adopting Jürgen Habermas's argument for the emergence of a late eighteenth-century public sphere, have argued that the meaning of letters in Protestant New England was "a technology of privacy underwritten by divine authority."[22] Extrapolating from the rigorous exegetical disposition of the Puritan divines and laity, these arguments suggest that a "Religion of the Closet" framed the relationship between persons and texts as a passive one of internalization. Michael Warner, in particular, deploys a flattened, apolitical conception of writing in seventeenth-century America—he goes so far as to argue that "expressly political publications are exceptional in the print discourse of the colonies before 1720"—in order to chart an eighteenth-century transformation whereby letters temporarily "become a technology of publicity whose meaning in the last analysis is civic and emancipatory."[23] Such a progressive teleology, while seemingly consistent with post-Revolutionary libertarian rhetoric in America, may misrepresent the structural features and causal relationships of what I am suggesting here was a dramatically different kind of transformation: that is, the historical trajectory by which a viable civic literary culture in early America dissolved, and whereby an embattled tradition of civic authorship was institutionalized and privatized alongside the consolidation of economic man.

In part, this was because by "naturalizing" free speech as a latent *attribute* of the private, rights-insulated individual rather than the instrumental *means* for meaningful political participation, eighteenth-century libertarianism also worked to enfeeble political commentary by taking it out of the political realm and circumscribing it within that of the "natural" subject. In this configuration, political commentary began to be seen, not as the means for embattled individuals to guarantee the virtue of the state but as the aggregate in print of a writing public freely seeking its own private interest. Given this state of affairs, the role of rhetorical contestation was no longer viewed as the realization of a virtuous state based on collective ideals but as the incarnation in political modes and institutions of a public's continually shifting opinion as expressed by accumulated interest. We might even go so far as to say that the vicissitudes of public writing in the modern era are encompassed by this formula. That is, when the model government was no longer that which sought some ideal of the good, but that which best realized the greatest interests of the greatest numbers, political faction was certain to replace the political conscience as the meaningful civic agent, and, paradoxically, public opinion was destined to supersede censorship as the primary obstacle to the ideal of the independent civic conscience.[24]

■ ■ ■

While Thomas Maule may have been the first to succeed in arguing for the political importance of a free press in a colonial court, he was by no means the earliest dissenting writer to exploit the ongoing tension between discretionary and delegated conceptions of civic authority forwarded by Puritan divines. And while the government's strict control of the only press in the colonies in the first three decades of Protestant America's founding, Stephen Daye's Cambridge press, prevented individuals from escaping the constraints imposed on them by their local circumstances, the Massachusetts theocracy discovered it could not prevent individuals from accessing the press—and hence a wide reading public—in England. This recourse posed a particular problem to the civil magistrates of New England, since by publishing criticism in London, colonial dissenters could exploit the issue of divided sovereignty, leveraging the political conditions in America by appealing to Parliament, colonial organizations, and noteworthy patrons, as well as to the catalytic power of popular public opinion. Consequently, the years up to 1662, when the General Court passed the first formal act for restricting the press through a policy of licensing and censorship, saw the flowering of a unique exchange of transatlantic civic criticism.[25] This was despite, or I should say, because of, the New England theocracy's effectiveness in suppressing printed commentary within the

colonies, an activity which again and again reemphasized the political nature
of public writing, and the concurrent lapse of censorship enforcement in England.

For instance, printed in London less than a year after an expatriated
Samuel Gorton published his notorious *Simplicities Defense against Seven-
Headed Policy* (1646), attacking Puritans for restricting rule only to "honorable,
learned, wise, [and] experienced" officials, John Child's *New England's Jonas
Cast Up in London* (1647) was such a clandestine attempt to reform the civic
affairs of the Massachusetts polity.[26] Representing his brother, Robert Child of
Massachusetts, John Child sought by printing the pamphlet to publicize the
efforts of his brother, William Vassal, and other petitioners who had attempted,
by means of a written summary of grievances, to enact a policy of religious toleration in New England and to grant civil rights to nonfreedmen. In this sense,
New England's Jonas attempted what an initial written petition to the General
Court of Massachusetts Bay had failed to accomplish, namely to argue for legislation assuring religious toleration for every "Turke, Jew, Papist, Arian,
Socinian, Nicklaytan, Familist, or any other."[27] This effort, which began with
a petition to the General Court of Plymouth, does not even appear in the official records there, apparently because Governor Prence, suspecting that in allowing the matter to come to a vote the petition would "eate out of the power
of godliness," suppressed it. When the General Court of Massachusetts subsequently delayed in acting on an appeal, convening a synod to discuss the more
abstract questions of how civil and ecclesiastical institutions were going to deal
with the problem of what they considered sedition, Robert Child and his associates circulated handwritten copies of their petition throughout the neigh-
boring colonies and as far away as New Netherlands, Virginia, and Bermuda in
an effort to stir up public sympathy.

What really gave the petition rhetorical power, however, was Child's
threat to appeal to Parliament on the basis that the petitioners were subject to
the Magna Carta and English common law rather than, as the magistrates of
the General Court repeatedly claimed, the laws of Massachusetts. After some
consideration, the General Court finally responded as they had when confronted with John Wheelwright's Fast Day sermon in 1637 and as they were to
do when faced with William Pyncheon's *Meritorious Price of Our Redemption*
(1650): they charged Child and his followers with sedition, based on the written petition's "false and scandalous passages." The magistrates concluded that
the petitioners were guilty of defaming the Court, of convincing others that
liberties and privileges belonged to everyone (rather than to those admitted to
such fellowship by the governor), of attempting to weaken the laws of Massa-

chusetts, of slandering the Church, of charging rulers with tyranny, and of attempting to incite others into disaffection. Child and his followers were subsequently examined by the General Court and fined.

Not to be deterred, Child circulated yet another petition throughout the
colonies, this time ostensibly addressed to Parliament, and purportedly "to be
in the name and on the sighs and tears of many thousands" of nonfreemen.[28]
Again the General Court responded, and Child and several others were arrested and fined additional sums. Child and an associate named Dand were arrested and searched a final time on the evening of what they hoped was to be
their departure to England with William Vassal, where the three men intended
to carry their petition to the Commissioners for Plantations. On the evidence
of various "seditious" documents found with Dand, the Court imprisoned
both men, and Vassal sailed to England alone where he composed *New England's Jonas* with Child's brother.

The pamphlet consisted of three interrelated sections. First, it accurately
reprinted the capital laws of the Massachusetts Bay Colony in an attempt to
convince an English audience of the severity of the New England penal codes,
particularly those banning public expression. A second section described the
persecution of Robert Child and other petitioners by Massachusetts authorities, pointing out the inconsistencies between New England and English rule.
A third section, finally, endeavored to refute the widespread belief that Vassal
and his party narrowly escaped a prognosticated catastrophe while crossing the
Atlantic by casting their petition into the sea.

With respect to the first two sections, *New England's Jonas* was an effort to
amplify in England what the petitioners had worked to accomplish in the
colonies: that is, an attempt to generate public support by framing their experiences textually in a persuasive fashion. The efforts Child and Vassal took ini-
tially to disseminate their petition widely are vitally important in this regard,
since the actions of the General Court reveal how sensitive authorities were to
the threat written or printed material posed to their institutional authority. Indeed, again and again in this and other instances of early American dissent, it
was textual evidence which served as the basis for warrant, incrimination, verdict, and punishment of sedition. But Child and Vassal were also aware that
publicity functioned to protect them from anonymity, and hence from certain
punishment. That is, the circulation of their views was also a defensive activity
in an attempt to limit the authority of the magistrates, who might find themselves reigned in by public sympathy.

Of course, the functionaries of the Massachusetts Bay Colony recognized
this dual threat to their authority, and they reacted by tightly controlling both

the content and the iconography of printed material. Thus, for instance, when Roger Williams was called before Governor John Winthrop in 1633 for writing a treatise critical of Plymouth colony, he was forced to author a letter submitting himself to the laws of the colony, including those governing dissent; he was required to pen a retraction of the statements made in the offending treatise; and finally, his book was symbolically burned in the marketplace.[29] Often, when it was impossible to enforce laws governing print or to obtain public statements of retraction from writers, Puritan authorities resorted to simply burning books in public, theatrically designating secular political texts as blasphemous even when the authors could not be apprehended. This was the magistrates' response to William Dell's *The Tryall of Spirits* (1653), for instance, a spiritist work which attacked ministerial prerogatives, two copies of which, according to Roger Williams, were burned in Massachusetts in 1654. Such symbolic gestures were deployed with some frequency throughout the seventeenth and well into the eighteenth centuries.[30]

The problem that *New England's Jonas* posed for the magistrates was that of what they were going to do about publications printed offshore where neither of the two registers by which the clergy dealt with transgressions in print (rhetorics and iconography) could be directly and effectively addressed. In the case of Vassal and Child's *New England's Jonas,* the authorities of the General Court were fortunate in that they had already dispatched their colonial agent, Edward Winslow, to protect the colony from the claims that Samuel Gorton had attempted to bring before the Commission for Foreign Plantations. When Gorton published his *Simplicities Defense against Seven- Headed Policy* in London in 1646, Winslow countered by responding with a systematic rebuttal of Gorton's assertions in his *Hypocrisy Unmasked* (1646), later revised as *The Danger of Tolerating Levellers in a Civill State* (1649). Recognizing that Vassal and Child were likewise attempting to circumvent the ecclesiastical authority of the Massachusetts Bay Colony by appealing to both administrative authorities and the English reading public, Winslow responded with his *New England's Salamander Discovered by an Irreligious and Scornfull Pamphlet, Called New England's Jonas Cast Up at London* (1647). In this pamphlet, Winslow cast doubt on the authorship of *New England's Jonas* in an attempt to discredit the account without impugning on Child's reputation; at the same time, Winslow reasserted that the Massachusetts government was "legall and not arbitrary, being as neere the Law of England as our Condition will Permit."

But while this strategy of textual containment by offering a deconstructive sequel was undoubtedly effective in some respects, what really gave Edward Winslow a rhetorical advantage over Vassal and Child came about as the result of a sermon John Cotton gave to his congregation—including some members who were to be passengers on the ship that was to carry Vassal to England—just prior to Vassal's departure. Cotton apparently suspected that Vassal intended to publish an account of the treatment that Vassal, Child, and the other petitioners had endured, and, as Winslow notes, he consequently presented a Thursday lecture by drawing from Canticles 2:15: "Take us the foxes, the little foxes, which destroy the vines." Vassal and Child concede in *New England's Jonas* that Cotton gave such a sermon, the aim of which was clear: "That if any shall carry any writings, complaints against the people of God in that country, it would be as Jonas in the ship" and that dissenters should "remedy of those things that were amisse, in that place, and tell it not in Gath, nor publish it in Askelon." Vassal and Child also maintain that Cotton informed the ship's captain that should any storms arise, he was to "search if they had not in any chest or trunk any such Jonas aboard," and if found he was not "to throw the persons over-board, but the writings." Winslow provides a similar albeit a somewhat more poetic account:

> When the terrors of the Almightie shall beset the vessell wherein they are, the heavens shall frowne upon them, the billowes of the sea shall swell above them, and dangers shall threaten them (as I persuaded myself they will) . . . I will not give the Counsell was taken concerning Jonah, to take such a person and cast him into the sea: God forbid: but I would advise such to come to a resolution in themselves to desist from such enterprises, never further to engage in them, and to cast such a petition into the sea, that may occasion so much trouble and disturbance.[31]

By making such a prophesy, it seems clear that Cotton worked to disable the claims of the petitioners by deploying a strategy similar in logic to burning books in the marketplace: he undermined the public's perception of the petitions before they could even circulate, and thus before there was a need to contain their contents at the level of rhetoric. Calling on the interpretive authority he possessed over his audience, Cotton leveled a clerical prophesy based on the prefigurative story of Jonah. Of course, Cotton was as fortunate as he was cagey in that Vassal's ship left for a crossing of the North Atlantic in early winter when the chance of the vessel encountering a storm was practically assured.

Cotton's sermon apparently had such an immediate impact that a "Mr. Thomas Peters had his goods and bedding on board to go, but hearing Mr. Cotton's lecture he took them out and went in another ship by way of Spain."[32] But more important, it worked to frame the experience of the ship's passengers to such a degree that when the vessel finally encountered rough seas some time into the voyage, the petition and other printed documents were immediately suspect. As Vassal and Child note:

> Whereupon, having great storms (as could not be otherwise expected) some of the passengers remembering Mr. Cotton's sermon, it seems were much affected with what he had said; and a woman amongst them came up from between the Decks about midnight, or after, in a distracted passionate manner, to Mr. William Vassall . . . she earnestly desired him, if there were any Jonas in the ship, that as Mr. Cotton had directed, it might be thrown overboard . . . He asked her why she came to him? and she said, because it was thought that he had some writings against the people of God: but he answered her, He had nothing but a petition to parliament that they might enjoy the liberty of English subjects, and that there could be no Jonas . . . After this she went into the Great cabin to Mr. Tho. Fowle [one of the petitioners] in like distracted manner; who told her he had nothing but a copy of the petition . . . [and] that if she and others thought that to be the cause of the storm, she and they might do what they would with it . . . So she took it and carried it between decks to them from who she came, and they agreed to throw it overboard, and it was thrown overboard.

■ ■ ■

While Vassal and Child asserted that the storm did not "leave us upon the throwing of this paper over-board," which they claimed was actually a duplicate, the incident apparently became such a sensation in widespread reports that it was the public debate over whether or not the casting of the written petition into the sea fulfilled John Cotton's prophesy, which seems to have provided the compelling exigency for Vassal and Child's pamphlet. The title of *New England's Jonas Cast Up at London* refers to the fact that the petitioners—and the original petition—arrived safe in London, being delivered from a near shipwreck off the coast of the Isles of Scilly a full fortnight after the supposed miracle. In other words, the title and the third and final section of Vassal and Child's pamphlet worked to reinterpret John Cotton's prophesy by recalling in the collective consciousness of a reading public how the story of Jonah ultimately played out: namely that Jonah survived in the belly of a great fish sent by God only to be vomited up on shore three days later to fulfill his obligation to preach to the dissipated city of Nineveh.

The fact that it was the interpretation of the "Jonas" story, and not the political claims of the petitioners, which became the primary site of contestation in the pamphlet, suggests the difficult position dissenting writers faced in voicing their claims. Vassal and Child's ability to lodge effective complaints against the New England orthodoxy rested, finally, on their ability to dismantle the typological prophesy constructed by Cotton by appealing to the sentiment of a wider reading public. Thus, they turned to what we might call "literary means" to secure political ends, reinterpreting in the realm of aesthetics a judgment made in that of the pulpit. In this light, perhaps the most striking aspect of this contest over ecclesiastical authority in early Massachusetts is that it took place, not before magistrates in a solemn New England meetinghouse, but in the transatlantic realm of printed texts over the status and interpretation of those texts on the part of the writers of those texts.

Nor were Vassal and Child an anecdotal exception. Aside from Roger Williams's famous pamphlet war with John Cotton over Williams's *The Bloudy Tenent of Persecution* (1644) and *The Bloudy Tenent Yet More Bloudy* (1652), there was a surprising number of dissenting writers who attempted to reform civil affairs in New England by making their "conscience" public to an English reading public. After enduring imprisonment in Lynn in 1651, the Baptist John Clarke managed to get his *Ill Newes from New England; or a Narrative of New England's Persecution* (1652) published in England, a dramatic pamphlet which openly challenged the relationship between church and state in Massachusetts. Rhetorically, Clarke's text was similar to Vassal and Child's. It began with a graphic account of the persecution of dissenters in New England, followed by the inconsistencies between English and colonial rule, and it concluded with a scriptural justification for reform of the laws on toleration. Clarke argued that the suppression of an individual's "conscience" was dangerous to government, since it made men "outwardly and hypocritically to conform" when in a virtuous commonwealth they should wish to join of free will. And, as Thomas Maule was to do in his trial for *Truth Held Forth,* Clark appealed to the civic-mindedness of his readers by arguing that "a forced conformity only bought the magistrates a little time against their state's utter corruption."[33] Just as they had in the case of Vassal and Child, the colony asked their English agent, this time Thomas Cobbet, to respond to Clarke's charges, which Cobbet did in *The Civil Magistrates Power in Matters of Religion Modestly Debated* (1653). And whereas John Clarke had argued for a voluntaristic conception of religious government in which the magistrates served as delegates of the individual consciences of the believers, Cobbet reaffirmed the discretionary authority of the civil leaders.

The efforts of such dissenting writers as these serve as an important reminder that McCluhanite historical models which assume that modes of early

American public discourse were marked by a linear transformation between, on the one hand, an organizing principle of orality (marked by ritual, kinship ties, prescriptive social bonds, and immanence) and, on the other, an organizing principle of printedness (marked by reason, social contracts, voluntary association, and representation) need to be closely interrogated. But perhaps more important, they dramatize a historical conjuncture between what we nominally term oral and print cultures, a conjuncture which reveals certain key assumptions about authors and texts in mid-seventeenth-century America.

With respect to texts, we might say that the pamphlets of dissenting writers like Vassal and Child reveal a world in which secular printed works were seen as political actions rather than ontological things, deeds meant to influence public affairs through public appeal by means of wide circulation. In the total field of printed material, these textual activities, because of their political power, tended to be classified by authorities into the categories of the "official," the "unofficial," or the ambiguous. Indeed, the interpretive mechanisms the church and state used to control the medium of print functioned to classify texts according to these three categories. Thus, when a Parliamentary committee sought to reinstate some of the control over the print trade it lost with the abolition of the Court of Star Chamber in 1640, it drew up precisely these three fields of books: the "good and vendible," those limited to certain audiences, and those books to be burned. But regardless of whether the intent of a text was to instantiate, influence, question, or alter the terms of existing social relationships, printed works held this public and political status.

As Sacvan Bercovitch, David Hall, Stephen Greenblatt, and others have pointed out directly or indirectly, the so-called intensive reading habits of Protestant culture, far from making the relationship between readers and texts one of internalization, may have actually worked to accentuate this symmetrical relationship between the interpretation of texts and sociopolitical activity in the public realm.[34] Biblical exegesis was no exercise in playful interpretation on the part of private readers; rather, it was a hermeneutical practice conducted in public by "authorized" individuals seeking to establish the contiguity between the textualized word of God and the social world of man. Authorship, at least in the way we think of it, as reasonably autonomous individuals expressing sentiments in written form to a largely anonymous public, was in this configuration an activity that was potentially so incendiary to the church and state that it was certain to bring close scrutiny. Blasphemy was punishable by death in Plymouth Colony, Massachusetts Bay Colony, and Maryland in the seventeenth century; and the Massachusetts authorities were quick to prosecute on the mere *suspicion* that defendants possessed unauthorized texts. As the Puritan reader Arthur Howland discovered in 1657 when he was sentenced and convicted for possessing seditious material in print, the General Court was quick to suppress the work of dissenting writers, particularly those which constituted what they saw as an invasion of competing religious sects. The Court passed an act in 1656 prohibiting any person from "knowingly import[ing] into any harbor . . . any Quakers bookes or writings concerning their diuilish opinions" and allowing that any such person who persisted in defending "the hereticall opinions of the said Quakers, or any of theire bookes or papers . . . [be] committed to the howse of correction . . . [then] banishment." Nor was the censorship of printed texts a simple denominational issue; it extended to orthodox as well as to dissenting writers. As early as 1638, for instance, Thomas Dudley, an assistant to printer Stephen Daye, turned a copy of a book written by clergyman Thomas Lechford over to John Winthrop, asserting that he "found the scope thereof to be erroneous and dangerous, if not hereticall . . . I haue sent you the book herew[i]th that in stead of putting it to the presse as he desireth it may rather be putt into the fire as I desire."

Thus, at least in the context of early seventeenth-century America, there may be a solid historical corollary to Foucault's theoretical account of the birth of the author. As Foucault notes in "What Is an Author," authorship was originally a site of penal appropriation: that is, "texts, books, and discourses really began to have authors . . . to the extent that authors became subject to punishment, that is, to the extent that discourses could be transgressive."[35] There are hundreds of cases of censorship and persecution in New England alone before 1760, ranging from imprisonment, to public humiliation, to fines, to book burnings. Historians like Clyde Duniway, Leonard Levy, and Philip Gura have carefully documented the conditions in the northern colonies, and the more Anglican southern colonies like Virginia (which banned printing presses until the 1720s) were even more effective in the seventeenth and early eighteenth centuries at suppressing political writing. Governor Berkeley's infamous—but by no means unusual—statement that he had God to thank that "there were no schools nor printing" and that he hoped that "we shall not have [either] . . . [since] learning has brought disobedience, and heresy, and sects into the world, and printing has divulged them and libels against the best government" found enough sympathy that several printers were soon after successfully tried for illegal printing. And when Lord Effigham arrived to take control of the colony in 1683, he was explicitly ordered "to allow no person to use a printing press on any occasion whatsoever."[36]

What is most interesting about pamphlets like *New England's Jonas* in this context is the fact that, by exploiting the inability of the New England clergy to suppress printed works abroad, dissenting writers like Vassal and Child stepped outside the usual geographical boundaries into an alternative, transatlantic formulation of authorship based on an appeal to a wider community of anonymous readers. And, in this sense, writers like Vassal and Child may be the true progenitors of what was to become idealized in the eighteenth century as the *res publica,* or Republic of Letters, that Fourth Estate which was championed as a means to monitor the political workings of the state. By saying this, I do not want to collapse the important theological differences between such a wide range of dissenters, nor to claim that writers found a breach in colonial authority to successfully exploit. This appealing vision of effective public writing is tempered by the fact that Edward Winslow's responses were undoubtedly effective in "containing" the efforts of Gorton and Vassal and Child. Perhaps more important, as Sacvan Bercovitch and Philip Gura remind us, focusing solely on the efforts of dissenters blinds us to the ways in which orthodoxies used the persecution of dissenters to bind popular consensus. Dissenting writers were often constructed as well-publicized pillories, their efforts providing a compelling rationalization for why various mechanisms of restraint were in place to begin with. Consequently, the notion of an early transatlantic sphere of civic critique suggested so tantalizingly by the efforts of Vassal and Child needs to be examined carefully in terms of its efficacy. But texts like *New England's Jonas* raise some important questions regarding our assumptions about early American print culture. Far from being antiquarian or privately pietistic, the publication of dissenting views, often dramatically literary in their representation of such social and political issues as corruption and religious persecution, signals a more dynamic conception of Protestant print culture than we have traditionally acknowledged, one that counterpoised the static institutions of the New England state with the dynamism of its constituent saints/citizens. We might even see in the effort to leverage political reform by way of an emotional appeal to an anonymous reading public the birth of an indigenous conception of authorship in America, one that deployed the amplifactory potential of printed discourse as the catalytic vehicle for meaningful civic agency and continual social and political reform.

TWO

The Rise of a Free Press and the Erosion of a Public Sphere: The Zenger Case Reconsidered

The years following Thomas Maule's trial in 1696 saw the gradual loss of the exclusive control of the colonial press on part of the New England theocracy. The importation of presses and printers to the mid-Atlantic colonies, which were often less sympathetic to the aims of the New England government, provided a new, domestic mouthpiece for dissenting writers like Thomas Maule. But while printers in the middle colonies found they could publish New England writers critical of their government, they found, as authors had in New England, that they had more difficulty with the writings of their own residents. William Bradford, Pennsylvania's first printer, serves as a good example. Bradford's initial publication, an almanac, was censored while still in manuscript, and Bradford was repeatedly warned not to print anything without a license. In 1689, Bradford was interrogated by Governor Blackwell for having printed Joseph Growdon's "Frame of Government," which was seen as an unlicensed publication "of a dangerous nature," and forced to depart to England. And soon after returning, Bradford, along with George Keith and Thomas Budd, was arrested for printing *An Appeal from the Twenty-Eight Judges to the Spirit of Truth,* a pamphlet which argued that Quaker ministers should not be magistrates and accused them of monopolizing power. Keith and Budd document the plight of the political writer in early Pennsylvania in their *New England's Spirit of Persecution Transmitted to Pennsylvania* (1693); after having been convicted by a court of six (out of eight) of the magistrates attacked in the pamphlet, Keith and Budd were sentenced to humiliation in the marketplace.[1]

34   However, despite such repeated attempts at censorship on the part of

colonial governments, the explosion of a domestic printing trade, together with a growing commercial trade in imported European books, posed an insistent challenge to the expediency of a priori modes of political restraint. The expansion of the printing trade had already forced the English government to turn gradually to a posteri modes of regulating the press (allowing the 1662 Licensing Act to expire in 1679, then abolishing the act altogether in 1695), and the first two decades in the eighteenth century saw the shift to similar means in the colonies, namely in the form of seditious libel laws. These laws, in turn, were qualified, if not weakened, over the course of the eighteenth century as the "truth" of an accused libel, irrelevant or even an aggravation in early libel cases, was increasingly accepted as a defense by juries. This development has been well documented by historians like Leonard Levy, especially in relation to the conditions of the press in the years leading up to the famous 1735 Zenger trial, and it appears to have been largely coextensive with the rebirth in popularity of radical Whig ideology which found expression in the colonies through reprints of Trenchard and Gordon's enormously popular *Cato's Letters* (c. 1720).[2] *Cato's Letters* was quoted in nearly every colonial newspaper and magazine by the time of the Revolution, and one historian has gone so far as to assert that "no one can spend any time in the newspapers, library inventories, and pamphlets in colonial America without realizing that *Cato's Letters* rather than Locke's *Civil Government* was the most popular, quotable, esteemed source of political ideas in the colonial period."[3]

But the rise of a press that was free from prior restraint did not develop evenly in eighteenth-century America nor, I would argue, did it precipitate out in concrete terms the idealized sphere of unhindered public criticism which was championed by Trenchard and Gordon's Cato. James and Benjamin Franklin's embattled efforts to create a colonial analog to such neo-Harringtonian organs as Trenchard and Gordon's *Independent Whig* suggest that an increasingly "free" press was still subject to arbitrary persecution in Boston in the first decades of the eighteenth century. Infuriated by the *New England Courant,* Increase Mather asserted in Philip Musgrave's rival newspaper, the conservative *Boston Gazette,* that he could "remember when the Civil Government could have taken an effectual course to suppress such a Cursed Libel." But even this statement belies the precariousness of the *New England Courant* in the 1720s. After all, Mather's comments came only twenty-five years after Maule was tried for *Truth Held Forth;* twenty years after Mather himself reportedly had Robert Calef's *More Wonders of the Invisible World* burned in Harvard yard; seventeen years after two irreligious and scandalous pamphlets were ordered to be burned in the street by the General Court; ten years after John Green was fined and put under bonds for publishing "a most prophane, filthy, and obscene discourse" and the book burned by the hangman; seven years after Bartholomew Green, James Cummins, Thomas Fleet, Nicholas Boone, and John Allen were examined to discover the author of *The Case of His Excellency the Governor and Council* and Samuel Tyley condemned as the author and copies of the book burned; six years after the General Council prohibited William Drummer from publishing an article on Massachusetts politics that was printed in the *London Flying Post* and reaffirmed its power to suppress any printed matter that displeased it; three years after Anglican John Checkley was prevented from publishing a tract critical of Calvinist doctrines; and one year after Governor Samuel Shute, disturbed by the growing licentiousness of the press, attempted to get from the General Council an endorsement of his instructions from England that no printing matter could be published without his license. Even putting aside emergency actions such as the General Council's May 13, 1725, order that "printers of the news papers of Boston be ordered upon their peril not to insert in their Prints anything of the Publick affairs of this Province relating to War," as late as 1751 Lieutenant-Governor Spencer Phips could still issue a proclamation ordering the arrest, with a reward of £10, for Robert Howland and Fobes Little for being the suspected authors of *A Sad and Deplorable Lamentation,* a text critical of the Massachusetts legislature.

Perhaps the greatest irony of early American libertarianism is that as the function of state censorship was transferred to the juridical realm of seditious libel, it was the acclaimed bastion of the people's liberties, the popularly elected colonial assembly, which replaced the General Court as the most suppressive body with respect to political dissent. One historian notes that in the early decades of the eighteenth century, "literally scores of persons, probably hundreds, throughout the colonies were tracked down . . . and brought to the house to make inglorious submission for words spoken in the heat of anger or for writing which intentionally or otherwise had given offense."[4] And Leonard Levy argues that had "Zenger attacked the New York General Assembly instead of a despised royal governor, he would have been summarily convicted. . .jailed, and in all likelihood, forgotten by posterity. Instead he was tried by a jury and acquitted because he symbolized a popular cause."[5]

Freedom of the press was increasingly seen as the freedom to participate in the popular dissatisfaction over the Crown's administration of the colonies, not the freedom to critique popular government, an institution that was increasingly seen as "of the people" and therefore by definition already the embodiment of the "common good." This was especially the case in the years just prior to and during the Revolution. Levy argues in this context that "no cause was more honored by rhetorical declamation and dishonored in practice than that of freedom of expression during the revolutionary period," reiterating Arthur Schlesinger's claim that in Revolutionary America "liberty of speech belonged to those who spoke the speech of liberty."[6]

Thus, aside from the concrete juridical restraints imposed by the doctrine of seditious libel—effective to a varying degree well into the years of the early Republic—public writers were forced to confront the less tangible philosophical obstacles imposed by the intimations of popular sovereignty.[7] In leveling dissent against a popular rather than an authoritative government, a writer could no longer rely on a classical conception of a government of the "one, the few, and the many" that justified—indeed required—the participatory civic conscience, the free citizen, to monitor the virtue of the state. This was because, it could be construed theoretically, the concept of popular sovereignty mystified both the idea of an external state capable of receiving criticism, and a differentiated civic conscience which could legitimately embody such discourse. This was especially true in the politically charged climate in the years leading up to the American Revolution, when colonial political leaders sought to consolidate antipathy toward English rule by conflating the assemblies with "the people," diminishing the distinction between colonial assemblies and colonial citizens.

In this respect, while the middle decades of the eighteenth century saw the flowering of neoclassical and civic-humanist rhetoric in America, namely through the immense popularity of *Cato's Letters,* such rhetoric was often deployed palimpsestically. In appropriating Trenchard and Gordon's emphasis on the importance of a free press for facilitating the examination of public officials by independent citizens, in neoclassical and Christian humanist thinking the necessary precondition for a moral and just state, colonial officials increasingly equated popular assemblies with an oppressed "people" in their efforts to cast the British authorities as the corrupted trustees of a despotic government. And, in doing so, they began to redraw the boundaries of the classical model of government. By the time of the Revolution, pamphleteers were casting the American public as a virtuous but embattled "citizen," and British officials the corrupted representatives of a fallen state.[8] This, of course, was to have profound consequences after Independence, once the authority of the English state was gone, and American leaders continued to assert the coextension of the people and popular government. In doing so, they not only continued to define themselves, tenuously, as the extrapolation of the people ("We the People") and in a negative relation to government; they continued to simplify the differences between the static collective interests of the people and dynamic moral goals of the state. American political thinking thus inherited a revolutionary bowdlerization of classical republicanism. And from the Revolution onward, America was to be a citizen without a state.

In this light, the transatlantic political development of contested colonial sovereignty, embedded in the socioeconomic conditions which were to mobilize the colonies toward independence, confronted dissenting writers with new constraints that were to hint at the conditions of modern authorship in America: namely the redefinition of public good into public interest, as expressed by public opinion; and the rise of political thinking which saw the ideal government as the embodiment of the aggregate of such interest. This later development, following upon political currents in Europe, was a radical revision of traditional conceptions of statecraft, and it offers a tentative explanation of how free public commentary could become honorable—even desirable—by the end of the eighteenth century after having been condemned as seditious, blasphemous, and libelous for centuries.[9] Albert O. Hirschman has discussed how a new theory of the state, born in the Renaissance and propounded by precursors to Adam Smith like Machiavelli, Spinoza, and Vico, attempted to replace the most obvious solutions to the age-old threat of the unpredictable passions of individuals (what Vico enumerated as ferocity, avarice, and ambition)—those of repression, coercion, and censorship. This new theory sought to harness such passions instead of repressing them, first by making them visible, then by opposing them as countervailing forces which could be directed toward the public good. This entailed making a clean break from "utopian" conceptions of a virtuous social order, what Machiavelli characterized as "imaginary republics and monarchies that have never been seen nor have been known to exist," and instead constructing a government based on the "effective truth of things." In this way of thinking, "interest" evolved as the new paradigm for politics, accompanied by the maxim that "interest will not lie." This was because, the thinking went, when individuals pursued their own interests, their actions became transparent and predictable, "almost as though [they] were wholly virtuous person[s]."[10]

The state in this context, as James Madison was to formulate famously in *Federalist 10*, was merely an administrative mechanism which controlled the effects of such aggregated interests, expressed in the political realm by competing factions. While Madison doubted that "enlightened statesmen [would] be able to adjust these clashing interests, and render them all subservient to the public good," he had enormous faith that the effects of faction could be effectively managed by a federal Constitution which directed "the great and aggregate interests . . . to the national" and the "local and particular [interests] to the

State legislatures."This was also the thinking behind *Federalist* 51, where Madison insisted on divided branches of government so that, structurally, "ambition must be made to counteract ambition."

The ideal of an individual civic "conscience" in this context, while increasingly free from a priori, then a posteri, restraint, found itself, by the end of the eighteenth century, philosophically speaking, without a government to criticize, since the American state was, seemingly by definition, the individual, rights-bounded citizen writ large—an institutional reflection of the American people.[11] In this light, it should come as no surprise that public commentary, far from being considered dangerous to the state, was increasingly figured as constitutive of it, particularly in such formulations as the *res publica*. This transformation bespoke of a fundamental cultural redefinition of the freedom to write publicly. Whereas in the classical tradition, civic authorship was seen as the liberty of the "free" citizen (white male property holder unfettered by economic dependence) to monitor the virtue of the trustees of the state, it was by the end of the eighteenth century defined as the freedom for individuals to give public expression to their opinions and interests, the sum total of which was thought to constitute the public realm. No longer considered an agent of social repression, the state was increasingly figured as the structure of an open theater, in which most individuals (usually still white male property holders but not just citizens or saints) were free to express their opinions and interests, and where a majority, expressed through popular opinion and determined by popular elections, carried the day.

This was, of course, theoretically speaking, since in its day-to-day functioning the state was not an extrapolation of an ideal public domain but a very real physical assembly of administrative institutions and officials. While libertarian rhetoric and the specter of a *res publica* construed the state as responsible to an open political arena governed by popular sovereignty, such idealizations masked the degree to which the American public was also becoming a passive *audience* to the staged and publicized performances of the denizens of that political theater. That is, at the very same time that individual citizens seemed to enjoy a new and remarkable freedom to participate in public life, public life was made more and more distant, refracted through the lens of popular sentiment, projected by an impersonal print sphere, and presented as the immutable workings of the public will. This was probably the case in early to mid-eighteenth-century America, where the access to the increasingly impersonal affairs of state was mediated by a few colonial presses, most of which still relied almost exclusively on government printing contracts and patronage for their survival.[12] And it was almost certainly the case once the colonial presses were capitalized by business interests, becoming, by the turn of the century, venerable institutions which tended to reflect such interests. Thus, we might go so far as to say that while the freedom of the press arrived in America under the anti-Court banner of the Fourth Estate, the victory it secured was not, by and large, for the freedom of the idealized independent civic conscience of classical political thinking; rather, it was a triumph for the freedom of the partisan press, what was to be the ascendant mouthpiece for modern factional politics.

Nowhere in eighteenth-century politics is the discrepancy between the vigorous rhetoric of libertarianism and the erosion of a viable civic print sphere more clearly and paradoxically seen than in the famous 1735 acquittal of printer John Peter Zenger for seditious libel. The Zenger case was enormously popular in both eighteenth- and nineteenth-century America as a rhetorical touchstone for colonial independence. During the trial, reports were reprinted in Zenger's newspaper, the *New York Weekly World;* and James Alexander's account of the case, *A Brief Narrative of the Case and Trial of John Peter Zenger,* first published in 1736, was reprinted fifteen times in the eighteenth century, making it what one book historian has called "the most famous publication issued in America before the *Farmer's Letters.*"[13] It was republished in London in 1752 to bolster the defense of the seditious libel case of William Owen and in 1765 during discussions of the case of John Wilkes, again in New York in 1770 during the failed attempt to convict Alexander McDougall of seditious libel, and it was reissued in Boston in 1799 in response to the Sedition Act. For nineteenth-century historians like James Grahame and George Bancroft, the trial epitomized the "notable struggle between [the colonists'] arbitrary ruler and their persecuted fellow citizen."[14]

The story of Zenger's imprisonment as it unfolded in the press must have been a story very familiar to those schooled in the oppositional ideology of the radical Whigs. The case was occasioned by the arrival in 1732 of William Cosby, who was to assume the role of governor of New York after his predecessor died and left the executive powers of the colony in the hands of Rip Van Dam, a New York merchant. A displaced bureaucrat who was determined to use his position to accumulate personal fortune, Cosby was immediately perceived by his constituency as "quick-tempered, haughty, unlettered, jealous, and above all greedy," especially when he began selling provincial offices to fatten his purse.[15] His efforts were quickly brought to a crisis point when he attempted to exact from Van Dam a traditional largess. Aware that he could not bring a common law suit for retrieving his honorarium in the Supreme Court of New York, where he would have to submit his claims to an already alienated jury of New Yorkers, Cosby attempted to enact an ordinance which would convene a more insulated—and hence more favorably disposed—Court of Exchequer. When the petition for the ordinance came up before the Supreme Court, however, Chief Justice Lewis Morris delivered a long opinion attacking the legality and propriety of such a court, going so far as to publish his sentiments. An enraged Cosby dismissed Morris from the court, provoking one of the wealthiest inhabitants and probably the foremost politician in New York.

As the historian Stanley Katz points out, while Lewis Morris was an extremely unlikely candidate to have led a popular political party—both an aristocrat and, as described by a contemporary, not by temper "fitted to gain popularity"—he was apparently able to capitalize on the widespread dissatisfaction with Cosby, molding a strong opposition party which advertised the missteps of the "tyrannical" governor while boasting of its attachment to George II, the House of Hanover, and the "Glorious Revolution." To strengthen the self-conscious association of the Morrisites between their cause and English opposition politics, they launched their own newspaper, the *New York Weekly Journal,* and hired John Peter Zenger as editor to stir up popular support. This proved to be essential, because New York's sole newspaper, William Bradford's *New York Gazette,* was "a paper known to be under the direction of the government, in which the Printer of it is not suffered to insert anything but what his superiors approve of."[16] Once in operation, Zenger's newspaper reprinted the essays of Trenchard and Gordon and other radical Whigs, published pseudonymous letters attacking the colonial government and its administration, and even printed sham advertisements which attacked the Cosbyites in more scandalous terms.

William Bradford (ironically, the same figure who had printed Thomas Maule's *Truth Held Forth* and the same printer who had been persecuted for his oppositional presswork in Pennsylvania) attempted to counter Zenger's use of radical essayists like Trenchard and Gordon with some of the popular English defenses of established order, even taking up a spirited defense of the virtues of the law of seditious libel. But such sentiments apparently did not sit well with a local reading public already generally suspicious of transplanted Royalist functionaries and specifically unhappy with the Cosby that was characterized in the *New York Weekly Journal.* As Katz points out, "[T]he leaders of the New York opposition found the slogans of free speech to their taste and interest," and they continued in their narrow political contest to characterize their attempt to regain political power as the right of the virtuous citizen to reform a corrupted constitutional monarchy.[17] A manifesto on the freedom of the press printed in numbers 2 and 3 of the *New York Weekly Journal* makes the rhetorical power of these sentiments clear. The essay argued typically that if such an overgrown criminal, or an impudent monster in iniquity, cannot be come at by ordinary justice, let him yet receive the lash of satire, let the glaring truths of his ill administration, if possible, awaken his conscience, and if he has no conscience, rouse his fear, by showing him his deserts, sting him with shame, and render his actions odious to all honest minds.

For nearly two months, the *New York Weekly Journal* argued in like terms at the same time that it attacked Cosby, both seeking to popularize the theory of the press as the safeguard of English and colonial liberties, and attempting to liberalize the more technical understanding of the law of seditious libel by asserting that truth was a legitimate defense against criminal expression. A reprint of Cato's famous letter on libeling was typical in this respect, asserting that "the exposing . . . of public wickedness, as it is a duty which every man owes to truth and his country, can never be a libel in the nature of things."[18]

The altercation came to a head in 1734 when Cosby succeeded in getting the Council to find several issues of the *Journal* seditious, subsequently ordering the newspapers burned and Zenger imprisoned. While Zenger's arrest threatened the most effective political tool of the Morrisites, it also played into the scenario over the threat to personal liberties that they had been capitalizing on in their effort to mobilize popular support against Cosby. When bail was set for Zenger by Cosby's new chief justice, James De Lancey, the members of the wealthy Morris faction refused to see Zenger released, apparently realizing that he was worth far more in prison than at his press. Thus, the stage was set for the Morrisites. The trial of John Peter Zenger, the culmination of a very local battle between two powerful New York political factions, was to be tried in the public's eye as the case of a virtuous local printer's plight for personal liberty against a repressive Royalist governor. That is, a narrow factional contest was to be elevated, in a propagandistic newspaper battle, to a more abstract debate that pitted the right of the disinterested civic conscience to monitor the virtue of the public's leaders against the partisan authority of the Crown.

The Zenger trial itself was something of a farce. When Zenger's first two lawyers, James Alexander and William Smith, attempted to turn the trial into an impeachment of the Cosby administration, De Lancey disbarred them, and he appointed attorney John Chambers, a governor's man, to represent the printer. Having moved for a struck jury, even Chambers could recognize that the list of potential jurors submitted by the clerk included former magistrates and tradesmen in the governor's employ. The Morrisites managed to get a new jury struck, and they replaced Chambers with Andrew Hamilton, then reputed to be the best lawyer in the colonies, and who himself had been engaged in the opposition to the proprietary governor of Pennsylvania. The law of

1735 was squarely against Hamilton. Legal precedent not only stipulated that the truth or falsity of a statement was irrelevant in a libel case, but also that the question of whether or not a statement was libelous was to be determined solely by the magistrates; the jury's role was simply one of determining whether or not Zenger published the statements. Hamilton, however, addressed the jurors directly, and he argued, on political rather than legal grounds, that the court's law was outmoded. Citizen's had a right to criticize their rulers, he maintained, because freedom of expression would prevent corruption "by making a governor sensible that it is in his interest to be just to those under his care." It was the social responsibility—indeed, the "natural right"—of each citizen to guard against the misuse of authority. This was particularly important in the colonies, he concluded, because representatives of the Crown, by their disproportionate power over courts and local assemblies, could not be held responsible for misdeeds. Hamilton's argument persuaded the colonists, and it took only minutes for the jury to return a verdict of not guilty.

Despite his deployment of the oppositional ideology of the radical Whigs, Hamilton's defense was by no means an attempt at legal reform, nor, according to most legal historians, was the case ultimately successful in securing the rights of individuals to criticize their government.[19] Rather, Hamilton's argument was a masterful articulation of the problem of divided sovereignty, and it was clearly a victory for the successful mobilization of public opinion on the part of the Morrisites. Stanley Katz concludes that

> the force of Hamilton's argument for free speech rested upon his sense of the difference between government in England and in America . . . American sovereignty appeared to reside in the people, especially as their assemblies came to dominate colonial government. The absenteeism of the king and his imperial administrators combined with the colonial experience of self- government, therefore, to produce an American sense of popular government . . . Hamilton, like the Morris party, sensed this popular spirit and mobilized it in defense of Zenger. Although his argument in the case . . . [and] his citations in support of truth as a defense are altogether unconvincing, and neither history nor law justified his glorification of the jury's role in libel cases. But the rhetoric . . . [of] free speech was designed to appeal to the twelve plain jurymen, and to accord with their experience of government. The law was against him, but the law was out of step with public opinion, and he saw to it that Zenger was tried by the public rather than by the law.[20]

Thus, while the Zenger case did little to liberate the independent civic conscience from retribution by the state, it was probably first in a number of other respects. It was almost certainly the first partisan oppositional newspaper in the colonies, and the first founded solely to amplify the politics of a single faction. And it was probably the first in America to stage a partisan political contest in the polemical terms of radical libertarianism. The case did not set a legal precedent, and in a short time it became clear that the "Morrisite party represented neither 'freedom' nor 'the popular cause.'" A few years after the trial, Cosby was dead, Morris was the speaker of the assembly, and a "liberated" Zenger—already a colonial symbol of the individual's right to criticize his government—became the assembly's establishment printer. Most historians now agree with Stanley Katz that Zenger and his associates were "neither political democrats nor radical legal reformers. They were, in fact, a somewhat narrow-minded political faction seeking immediate political gain rather than long-term governmental or legal reform."[21]

The Zenger case powerfully demonstrates how a fragile civic print sphere, despite—perhaps even because of—the pervasive rhetoric of libertarianism, may have been on its way to becoming more a national fantasy than an actuality by the middle of the eighteenth century. The final victory for unrestrained political expression through a free press, to be given formal and prominent expression in the provisions of the First Amendment, masked the degree to which the freedom of the press was becoming an issue of the freedom of political faction or interest rather than the freedom of a disinterested civic conscience to participate in the public realm. As colonial presses were increasingly privatized, and as they began to represent powerful political and economic interests, the idealized civic conscience of classical republicanism and Christian humanism was left to access the public sphere by way of an increasingly complicated printing trade, one which substituted the obstacles of state censorship with the vicissitudes of factional politics and, by the end of the eighteenth century, the contingencies of literary economics. At the same time, as a citizenry educated on the pre-Revolutionary tenets of popular sovereignty began to imagine and experience government, in abstract terms, as the collective will of the people—as expressed through what Benedict Anderson has called the "imagined community" of print-capitalism—they found themselves without the sense of a concrete government on which to level criticism.[22] And in this sense, they were circumscribed by the very same "free press" which promised to liberate them. The Zenger case, publicly a contest over access to a supervisory public sphere, privately an internal battle between competing political factions, suggests how an American public was becoming the audience to a fictional transformation of the public sphere, one in which civic authors were left celebrating what they increasingly intuited was a hollow victory to participate in public affairs.

THREE

Benjamin Franklin's Autobiography *and* Republican Print Rationality

If the Zenger trial was to become the cause célèbre for libertarians of the nineteenth century, Benjamin Franklin was to be canonized as the representative writer for whom this victory was secured. Widely considered to be the "founding father" of modern print culture in America, one would be hardpressed to find another writer of the eighteenth century who articulated the rational virtues of an objectifying commercial print culture with more enthusiasm or clarity.

But there is a peculiar moment in the *Autobiography* where Franklin, after attributing the efficacy of George Whitefield's itinerant preaching to the fact that practice through repetition had allowed him an advantage over local ministers "who are stationary," asserts that the decline of Whitefield's reputation after his death was the result of his writing. He notes that while "unguarded expressions and even erroneous opinions del[ivere]d in preaching might have been afterwards explain'd . . . qualify'd . . . or they might have been deny'd," *litera scripta manet* [the written letter remains]. I am of the opinion, if he had never written any thing he would have left behind him a much more numerous and important sect. And his reputation might in that case have been still growing, even after his death."[1] This is an unusual moment in the *Autobiography,* indeed in the canon of Franklin's writing, since it comes from the very same individual who asserts so emphatically that "prose writing has been of great use to me in the course of my life . . . a principal means of my advancement," whose written life is ostensibly offered to posterity for imitation, and whose biography might be read as a chronicle of the way in which individual expression by, 45 through, and within texts consistently obtains both tangible and intangible (in the sense of, say, reputation) social currencies (60).

In some sense, Franklin's assessment of Whitefield's writing is a conclusion predicated by Franklin's own theories of communication and cognition, theories that fashioned orality and printedness as poles at the extremes of intersubjective discourse. The interpersonal relationships of orality were, in Franklin's epistemological worldview, relationships of dominance and submission, whether the acceptance of the terms of these relationships engendered such benign effects as Franklin's compulsion to surrender the contents of his pockets to Whitefield's collector's dish, or whether they served to bind individuals to deleterious personalities or irrational cultural institutions, such as to Josiah, or James, or the church. In contrast, the intersubjective commerce of printedness, according to Franklin's various formulations, constituted relationships of exchange, the "public" medium of print being a free and open space in which the ideals of truth and value could be established by a mechanism of "free" intercourse regulated only in terms of the "style" in which self-interested communicators conducted themselves. As Franklin suggested in his "Apology for Printers," when all writers had the advantage of being heard by the public through publication in the public realm, and "when truth and error have fair play, the former is always an overmatch for the latter."[2]

Within the logic of this communicative model, it is easy to see why Whitefield's authorship failed him. Whitefield's commitment in writing was also a commitment to the "visible marketplace" of the print medium where the impermanent and subjective idiosyncrasies of the individual—such as personality, skills, and authority—were evacuated and replaced by the object of public discourse, the text. Separated from both the medium and the message, Whitefield lost even the *potential* to assert a physical presence—his professional trademark, so to speak—which might continue to compel public assent. Yet his writings, finite and determinate, continued to circulate according to their own logic in the public print sphere, open to the devaluating effects of exchange with a potentially infinite number of critiques. Through publication, we might say, Whitefield allowed his characteristically oral discourse to enter into a controlled, contestatory exchange relationship with his critics, much in the same way that laissez-faire producers came to allow their commodities to be exchanged on the open market under the preconditions of a juridical system of justice. The net result, as Franklin notes arithmetically, was the "appearance of reason" which decreased "the number of his votaries, and prevent[ed] their encrease" (180).

In short, Franklin's textual economy, what I will argue here was a synecdoche for what precursors to Adam Smith called *le doux commerce* and a parallel to Franklin's own physiocratic theories of what Quesnay called "the physiology of the social order," precipitated out a negative value for Whitefield's religious doctrines, carrying with it the value of Whitefield's ministerial reputation.[3] Yet herein lie what I hope to argue is the fundamental paradox of the *Autobiography,* a paradox Franklin himself alludes to in the paragraph immediately following his critique of Whitefield when he asserts that, in contrast to Whitefield's reputation, "my business was now continually augmenting . . . I experienc'd too the truth of the observation that *after getting the first hundred pound, it is easier to get the second:* money itself being of prolific nature": namely if the objectification of the self through writing served as the principle means of Franklin's advancement and, like capital, augmented its value independently of the individual, that same objectified self was, as in the case of Whitefield's writings, equally subject to subsequent devaluation (180).[4] While in Whitefield's case Franklin suggests that such a downward correction was important in establishing the "actual" underlying social value of the preacher's religious doctrines, the instability of Whitefield's reputation also pointed to a larger and more abstract problem concerning authorial control: when individual writers like Whitefield surrendered their productions to the public print sphere, they could no longer maintain authorial sovereignty over their successes or failures. Instead of merely representing in typography the product of the individual writer's intellectual labor, printed works seemed capable of taking on a life of their own, coming instead, as in the case of Whitefield, to represent their evacuated authors.

This was a philosophical problem Franklin took up in a slightly different context in *The Way to Wealth*, where Poor Richard's best-selling maxims, recited by the far less engaging Father Abraham, are ignored by his auditors. In this case, however, the relationship is something of the obverse: the Father Abraham story reveals how an intractable traditional culture could continue to threaten Franklin's ideal of a purely "rational" print realm by merely appropriating and embodying such objectified discourse. Poor Richard's popular maxims become meaningless to their audience in *The Way to Wealth,* not because their content has been altered but because they have been devaluated in their appropriation by a sententious Abraham. If the case of Whitefield exposed the instability of the author, the case of Father Abraham demonstrated the precariousness of this subsequent disembodied text.

Both the instance of writing evacuated of its authorial presence (Whitefield) and that of objectified writing embodied by an imposturing authorial presence (Father Abraham) serve as important qualifications to Franklin's more characteristic enthusiasm for the virtues of republican print culture. Michael Warner has recently explored Franklin's idealization of print in an effort to locate him within what he calls the emerging rationalist discourse of "republican print ideology," a discourse grounded in the assumption that "print—not speech—[was] the ideal and idealized guardian of civic liberty . . . [because it represented] a public vision from a nonparticular perspective." He suggests that Franklin worked systematically in his writings to repudiate "*personal* authority in favor of a general authority based in a negative relation to one's own person," to evacuate the bodily and hence corruptible writing subject from his or her textual productions, so that reason and virtue might shine forth. Warner goes on to tie Franklin's individual project to the more general emergence of a bourgeois public sphere in colonial America, arguing that Franklin provides some of the philosophical assumptions that allowed the emergence of a "supervising agency" of an "abstract public," or what Fielding coined as the Fourth Estate, similar to the one Jürgen Habermas has observed in his study of eighteenth-century Europe.[5]

But Warner's account elides Franklin's anxieties about the objectifying tendencies of print culture as well as his fear of the political consequences of a print sphere evacuated of authors. Franklin's speculations on Whitefield and Father Abraham suggest a vague understanding of some of the consequences of aligning the activity of public writing with eighteenth-century theories of commerce. Moreover, they hint at Franklin's perception of the beginnings of a phenomenom Georg Lukács was, almost two centuries later, to term "reification": what Lukács defined as perhaps the "central structural problem" of the modern age, whereby social phenomena "take on the appearance of things" and where people's productive activity "appears as something strange and alien to them." Lukács posited two consequences of reification: on the one hand, it obscured people's productive activity and made what they produced appear as though it were a given, an "external and objective reality operating according to its own immutable laws"; on the other, it estranged or alienated human activity by mystifying its participation in the forces of history, making people passive and contemplative in the face of that objectified and rationalized reality.[6]

I want to argue here that Franklin not only comes upon this problem in his discussions of authorship and writing, but that this discovery also leads him to question—albeit rhetorically—some of the basic tenets of the Enlightenment. Specifically, Franklin interrogates the recession of the individual subject as the result of an increasingly rationalized social realm, and the corresponding rise of the fiercely individualistic public personality who, born a *tabula rasa,* boldly and paradoxically wrote the self into and out of existence within this world. This paradoxical relationship holds, I will suggest, because in a world governed by discoverable laws, the individual subject becomes as much a *product* of ascertainable mechanisms (say, e.g., Hobbes's laws of pleasure and pain or Smith's laws of supply and demand) as he or she, as a historical actor, produces them (say, in Franklin's case, by writing). We might even think of this as the central opposition in the *Autobiography,* since Franklin's narrative is simultaneously the principal means by which Franklin writes his historical self into existence, hence the *Autobiography,* and at the same time it is a means by which he evacuates evidence of his historical contingency, replacing his idiosyncratic life with both a rational methodology—his maxims, habits, and virtues—and a notion of representativeness.

To set out this claim, the first section of this chapter outlines both a thematic and a historical argument. It maintains that the plot of the *Autobiography*—beginning in an early eighteenth-century cultural setting with few books and an extremely effective state apparatus for controlling the production and circulation of print—*reflects* a transformation in the conditions of public writing. The *Autobiography* opens by detailing a residual understanding of public writing as an effective means for individuals to participate in familial and civic affairs. This gives way by the end of the narrative to a new, dominant ideology which, while championing participatory authorship, increasingly figures writers and texts as objective aspects of cultural production. I argue that it is this final state of affairs which occasions Franklin's apprehension of a cultural phenomenon later theorists were to term "reification."[7]

The second part of this chapter will discuss the objectification of words, texts, and, ultimately, writers, claiming that the *Autobiography,* based on emerging eighteenth-century economic theories, can be read as a theoretical exposition of an understanding of human behavior based on idealizations of the market. Within this model, the circulation of printed texts mirrored that of money; both were figured as rationalized vehicles for bearing the social currency of individuals. Questioning the progressive ideology of the rise of a "free press," this section suggests that the widespread glorification of print discourse in the second half of the eighteenth century (a valorization in which Franklin played an indispensable role), and what recent critics have called in different formulations "republican print ideology," served as a synecdoche for nascent theories of a rational, self-regulating economy, a synecdoche (couched in the ethical rhetoric for a "free press") which helped to generate the social assent necessary for the turn to a market culture.[8] In doing so, this argument attempts to qualify recent technodeterministic theories, based loosely on Habermas's theoretical work, that the proliferation of print in colonial America opened up a so-called public sphere which, in turn, revolutionized relationships between individuals and the state.[9]

The third section, finally, suggests, by anecdote, some of the sociological consequences for readers posed by the rise of "republican print ideology," and enumerates the problems this ideology posed for the practice of authorship and the social function of texts in the early Republic.

■   ■   ■

Recent critics have noted several general thematic movements in the plot of Franklin's *Autobiography* which suggest that the text interpolates the abstract relationships of capitalism and modern selfhood. Mitchell Breitweiser, for example, notes that Franklin "participates in the widespread rethinking of filial relations," that his project works for "the denial of impulse in the interest of a detached calculation and fidelity to distant ends," and that "Franklin's own self-definition in the *Autobiography* is resolutely negative and contrastive, a repeated evocation of "roads not taken."[10] Michael Gilmore also suggests that Franklin turns to a series of "cautionary doubles" to construct a conception of the self through negation, while Myra Jehlen asserts that the *Autobiography* recounts "the birth of modern selfhood, recapitulating . . . the ontogeny that transformed feudal continuities between individual and society into free-market dialectics."[11] Other twentieth-century critics have, predictably, emphasized Franklin's theories of individuality, acquisition, and calculating rationality, positioning him—as Perry Miller, David Levin, and Robert Sayre all have—as a protocapitalistic counterbalance to the metaphysical spiritualism of figures such as Cotton Mather and Jonathan Edwards.[12] In the nomenclature of New England Puritan studies, Franklin is usually cast as the grimy figure for whom the doctrine of "works" finally and irrevocably superseded "grace," marking what Perry Miller called the "divided heritage of puritanism": that theological breach which finally sundered the tenuous social construction of visible sainthood and paved the way to a market culture.

Max Weber established this line of investigation in his famous critique of Franklin's utilitarian ethic, claiming that the organizing principle of acquisition, once merely the means to basic material and metaphysical ends, became an end in itself in Franklin. Weber based his analysis on what he termed a sudden reversal of a "natural relationship" between man and the material world he found present in Franklin's text.[13] For Weber (and a clear majority of critics in the seemingly inexhaustible body of criticism on Franklin), the idea of a premodern "natural economy" in which there was an intimate relationship between producers and products was a compelling antithesis to the emergence of what D. H. Lawrence called sarcastically Franklin's "barbed wire enclosure of freedom," a sinister version of the sociological phenomenon C. B. MacPherson termed somewhat more optimistically "possessive individualism."[14] This dialectic between a residual "natural economy" of subsistence and an emergent "money economy" of acquisition continues to inform much of the work on Franklin which sees the *Autobiography* as either anticipating, generating, reflecting, or mediating these two epochal poles.

I too want to suggest that the *Autobiography* represents in some sense a historical analysis of residual and emergent modes of social organization in colonial America. In contrast, however, I want to assert that Franklin figures these historical abstractions in terms of certain sets of relationships between writers, readers, and texts. There are several compelling reasons why Franklin should have chosen to do so. First and foremost, there seems to be a conceptual link between Franklin's calculating rationality and his "project of supplanting speech and immediacy with writing and generality."[15] As I will argue below, there is a wide register of parallels and simultaneities between Franklin's understanding of money and commerce and his philosophy of print and textual circulation. In addition, as Mitchell Breitweiser has noted, Franklin the writer was "thoroughly involved with money personally (in his business), technically (in his printing of currency), and theoretically (in his speculations on the nature of money)."[16] Finally, as Franklin tended to view colonial economics in terms of the activities that brought him his success, it should come as no surprise that he consequently considered the medium of exchange in terms of print, abstract labor in terms of writing and printing, the market in terms of readers, and commodities in terms of texts. Conversely, Franklin's self-conscious decision to enter into an emerging printing trade carried him into what was arguably the earliest domestic capitalistic industry in America. After all, the printing trade was the first capitalized business to subscribe to the modern industrial practices of utilizing interchangeable parts (types), establishing standardization (typography), employing a division of labor according to tasks, and applying the principles of mass production and distribution from a central geographical location.[17]

We might say that the "natural economy" in Franklin's formulation was based on a state of affairs in which a complete liberation of the subject could not be obtained, because intimate—as opposed to rational—relationships bound individuals to other individuals, families, or institutions. These intimate relationships, usually established and maintained by oral communication, were predicated on a hierarchical system of domination and submission, either benign, as in the case of the subject submitting to the good of the whole, or tyrannical, as in the instance of an individual's unwarranted consent to an irrational or destructive social authority. The distinguishing feature of such intimate relationships, as characterized by Franklin, was a complete dependence on the "personalities" of the individuals involved.[18]

Ostensibly, the *Autobiography* underwrites intimate as opposed to rational relationships, since Franklin's initial self-professed intention is to provide a kind of oral "recollection" of his life for the instruction of posterity. The opening rhetorical gambit in the *Autobiography,* after all, is the intimate gesture to the possibility of intergenerational continuity. Composing Part One for his illegitimate son William, Franklin hoped that the circumstances of his life would be "fit to be imitated" by his offspring, and that his son William would submit to the textualized figure of his father (43). The activity of writing in this residual formation thus was characterized by its particularized and localized utility. It functioned conservatively as an alternative for—or even an extension of— the intergenerational transmission of familial and cultural scripts.

Of course, in Franklin's case, the effective transmission of such instruction was obstructed by the real-world particularities of his relationship with his son William, singularities we might see as manifestations of what Jay Fleigelman has summarized as emerging characteristics of familial relationships in the years prior to the American Revolution: namely "the growth of a newly emergent class of property-less and mobile young men"; "the gradual replacement of land as the primary medium of value by more portable forms of capital"; and an increase in "premarital sex and a sharp rise in premarital [and also extramarital] conceptions."[19]

Given such widespread obstacles, it should come as no surprise to discover that the *Autobiography* was not unique in its public effort to supplant the paternal with the textual. Similar threats to familial contiguity, also posing difficulties for the maintenance and continuity of traditional family relationships in England, for instance, compelled popular dictionary maker Thomas Sheridan to recommend that parents write to their children upon their leaving the home. Such a document would consist of "an abridgement of the maxims and lessons of prudence and virtue . . . a brief view of the doctrines and precepts of Christianity . . . an abstract of the most forcible and convincing arguments for the truth of Christianity . . . [and] directions in case of fatal defection from virtue and religion." Realizing that such efforts were beyond most parents, James Burgh, an acquaintance of Franklin, subsequently published a similar anthology, entitled *Youth's Friendly Monitor or the Affectionate School Master* (1754), which contained a "farewell lecture to the young people on the entrance into a busy world" and which became popular in both England and

America. Billing itself as a substitute for domestic education, this collection played off of Michael and Adam in *Paradise Lost,* where, Fliegelman notes, "self-sufficient independence made possible by the right education replaces the circumscribed paradise of a well-ordered family."[20] Franklin's epistolary project was, at least in part, a similar means of fulfilling his parental responsibilities, obligations threatened by geographic distance of space—Franklin wrote from Twyneford, England—and the emotional distance of his son's illegitimacy, age, and politics—William was nearly forty years old in 1771 and the Royalist governor of New Jersey.

But if public writing was championed in early to mid-eighteenth-century guidebooks as an active means by which to continue to extend paternal authority within a culture increasingly in flux, it also was figured as an effective way for individuals to participate in ecclesiastical and civic affairs.[21] This, of course, did not develop evenly, as a long and rigorous tradition of censorship in colonial New England attests. The New England orthodoxy, at the same time it acknowledged its philosophical roots of underwriting continual social and political reform, worked to limit the activity of public writing to the function of the medieval *auctor,* a term which denoted "authority" and "respect" rather than agency and subjecthood. As Donald Pease suggests, traditional *auctors* derived their power from their ability to "sanction the moral and political authority of medieval culture" by providing the terms by which scribes could "organize otherwise accidental events into an established context capable of making them meaningful."[22] The *auctor's* task was to provide the principal terms through which exegetes could transpose everyday events of the world into a preexisting cosmology. Or, to put this more crudely, the *auctor,* far from a modern social or cultural agent, served as an instrument for the immanent workings of the divine, articulating rather than formulating or creating the rules and principles by which God ruled the kingdom of man. Franklin even alludes to the Puritan version of the medieval *auctor* who derived his authority from divine revelation when he notes that he can trace his family lineage in Cotton Mather's *Magnalia Christi Americana,* a text which sought through typology to organize the secular history of New England into the chiliastic prefigurations of the Bible. In this context, Franklin notes that his mother Abiah Folger's father, Peter Folger, is invoked by Mather's book as "a godly learned Englishman" (51).

Yet Franklin is quick to point out the political heritage in that Folger also "wrote sundry small Pieces," one of which, written in "the homespun Verse of that Time and People, and address'd to those then concern'd in the Government there . . . [argued] in favor of Liberty of Conscience, and in behalf of the

Baptists, Quakers, and other Sectaries, that had been under Persecution" (51–52). Franklin goes on to suggest that Folger attributes "the Indian Wars and other Distresses, that had befallen the Country to that Persecution, as so many judgments of God . . . [and that Folger exhorted] a Repeal of those uncharitable Laws" (52). Franklin concludes, "The Whole appear'd to me as written with a good deal of Decent plainness and manly Freedom. The six last concluding Lines I remember:

> because to be a Libeller (says he)
> I hate it with my Heart.
> From Sherburne Town where I now dwell,
> My Name I do put here,
> Without Offence, your real Friend,
> It is Peter Folgier. (52)

The "author" of this piece of civic and ecclesiastical criticism is, in striking contrast to Franklin's various dependent, feminized, and masked personae (Silence Dogood, Poor Richard, etc.), constituted not by Folger's anonymity but by his visibility, a visibility which in turn underwrites his "manliness" and freedom. As Franklin acknowledges, since Folger's "censures proceeded from *Goodwill* . . . therefore he would be known as the Author" (52). It is precisely because Folger writes with intentions of public good-spiritedness that he is eager to link his writing with his identity, going so far as to not only provide his given name and surname but to announce his location of residence. In fact, it is precisely this willingness to merge writing and writing subject Folger hopes will protect him from redress or retribution, say, for example, the clearly articulated fear of being charged for seditious libel.

Effective public writing as Franklin figures it through Folger—in contrast to both Puritan formulations of the *auctor* and enlightenment notions of an evacuated public print sphere—was an activity *invested* with personality; that is, it reflected the deliberative intentions of an independent subject, and it was directed outward toward an increasingly anonymous public for the promotion of the "public good." Of course, in his subsequent account of the imprisonment of his brother James for publishing a critique of the state's policy on piracy, Franklin suggests the problem of this identification of writing and writing subject. As I have already suggested, both the state and church in colonial New England played an unusually active role in regulating the print trade, suppressing questionable productions in print, and punishing writers and printers who threatened dominant ideologies and practices. The New England theocracy probably took an even more active role than Franklin intimates in his account.[23] Still, despite the ubiquitous rhetoric for a free press, the specter of censorship stalks Franklin's account of public writing in early America. Franklin notes how James is imprisoned for his publication of the *New England Courant,* first forbidden to print anything without prior approval, and eventually pressured into leaving Boston for Rhode Island; Franklin leaves Boston in part because he has made himself "obnoxious to the governing Party" and thinks "from the arbitrary Proceedings of the Assembly in [James's] Case" that he too might be persecuted; and when he first meets William Bradford, Franklin notes parenthetically that he "had been the first printer in Pensilvania, but remov'd from thence upon the Quarrel of [Governor] Geo. Keith" (71).

At first glance, such supervision by the state would seem antithetical to the efficacious extension of the thoughts of individual writers. Annabel Patterson has argued as much in her study of censorship and eighteenth-century English literature, suggesting that early English writers first turned to literary tropes and other "modern" techniques of authorial displacement in part as an effort to avoid the consequences of authorship imposed by the state.[24] Yet Franklin suggests that it is precisely this dialectic between authorial agency and regulating institutional authorities which guaranteed that writing *could* threaten— and thus alter for the better—existing states of social affairs.[25] In other words, it was the very threat of repression which gave writing its power. For instance, in perhaps the most memorable scene of reading in the *Autobiography,* Franklin turns to the collective memory of the persecution of Protestants in Europe to demonstrate the link between persecution and textual power, noting how his family successfully resisted English authorities who, under the edicts of Queen Mary, attempted to convert them from Protestantism:

> They had got an English Bible, and to conceal and secure it, it was fastened open with Tapes under and within the Frame of a joint stool. When my Great Great Grandfather read in it to his Family, he turn'd up the Joint Stool upon his knees, turning over the Leaves . . . One of the Children stood at the Door to give Notice if he saw the Apparitor coming, who was an Officer of the Spiritual Court. In that Case the Stool was turn'd down again upon its feet, when the Bible remain'd conceal'd under it as before. (50)

Such championing of Protestant piety over the watchful eye of the state would seem odd for a secular figure like Franklin. That is, unless we think of the Bible in Franklin's anecdote as a material text rather than a set of sacred religious beliefs. It is the Bible rather than the doctrines of Protestantism which emerges victorious in Franklin's account, a text which could threaten a conventional state of affairs by interpellating and maintaining a community of resistant readers.

This "connected" and "subjective" formulation of authorship is gradually supplanted in the *Autobiography* by Enlightenment formulations of print rationalism. Consequently, beginning with the anticipation of Franklin's departure from his family in Boston, printed material takes on a life of its own. At sixteen years of age, Franklin happens "to meet with a book" on dieting by Tyron (63). This odd personification is followed by others. When intent on improving his facility with language, Franklin arranges to be "met with an English Grammar" (64). And when he rescues a copy of Bunyan's *Pilgrim's Progress* from a drunken Dutchman who has fallen into the Kill van Kull in New York harbor, Franklin finds it "finely printed on good paper with copper Cuts, a dress better than I had ever seen it wear in its own language" (72).

But if young Franklin begins to conceive of books, even rhetorically, as objectified "persons" to be met and conversed with, he also makes it clear that they are at the same time commodities to be held either as a form of abstract currency, invested for the accumulation of various forms of capital, or exchanged for assorted goods or services. For instance, what ultimately gives Franklin the liberty to leave Boston for Philadelphia is his ability to sell "some of [his] books to raise a little money" (71). Nor is this "exchange value" limited to tangible currency. If the objectification of texts functions, even anecdotally, to offer up books as surrogates for interpersonal relationships, it also works to generate a form of social currency which facilitates real acquaintances. Again and again, the possession of books, either in terms of literal ownership or in readerly familiarity, provides Franklin with a kind of portable currency. For instance, it is when Dr. John Brown discovers that Franklin "had read a little" that he becomes "very sociable and friendly" (73–74). Similarly, it is only when Governor Burnet of New York learns that "a young man . . . [has] a great many books" that Franklin is invited to see the governor's library and to carry out "a good deal of conversation about books and authors" (85). Finally, it is an exchange of books which establishes the friendship between Franklin and a member of the opposition in the General Assembly of Pennsylvania. As Franklin notes:

> I did not . . . aim at gaining his favour by paying any servile respect to him, but after some time took this other method. Having heard that he had in his library a certain very scarce and curious book, I wrote a note to him expressing my desire of perusing that book, and requesting he

would do for me the favour of lending it to me for a few days. He sent it immediately; and I return'd it in about a week, with another note expressing strongly my sense of the favour. When we next met in the House he spoke to me (which he had never done before) and with great civility. And he ever after manifested a readiness to serve me on all occasions, so that we became great friends, and our friendship continu'd to his death. (172)

This scene alludes to the phenomenon theorists have described as "reification" with stunning clarity, since the relationship Franklin establishes with the assemblyman is predicated solely in the indirect terms of the exchange of goods. We might say that Franklin does not borrow the actual book but the "phantom" value it confers in its circulation.

The exchange of even such illusionary values in the interest of establishing interpersonal relationships is not limited to books alone. Writing also seems to carry with it abstract value. Readers will recall that Governor William Keith of Pennsylvania calls for Franklin only after he intercepts Franklin's letter to his brother-in-law and decides that Franklin was "a young man of promising parts, and therefore should be encouraged" (80). Notwithstanding the failure of Keith's "Letter of Credit" to set Franklin up with printing materials in England, it confers, indirectly, enough standing to introduce Ralph and Franklin to the "Gentlemen" on their vessel, this despite their having been "considered as ordinary persons" earlier (93). Other instances include the circulation of Franklin's pamphlet, *A Dissertation on Liberty and Necessity, Pleasure and Pain,* which brings him into an acquaintance with the English surgeon William Lyons, the political theorist Bernard Mandeville, and even gives him the prospect of meeting Isaac Newton (97).

In all these cases, Franklin suggests that relationships based even incidentally on the circulation and free exchange of texts obtained more meaningful personal attachments than those based on affect. This is frighteningly demonstrated in Franklin's account of Collins who returns with Franklin to Philadelphia after Franklin's failed attempt to solicit financial support from his father. Obviously disenchanted with family relationships as a result of his father's reluctance to underwrite his printing venture, Franklin notes with some irony that Collins "set out . . . leaving his books [not, as we might expect, his family or friends] to come with *mine* and me to New York" (82–83; emphasis mine). And if in Franklin's striking inversion texts substitute for intimates, positing the abstract currency of books as a more meaningful and reliable kindred, he also inverts the familial affections of his father and mother, asserting caustically and depreciatingly that all he could obtain in terms of support were promises and "some small gifts as *tokens* of [his father's and] mother's love" (83).

If the possession of texts facilitates or even substitutes for actual interpersonal acquaintances by obtaining a form of abstract currency, the activity of public writing also becomes the means by which Franklin eschewes the irrationality and unpredictability of relationships based on kinship or affect. This is most powerfully illustrated in the opposition Franklin sets up between Josiah Franklin's desire to offer his son as a tithe to the church and the avocation of writing which ultimately frees Franklin from the clergy. But it also finds expression in Franklin's theories of self-effacement and humility which are tied inextricably to public writing. Readers will remember that Franklin gets his start in journalism at the *New England Courant* by disguising his authorial labor in an effort to escape the personal prejudices of his brother James, noting that since Franklin's "brother would object to printing any thing of [his] in his paper if he knew it to be [his], [Franklin] contriv'd to disguise [his] hand . . . writing an anonymous paper" (67). This paper, of course, was the first of the *Dogood* letters, and it clearly parodies the residual characteristics of public writing in which the writer and the text were intricately linked. At the same time, interestingly, it thematizes the loss of the intimate relationships of the family as coincident with the birth of such a modern author. Silence notes that

> since it is observed that the generality of people, now a days, are unwilling either to commend or dispraise what they read, until they are in some measure informed who or what the Author of it is, whether he be poor or rich, old or young, a scholar or a leather apron man, &c. and give their opinion of the performance, according to the knowledge which they have of the author's circumstances, it may not be amiss to begin with a short account of my past life and present condition, that the reader may not be at a loss to judge whether or no[t] my lucubrations are worth reading . . . My entrance into this troublesome world was attended with the death of my father . . . as he, poor man, stood upon the deck [of a ship carrying them to America] rejoycing at my birth, a merciless wave . . . carry'd him beyond reprieve.

Silence goes on to account how she is soon bound out as an apprentice, after which her "mother departed this life, leaving me as it were by my self, having no relation on earth." Despite the loss of her father and mother, however, Silence concludes that she is left in "the best of company, *Books.*"[26]

When Franklin the author cannot enter a fictional world to eliminate intimate relationships subject to such external "irrationality" as a "merciless wave" or such circumstantial conditions as Silence Dogood's mother's "indigency," he devises various writerly methods and conceits to offset the influence of the personal. Critic Michael Warner has provided a compelling reading of this authorial methodology, suggesting that Franklin's attempts to de-emphasize the writing subject was part of a general attempt on the part of eighteenth-century thinkers to take legitimacy out of the hands of the corruptible individual and place it in the realm of universal laws. There seems to be great explanatory power in this line of analysis. Franklin repeatedly adopts the mask of a "*publick-spirited Gentleman;* avoiding . . . according to [his] usual rule, the presenting [the self] to the publick as the author of any scheme for their benefit" (193). Moreover, this evacuation of the physical writer from the text seems to be strikingly consistent with Franklin's famous thirteenth virtue, "Humility: Imitate Socrates and Jesus."

But while Franklin's *Autobiography* champions print as the ideal "guardian of civic liberty" because it exposes "corruption in its lurking holes . . . without occupying a lurking hole of its own . . . [representing] a public vision from a non-particular perspective," Franklin does not seem to advocate the evacuation of the writing subject solely in the interest of enabling civic virtue.[27] It is the *guise* of self-effacement and not self-effacement itself which is so important to Franklin. Franklin himself makes this qualification clear in his discussion of "humility," asserting that he "cannot boast of much success in acquiring the *reality* of this virtue: but [he] had a good deal with regard to the *appearance* of it" (159). So he "dropt [his methods] of abrupt contradiction and positive argumentation, and *put on* the humble enquirer and doubter" (64). As he notes later in the text, "I therefore put myself as much as I could out of sight . . . [since] the present little sacrifice of . . . vanity will afterwards be amply repaid" (143).

In this formulation, the recession of the individual writing subject does not serve as a precondition to the promotion of virtuous civic dialogue; rather, it merely facilitates interpersonal and economic exchange because it evacuates the idiosyncratically personal, the emotional, and the irrational from the medium of communication. Franklin figures this in terms of repressing the passions of both communicants. He notes that when someone asserted something he "thought an error, [he] deny'd [him] self the *pleasure* of contradicting him abruptly." Instead, he effects a change "in [his] manners," using such conciliatory phrases as "I conceive" or "I imagine" rather than "certainly" and "undoubtably." The result, he suggests, is that "the conversations [he] engag'd in went on more pleasantly" (159). We might add to this "more rationally" and "more predictably," since by reorienting the catalyst for human action from beliefs to manners [and, we might add, given Franklin's obsession with notions of repetition, custom, and convention, *habits*], Franklin strives to eliminate the bugaboos of impulsivity, caprice, and illogicality.

■ ■ ■

In its emphasis on establishing a system of rational and therefore predictable relationships by evacuating them of their "personality," Franklin's philosophy of print bears an uncanny similarity to the fin de siècle sociologist Georg Simmel's monumental study of the philosophy of money. Like money, the physical or intellectual possession of books requires no specific qualities; the abstract character of printedness makes it possible for all kinds of activity and all types of talent to lead to its attainment. Even a journeyman printer like Franklin can lay his hands on an odd volume of the *Spectator* and acquire "a stock of words" with which to aspire to become "a tolerable English writer" (62). Since textuality, like money, lacks fixidity, it adapts itself to almost any demand or purpose. It allows the individual to reach beyond the confines of geography and station, to extend influence beyond the limitations of the local and circumstantial. At the same time, through standardization (in terms of typography and in terms of literary forms and genres), it encourages the illusion of objectivity, rationality, and permanence.

In his *Philosophie des Geldes* (1900), Simmel proposed several widespread cultural changes which were obtained by the development of a money economy, namely a shift in conceptions of the liberty of the subject, an alteration in the activity of the possession of materials, a metamorphosis in the nature of property, and a fundamental shift in the relationships between subjects and objects. The cultural characteristics of Franklin's "print economy" anticipates with uncanny resemblance aspects of these four features. This verisimilitude should not be at all surprising. As a writer and printer in the first half of the eighteenth century, Franklin not only straddled the beginnings of a modern money economy; he theorized and wrote on this economic development extensively.[28]

Many critics, for instance, have noted Franklin's adoption of various surrogate father figures in the *Autobiography,* usually interpreting these substitutes either biographically or psychoanalytically. But we might also see them as a reflection of Franklin's attempt to eschew the "totalizing" residual relationships rooted in a communicative model of orality, underwriting instead the more voluntary contractual relationships that are characteristic of print culture. If, as Simmel suggested, the subject in what he termed a "natural economy" depended on the personal services of a small number of individuals, this subject was bound to the whole extension of the personality of these individuals. Yet with the introduction of a money economy based on rational exchange, the individual was freed from the potential tyranny of such dependency. This was because money created an abstract relationship between the productive aspect of individuals while largely excluding other characteristics of their individuality. As Simmel pointed out, a money economy made a single person dependent on countless individuals, and this dependency was a contingency potentially limited to a single economic function (as possessors of capital, producers of goods, etc.) as opposed to the whole personhood of such individuals. Whereas in a residual economy the small circle of persons on which an individual was reliant was a "personal" circle, the large circle on which a person was dependent in a money economy was not a personal circle but a circle of economic functions. As Simmel noted, a person depended on more people but less on specific individuals. Moreover, this person was dependent on the function and not the bearer of the function. He or she had the freedom to choose bearers, offering independence and a sense of self-sufficiency. As Simmel concluded, this person's freedom finally consisted in his or her ability to change the individuals on whom he or she depended.[29]

It would not be too facetious to assert that Franklin's project in the *Autobiography* is to demonstrate how one might go about expanding one's circle of dependency through various uses of print, to make, say, the whole Anglo-American social realm the possible limits of one's freely entered-into circle of "functional" relationships. The freedom of the individual in the *Autobiography,* notwithstanding the philosophical importance of Franklin's deism, is figured repeatedly as the rather pragmatic freedom to select which relationships an individual enters into for mutual benefits, which relationships an individual exchanges for more useful acquaintances, and which relationships an individual avoids as "errata" because one or both parties stood to lose something in the intercourse. This freedom is tied to authorship and textuality in two important respects. On the one hand, Franklin's literacy gives him transportable currency in the sense that it enables him to carry his authorial skills and his more abstract "reputation" and social standing to a variety of geographically diverse settings. On the other hand, Franklin's skills at the printing press allow him to freely enter into existing productive relationships in different geographic locations of what was one of the first capital-intensive machine industries: the printing and publishing trade. In this second sense, we might see the unlimited circle of "useful" relationships, as Franklin does, as a feature of society made possible by the division of labor, a development which found some of its origins in the mass production of texts, and a feature Franklin describes in detail in James's (Boston), Keimer's (Philadelphia), and Watt's (London) printing shops. If, as

Adam Smith argued, the division of labor in society contracted the sphere of an individual's productive activity, say, to use the famous example in *The Wealth of Nations,* to drawing out or cutting the wire of a pin, it also expanded his or her circle of interdependent relationships, since such specialization meant that an individual was increasingly dependent on other "specialists" for satisfying material needs. As Smith noted approvingly in a long paragraph detailing with excruciating precision the myriad of the interdependent relationships of production, "Observe the accommodation of the most common artificer or day laborer in a civilized . . . country, and you will perceive that the number of people of whose industry is a part, though but a small part, has been employed in procuring him his accommodation, exceeds all computation."[30]

Franklin makes Keimer's Philadelphia print shop a study in the benefits and consequences of the division of labor. Interestingly, Franklin's critique of Keimer at the outset is based on Keimer's residual refusal to separate the activity of writing from the physical production and reproduction of texts. As Franklin notes, Keimer "could not be said to write [verses], for his manner was to compose them in the types directly out of his head" (78). Franklin also criticizes Keimer's reluctance to divide up the labor in the workshop, suggesting that since "there being no Copy [and] but one pair of cases, no one could help him" (78). This state of affairs, of course, would prevent Franklin from entering into a rational relationship based on exchange, which it does, and Franklin soon figures Keimer as a man guided by his idiosyncratic "passions" rather than by rational, productive habits. This he does by focusing, as he does elsewhere in the *Autobiography,* on the purely consumptive activities brought on by Keimer's appetites. For instance, Franklin recalls how Keimer "was usually a great glutton . . . [and] he long'd for the flesh pots of Egypt . . . [inviting Franklin] and two women friends to dine with him . . . [but eating] it all up before [they] came" (89). In this sense, Franklin's relationship with Keimer, like those with Ralph and Collins, promises to bind him into an unproductive association subject to the irrationality of the passions. By the time Franklin returns from London, however, Keimer has transformed his printing shop into a full-fledged capitalist enterprise, hiring as "hands" at "extream low wages" Hugh Meredith, Stephen Potts, Georg Webb, David Harry, and an Irishman named John as, respectively, "pressmen, bookbinder, and compositor" (108).

But if the division of labor in Keimer's printing shop promises Franklin a new sense of independence, self-sufficiency, and freedom from the influence of Keimer's personality by establishing functional as opposed to personal relationships, it also threatens that independence and autonomy by transforming the human laborers into an interchangeable set of functions. This, paradoxically, makes Franklin's value to Keimer wholly contingent on Franklin's ability to resist being reduced to an identifiable—and thus reproducible—set of functions. As Franklin notes philosophically when Keimer rehires him, "I soon perceiv'd that the intention of engaging me at wages so much higher than he had been us'd to give, was to have these raw hands form'd thro' me, and as soon as I had instructed them, then, they being all articled to him, he should be able to do without me." This is in fact what happens, and Franklin suggests that as his value to Keimer declines, so does the nature of their relationship. "But however serviceable I might be," Franklin declares, "I found that my services became every day of less importance, as the other hands improved in the business . . . [Keimer] grew by degrees less civil, put on more of the master, frequently found fault, was captious and seem'd ready for an out-breaking" (110). Predictably, this falling out is arrested only when Keimer receives a contract to print currency "which would require cuts and various types that [Franklin] only could supply" and sends Franklin "a very civill message, that old friends should not part for a few words" (112).

If the abstraction of money in the form of wages and profit relates the disparate personalities, philosophies, ambitions, and labors of Keimer and Franklin much in the same way that texts and writing have the potential, by evacuating the personal, to establish rational relationships between similarly dissimilar parties, Franklin's realization of the contingency of such relationships given the interchangeability of economic functions obtained by the social division of labor exposes a fundamental problem. Namely once interpersonal relationships are evacuated of their emotional or psychological constituents, replaced by their objectified "values" in terms of either currency (representing labor value or use value) or textuality (representing public reputation or status), the "whole" individual, with his or her passions, desires, and "character," is threatened with impermanence or effacement. This is because this abstract social "value" is subject to wildly unpredictable inflation and deflation given the circumstances of the marketplace. We can think of the "objectified" printer Benjamin Franklin who falls in value once Keimer finds a replacement, or the objectified writer George Whitefield who suffers a decline in reputation once (dead) he can no longer assert his physical presence as symmetrical illustrations of this depreciation.

Yet an assertion that the individual faces potential effacement in Franklin's money/print economy might seem contrived given our general impressions of the *Autobiography*. After all, one would be hard-pressed to find a more egoistic figure in the annals of American literature than Benjamin Franklin. The *Autobiography* is, after all, the archetypal story of the radical individualist who boldly writes himself into history, the prototypical example of the American *self-made man*. But, as Simmel suggested, the objective characteristic of money is an important and paradoxical aspect in the development of extreme individualism since, because it has no inherent characteristics of its own, its possession allows the individual who makes use of it the expression of his full individual peculiarity.[31] Whereas an individual who owns a plot of land, for instance, is limited in exercising his "personality" through such a possession by its concrete physical limitations, the fungible nature of money allows full reign of the egoistic impulse. While tangible possessions to some extent determined individuals, their equivalents in such intangible currencies as money (and, I will suggest, texts) allowed individuals complete freedom to express themselves through the realm of objects however and whenever they wished. This freedom to constitute the self through the selective consumption of material goods, of course, becomes a central facet to the ideology of the rising bourgeoisie: namely the freedom to purchase and display those objects which reflect the social status, individual taste, and character of the purchaser.

There is a clear example of this opposition between the possession of real and abstract property in the *Autobiography* when Franklin seems to chastise, then praise, his wife for purchasing a luxurious China Bowl. Franklin responds with characteristic frugality that it is an example of how "luxury will enter families, and make a progress, in spite of principle . . . [It] had been bought for me without my knowledge by my wife, and had cost her the enormous sum of three and twenty shillings, for which she had no other excuse or apology to make, but that she thought her husband deserv'd [it] . . . as well as any of his neighbors. This was the first appearance of plate and china in our house, which afterward in a course of years as our wealth increas'd augmented gradually to several hundred pounds" (145). At first, Franklin, always concerned about the social value of his public persona, worries that the possession of the bowl will counter his self-constructed reputation for thriftiness, noting that he and his wife "kept no idle servants [and their] table was plain and simple" (145). What redeems the purchase, however, is its self-augmenting exchange value: in other words, its abstract worth in currency on the open market.

This anxiety about the potential for the possession of material objects to "express" the corporeal possessor, here countered by Franklin's musings on the China Bowl's abstract exchange value, surfaces at other points in the *Autobiography*, usually in terms of the public appearance of the corporeal self, the public appearance of mental or physical labor, and especially the public appearance of texts. It would be hard to overemphasize the importance of (and his anxiety about) public "appearances" in Franklin's writings. For instance, upon disembarking at Philadelphia, Franklin notes how he insisted on paying for his passage with his last copper shilling even though the owners of the boat attempt to refuse it. "I insisted on their taking it," Franklin explains, "a man being sometimes more generous when he has but a little money than when he has plenty, perhaps thro' fear of being thought to have but little" (75). When he returns to Boston to solicit capital for his printing venture, Franklin is keenly aware of how he enacts what he terms a "raree-show": "I was better dress'd than ever while in his service, having a genteel new suit from head to foot, a watch, and my pockets lin'd with near five pounds of sterling in silver." Franklin shows off his hard currency to James's journeymen, also "taking the opportunity of letting them see [his] watch" (81). Then, of course, there is the famous scene where Franklin notes how the appearance of his seemingly endless physical labor secures him public credibility, recalling how one night he worked late to finish a printing job and "this industry visible to [his] neighbors began to give [him] character and credit" (119). He reinforces this scene by noting several pages later that

> in order to secure my credit and character as a tradesman, I took care not only to be in *reality* industrious and frugal, but to avoid all *appearances* of the contrary. I drest plainly; I was seen at no places of idle diversion; I never went out a-fishing or shooting; a book, indeed, sometimes debauch'd me from my work; but that was seldom, snug, and gave no scandal; and to show that I was not above my business, I sometimes brought home the paper I purchas'd at the stores, thro' the streets on a wheelbarrow. Thus being esteem'd an industrious and thriving young man, and paying duly for what I bought, the merchants who imported stationary solicited my custom, other's proposed supplying me with books, and I went on swimmingly. (126)

But if the mere "appearance" of Franklin's body and labor becomes a kind of currency in a society in which actual workers and work were being obscured by the division and specialization of labor, Franklin also hints how such phantom appearances could also become liabilities. For instance, the recurring appropriation of Franklin's name by others in the *Autobiography* suggests Franklin's anxiety about loosing control of the abstracted self (represented, say, in print or in reputation) circulating independently of the corporeal subject. As Franklin notes, James uses the emerging idea of an abstract "corporation" to transfer the title of the *New England Courant* to his brother to avoid punitive action by the state (69). As late as three years after Franklin leaves for Philadelphia, James continues to publish the *New England Courant* under his brother's name. James Ralph also appropriates Franklin's name, but for a more mundane application. "Unwilling to have it known that he once was so meanly employ'd [as a schoolteacher]," Franklin notes, " [Ralph] chang'd his name, and did me the honour to assume mine" (36).

Nowhere is this anxiety of objectification more clearly articulated than in Franklin's discussion of the most prominent material basis for the appearance of his public self: print. If the recession of the corporeal writer in print worked to counter the deleterious effects of the conflagration of human passions, positing the exchange of disembodied texts as a more rational and predictable means for conducting secular affairs, it also worked to alienate the individual writer from his own productions. This estrangement had two components: because, as Franklin suggests, the author's productions in print obtained an external objective reality and operated according to their own immutable laws of exchange, what we might call a "logic of print," they no longer seemed to acknowledge the fact and or circumstances of their production; on the other hand, because this objective "print" reality both obscured and mystified the human activity which created it, authors were left passive with the sense that they were outside such an objective realm.

This brings us back to Franklin's discussion of Whitefield whose reputation suffers as the result of his writings. If the objectification of the self in writing allowed an individual more sovereign control over the public self, it also threatened to render the individual a passive observer to the circulation of this apparent identity. In a letter included in the *Autobiography,* Benjamin Vaughn reveals this problem, warning Franklin that he may not be in control of his own memoirs. "Your history is so remarkable," he cautions, "that if you do not give it, somebody else will certainly give it; and perhaps so as nearly to do as much harm, as your own management of the thing might do good" (135). But Franklin himself, despite his repeated fantasies of existing as a text, also identifies the problem of the objectification of the self in print, suggesting, in a discussion of the Quakers, how print functioned to alienate the representation from the represented. He notes that the embarrassments the "Quakers suffer'd from having establish'd and published it as one of their principles, that no kind of war was lawful, and which being once published, they could not afterwards, however they might change their minds, easily get rid of" (190). In other words, once publicized, the Quaker's immutable writings circulated independently of their own historically changing views, determining rather than reflecting or facilitating their beliefs. If the development of an abstract print economy, like the emerging pre-Revolutionary money economy, promised to "free" the individual from persecution from the state, to liberate the subject from the tyranny and irrational unpredictability of intimate relationships, and to allow the individual to self-fashion him- or herself through the acquisition of representative material goods, Franklin hints that this development also occasioned a potential loss of freedom in the sense that the subject became passive—even prey—to his or her own productions.

■ ■ ■

In an 1802 *Portfolio* article, republican journalist Joseph Dennie's conservative nom de guerre, Oliver Oldschool, recalled his first exposure to Franklin's writings as part of an attempt to desacralize the Founder's philosophical authority. As it is a fascinating condemnation of Franklin's juxtaposition of economic and authorial production at the same time it is a critique of Franklin's project of substituting the personal with the textual, I will cite it at length:

> I remember, when I was a boy, somebody put into my hand the life and essays of Dr. Franklin. At the time this man lived, and particularly when his *philosophy,* and his newspaper ethics and economics were diffused over the continent, it was the fashion for Vanity to "rejoice and be exceedingly glad" in the possession of such treasure. I have heard somewhere of a book, for the use of apprentices, servant maids, &c. entitled "The *Only* Sure Guide to Love and Esteem." In like manner it was thought that there was no other road to the temple of Riches except that which run through—Dr. Franklin's works . . . Every miser read his precepts with rapture, and Franklin was pronounced not only wise, and good, and patriotic, and all that—but an *original writer!* Such a strange opinion as the last never could have been entertained, except in a country, from its newness, paucity of literary information, and the imperfection of its systems of education, puzzled to distinguish an original from a copy . . . As a writer, [Franklin] plundered his thoughts and his phrases from others . . . Yet every American who had read or spelt through two or three papers in the *Spectator,* talked of the doctor's genius, and philosophy, and simplicity in writing . . . This pseudo philosopher has been a mischief to his country. He was the founder of that Grub-street sect, who have professedly attempted to degrade literature to the level of vulgar capacities, and debase the polished and current language of books . . . Above all, he was author of that pitiful system of economics, the adoption of which has degraded our national character . . . there is a low and scoundrel appetite for small sums, acquired by base and pitiful

means; and whoever planted or cherished it, is worthy of no better title
than the foul disgrace of the country.

For Dennie, Franklin the writer was indistinguishable from Franklin the economist, not just in the suggestion that Franklin's "pitiful system of economics"
was ultimately a kind of degrading doctrine for his "Grub Street sect" of writers, but also in that his "treasure," his posthumous writings, continued to point
readers, particularly readers of the lower orders, towards a "temple of riches."
Dennie criticizes Franklin's writings for replacing a moral economy, based on
a liberal education and familial relations, with a totalizing economic philosophy based in print on false notions of "originality," "transcendence," and
"autonomy." In fact, Dennie devotes most of the article to the task of demonstrating how Franklin's writings were ingloriously culled from other sources,
suggesting that Franklin's authorial currency was overvalued, based on the
conceits of Franklin and the naiveté of American readers.[32] Dennie notes, for
instance, that in evaluating the simple style of Franklin's writings, unlearned
readers were deceived: "Ignorance and unskillfulness, as they are wont, naturally wondered at what bore the semblance of specious novelty. Like those children, described in *Shenstone's* Schoolmistress, 'They in gaping wonderment
abound, And think he was the greatest wight on ground.'"[33]

Dennie gets right to the heart of reification when he suggests this stupe-
fied paralysis of readers when confronted with Franklin's "novel" writings.
Writing only eleven years after Franklin's death, Dennie suggests that Americans had come to consider Franklin's rather pragmatic intellectual labor, consisting of borrowed material, as something, to paraphrase Lukács, strange and
alien, something operating according to its own immutable laws of genius and
transcendental originality. Thus, Dennie ties the cultural process of the sacralization of writers to the mystification of intellectual labor, a mystification only
encouraged by the privation of secular texts in America. Dennie notes depreciatingly that "every American who had read or spelt through two or three al-
manacs, or two or three papers in the *Spectator,* talked of the doctor's genius,
and philosophy, and simplicity in writing."

Dennie's condemnation of the sacralization of Franklin's *Autobiography*
was, of course, unusual, as was his attack on Franklin. While it probably could
not compete in terms of popularity with Franklin's collection of economic
maxims from *Poor Richard's Almanac,* the *Way to Wealth,* Franklin's *Autobiography,* part of which was first published in English in 1793, went through at least
a hundred editions in the nineteenth century, and it was, and continues to be, a
resilient bestseller in the West.[34] But if Franklin hints at some of the conse-

quences of reification for the author in his philosophy of print, Dennie's critique points out more explicitly some of the problems reification posed for literary consumers. While the explosion of an increasingly anonymous print culture worked to cleave writers from their texts, Dennie suggests that something analogous occured between texts and readers. Namely he alludes to the fact that what originated as a useful item produced to fulfill a specific purpose or function, say a familial guide to love and esteem, became a "treasure," a book which was "The *Only* Sure Guide to Love and Esteem" (emphasis is Dennie's).[35] In other words, it became the embodiment of an objective reality which confronted the reader not as a temporal phenomenon but as something mysteriously external and eternal. It is this illusion of objective reality that Dennie struggles to topple by attempting to dismantle the proto-Romantic ideology of Franklin's "originality" and "genius."

But Dennie fought against a whole nation which was redefining its writers as either the passive embodiment of the genius of a native spirit or the homogeneous producers of useful intellectual property rather than participants in the public realm. The much disparaged 1790 Federal Copyright Act, which was the first piece of federal legislation to secure property rights for American authors, made the importance of encouraging the manifestation of the utilitarian "spirit" of the arts explicit in its original title: "A bill to promote the progress of science and useful arts."[36] Most of the state copyright bills which preceded the 1790 act were couched in similar objective terms. The 1783 New Hampshire bill, for instance, was entitled "An act for the Encouragement of Literature and Genius," again emphasizing the cultural imperative to facilitate the incarnation of American intelligence at the same time it reduced authorship to a mode of cultural production. As William Charvat points out, this legislation actually stifled American literary activity by requiring printers and publishers to pay royalties to American writers, expenses they did not have to incur if they merely reprinted European works.[37] But if the copyright acts did not work to put money in the pockets of American authors, they did help to establish the nominal value of "American Literature," elevating it to an external "thing" worthy of protection at the same time that American writers were increasingly left anxious and contemplative about their status as social and political participants.

FOUR

Liberalism and Republication: The Problem of Copyright for Authorship in America

Joseph Dennie's anxiety that the mystification of authorial activity threatened the communicative function of authorship reflected a viewpoint that was far from a commonplace to most observers in republican America. The consolidation of the idea of literary property, brought about by the 1790 Federal Copyright Act, was accorded a heroic role by contemporaries in what was seen as the effort to protect the rights of authors from the uncertainties of the marketplace. Building on the juridical polemics of this effort in England, of which most of the American jurisprudence is derivative, recent critics like Mark Rose have even gone so far as to link the move to secure proprietorship in literary works to the very emergence of the modern author. Yet despite the fact that the move to copyright was ultimately successful, and despite the fact that almost every major writer in America between the Revolution and the Civil War went on record in favor of the strongest copyright protection possible, enough evidence exists to suggest that many of these same authors knew that the incorporation of the legal fiction of literary property signaled a radical redefinition of what it meant to write to a reading public. Moreover, many of these writers were anxious about the larger implications of such a transformation.

Take the example of Washington Irving. Irving sets up a dramatic contrast in what are arguably the two most symmetrical and at the same time asymmetrical narratives in *The Sketch Book* (1819), "The Art of Bookmaking" and "The Mutability of Literature." In the former, Irving's protagonist steals into the reading room at the British Library where he observes modern authors "in the very act of manufacturing books . . . [drawing] buckets full of classic lore . . . to swell their own scanty rills of thought." Disabused of the notion that the intellectual laborers are Magi "so versed in forbidden lore as to be able to soar above the heads of the multitude," he concludes that the writers are largely assemblers in the realm of ideas, manufacturing their wares by "dipping into various books . . . taking a morsel out of one, a morsel out of another." The narrator rationalizes this conception of literary production by wondering whether "this pilfering disposition [might not] be implanted in authors for wise purposes . . . the way in which Providence has taken care that the seeds of knowledge and wisdom [will] be preserved from age to age." Suggesting that the imperative for the free circulation of ideas might preempt a romantic ideal of the sanctity of individual creativity and its attendant call for perpetual ownership rights, Irving's narrator deploys the rhetoric of Manifest Destiny to survey the potential cultural benefits of such a utilitarian conception of literary activity:

> What was formerly a ponderous history revives in the shape of a romance, an old legend changes into a modern play, and a sober philosophical treatise furnishes the body for a whole series of bouncing and sparkling essays. Thus it is in the clearing of our American woodlands; where we burn down a forest of stately pines, a progeny of dwarf oaks start up in their place.

These philosophical reveries are interrupted, however, when Irving's observer slumbers and imagines a scenario in which the individuated dead authors immortalized in portraits on the library walls come to life to reclaim the "rifled property" in which the modern writers have clothed themselves. After a comical scene in which a dozen old authors literally strip a modern professor of his literary clothes, the narrator awakens to be expelled from the "literary preserve" by a librarian for "poaching" without permission.

In "The Mutability of Literature" Irving's protagonist is admitted into yet another library, this time at Westminster Abbey, where he again muses on the status of texts and textual production. In contrast to the commercial atmosphere of the British Museum, however, the narrator considers the abbey as "a kind of literary catacomb, where authors, like mummies, are piously entombed and left to blacken and smoulder in dusty oblivion." Here the integrity of the works of "old polemical writers" are protected in perpetuity by the vergers, a kind of extreme case of protracted property rights in writing. Once again, Irving's narrator falls into an imaginative stupor and dreams that a small *quarto* comes to life to complain about its neglect. "I was written for all the world," the text asserts, "intended to circulate from hand to hand." The text goes on to point out the irony of the fact of its printedness and its subsequent obsolescence, asserting that its loss is even more poignant given that it was "ushered into the world from the press of the reknowned Wynkyn Worde . . . [and] written in [its] own native tongue, at a time when the language had become fixed." The narrator, in turn, rationalizes that the mutability of texts and language are good things in an age of "excessive multiplication . . . [where] the inventions of paper and the press have made everyone a writer and enabled every mind to pour itself into print and diffuse itself over the whole intellectual world." Besides, he notes, taking the example of Shakespeare, "there rise authors now and then who seem proof against the mutability of language because they have rooted themselves in the unchanging principles of human nature." To this the text breaks into a plethoric fit of laughter and, through sarcasm, demystifies and historicizes the reified category of the genius poet. "So you would persuade me that the literature of an age is to be perpetuated by a vagabond deer stealer!" it exclaims, "by a man without learning; by a poet foresooth—a poet."[1]

The symmetry and asymmetry in these two sketches are striking. In each, Irving's protagonist enters a literarium (one "quasi-public," one private) where he speculates on the nature of authorship. After rationalizing in "The Art of Bookmaking" for what we might call a utilitarian conception of literary activity (greatest good for the greatest number) and in "The Mutability of Literature" for a Lockean conception of authorship (perpetual and exclusive ownership rights) based on the transcendent creative powers of the genius poet, the narrator lapses into an imaginative state where the justifications of each conception of authorial activity are undone by the fictional incarnation of what each explanation has really attempted to suppress: in the utilitarian conception, the unique, individual *author,* and in the Lockean description, the historically contingent material *text.* These voices, in turn, question the narrator's—and by extension the reader's—seemingly commonsensical assumptions about authorship and literary property. We might say that in each narrative what begins as Geoffrey Crayon's logical justifications for existing juridical definitions of literary property are ultimately destabilized by the power of the free imagination to transcend the purely rational and to call to mind alternative states of affairs which expose those seemingly "natural" definitions as either apologies for the market or illusions about permanence.

That Washington Irving should have an interest in destabilizing what I will argue below were the two fundamental legal conceptions of literary property in nineteenth-century America by fanciful "sketches" is not entirely surprising. As Robert Ferguson has reminded us, Irving's first foray into writing after giving up the practice of law was to satirize Jeffersonian America's "blind devotion to legal theory" in his whimsical *A History of New York* (1809). Ferguson argues persuasively that "Dierdrich Knickerbocker is the natural enemy of Publius, Novanglus, the Pennsylvania Farmer, and other rational, legal spokesmen . . . [and that] Irving's comic historian easily ridicules the high seriousness of these republican mythmakers . . . [dismantling] the sense of country that they built from the legal humanism of the Enlightenment." Knickerbocker is especially critical of the "naturalizing" tendency of the explanatory power of legal doctrines. "[Legal] theories are at best but brittle productions," he asserts at one point, and they only distort and create illusions while "gravely accounting for unaccountable things."[2]

That Irving, who left the law in part as an attempt to obtain the intellectual independence of authorship, should chose to interrogate the legal conceptions of literary property is also not surprising. As Stanley T. Williams noted in his *The Life of Washington Irving* (1935), the immediate biographical context of *The Sketch Book* was the 1818 failure of P. and E. Irving, the family's merchant business and the source of Washington Irving's financial self-sufficiency. Suddenly confronted with that fact that, as Irving put it, his "future career must entirely depend very much upon [him]self," Irving composed the *Sketch Book* in large part to secure fiscal independence and security. Thus the very composition of the *Sketch Book* was linked explicitly to the demands of the marketplace, this despite Irving's desire to view a literary vocation, as he had in *A History of New York,* as a means of independent social and philosophical criticism. We might even see what Jeffrey Rubin-Dorsky has described as Irving's lifelong "crisis of identity" and subsequent drifting in the Old World as the sustained attempt to discover either a model or means for balancing these two imperatives: the asymmetrical desires for financial and intellectual independence.

Irving does not find much hope for reconciling these conflicting desires in his explorations of either of the two dominant juridical conceptions of literary property. In fact, as I will argue below, Irving's fictional speculations reveal how the seemingly "natural" ideas circulating in the public consciousness about what activities authors performed and what those performances yielded materially were really based on two independent philosophical constructions which marked the law's attempt to extend the ideology of the market to the communicative and intentional activity of authorship. Occilating between a utilitarian position which posited the value of free and wide circulation of texts over individual property rights in literature, and a Lockean position which underwrote the sanctity of individual ownership of literary work as a priori to the imperatives of either the public or the market, Irving actually re-constitutes—in fictional form—an intractable rift in American legal thinking with respect to definition of authorial activity.[3] This was a fissure, in turn, de-marcated by two largely incompatible legal structures which, despite their in-consistency, had existed side by side in Anglo-American jurisprudence since before the Statute of Anne Act of 1709: namely statutory rights for ownership in literary works for limited periods of time based on civic and market imper-atives; and justifications for perpetual ownership based on "natural" rights of persons to property in their individual labor, which often turned to precedents in common law for support.

The former, the statutory conception, tended to view literary works as useful "inventions," assembled from previously existing materials in some "original" way—that is, different from any previous arrangement. Along these lines, literary activity was linked to mechanical invention, an alignment which explains the concomitant development of patent and copyright law in early America. Article 1, section 8 of the 1787 U.S. Constitution reinforced these mutually self-constituting theories of literary and mechanical invention by giving Congress the power to "promote the progress of science and useful arts by securing to authors and inventors the exclusive right to their respective writings and inventions."[4] Taking the free circulation of useful knowledge as its ultimate goal, the utilitarian position, underwritten by statutory laws, was preoccupied with the problems of political economy; that is, statutory con-ceptions of copyright were concerned with establishing and maintaining the free commerce in—and wide dissemination of—literary works. This, of course, was the aim of the 1709 Statute of Anne in England, the model for the 1790 Federal Copyright Act, a statute initiated by booksellers rather than au-thors in an effort to encourage the publishing trade by assigning limited and alienable ownership rights without either creating monopolies or allowing unauthorized reprinting.

Authorship in the statutory construction was almost always seen in terms of abstract labor; that is, authorial activity was considered apart from its specific concrete and historically contingent characteristics. This focus was one reason why writing and mechanical invention, obviously different activities substan-tively, were taken by statutory formulations to be analogous—at times, even homologous. As perhaps the greatest nineteenth-century defender of utilitar-ian rights, the French bookseller Antoine Renouard, argued, "industry has mingled itself with literature . . . literary men no longer as formerly have a sep-arate existence . . . letters now lead to fortune [and] to employment." The equalization of intellectual and material labor in statutory thinking found a corollary in the leveling of the products produced by such generalized labor. Not only were texts figured materially as a semantic type of the more general category of "invention"; their importance was almost always seen in terms of their *cumulative* and homogeneous benefit to the nation through free exchange rather than in terms of their heterogeneous and incomparable use values. This is in keeping with what J. G. A. Pocock has noted was a change in the philosophy of property among economic thinkers during the course of the eighteenth century. Property, Pocock explains, "moved from being the object of ownership and right to being the subject of production and exchange . . . no longer defined within an unchanging structure of norms . . . [property] was understood to exist within a historical process." This redefinition was accompanied by what Pocock and Albert O. Hirshman have called the "ideology of eighteenth-century commerce," or *le doux commerce,* a set of beliefs which valorized the circulation of commodities as the progenitor of refined and cultivated society and which heralded exchange as both the most effective arbitrar of cultural values and the essential means to meaningful and peaceful social cohesiveness.

By contrast, Lockean notions of literary activity, underwritten by the similarity in ideas of many common law precedents (a similitude reflected, for example, in Blackstone's *Commentaries*), offered a more integrated conception of authorship. The Lockean notion of property suggested that writers created "unique" artifacts—that is, different from any previous or possible forthcoming production—which could neither be broken down into their component parts nor entirely alienated from their creators.[5] Under common law, property existed neither in the physical book nor in the ideas communicated by it but in a penumbral and indivisible "identity" consisting of the author's unique combination of style and sentiment. As Blackstone argued, the identity of a literary composition obtained

> intirely in the sentiment and the language; the same conceptions cloathed in the same words, must necessarily be the same composition: and whatever method be taken of conveying that composition to the ear or the eye of another, by recital, by writing, or by printing, in any number of copies . . . is always the identical work of the author which is so conveyed; and no other man can have a right to convey or transfer it without his consent, either tacitly or expressly given.

But whereas Blackstone's *Commentaries* had allowed for the alienability of property in cases where it was in the interest of the common good, late eighteenth- and early nineteenth-century proponents of the Lockean position tended to argue that civil society did not have a right to interfere with property under any circumstances. Taking the protection of an individual's natural right to property in his or her labor as its ultimate goal, the Lockean position privileged the rights of writers to the products of their activity over the concerns of public utility (access to and wide dissemination of "useful" knowledge) and the market (the unrestricted circulation of literary goods).

In contrast to what I am designating as the utilitarian rationale, the Lockean understanding of public writing tended to figure authorship in terms of concrete—albeit often generalizable—labor. The creation of literary works was thought to be highly individuated, the outcome of individual, proprietary personalities exercising themselves to generate unique, possessible artifacts. Against utilitarian conceptions which sought to make authorship intelligible by expanding the activity of writing within the geographic context of the nation's political economy, Lockean constructions contracted the idea of authorship to the confines of the philosophical imperatives of enlightenment rights to property in labor and, later, to what C. B. MacPherson has called the doctrine of "possessive individualism." Or, to put this outline more baldly, whereas, in the provisions of statutory laws, books were usually figured as circulating commodities, authors as assemblers or inventors, and literary activity as the national production of "useful" knowledge, a concurrent understanding of books as possessible artifacts, adapting and altering a common law understanding of property as a set of ownership rights, designated authors as individual creators, and literary activity as the requisite artisanal labor, or, often, the exercise of a unique "personality," leading to the acquisition of permanent and inalienable ownership rights.[6]

There is some debate about whether or not the seminal 1790 United States Copyright Act, the first federal legislation governing literary property in America, underwrote a utilitarian position by limiting the time an author could hold rights to his or her works to a maximum of twenty-eight years, or whether it assumed exclusive, perpetual rights and merely provided a statutory means for practical enforcement. This, of course, is essentially the same question which occasioned in England the two conflicting interpretations of the famous 1709 Statute of Anne Act: *Millar v. Taylor* (1769) which decided common law rights were not superseded by the statute, and *Donaldson v. Becket* (1774) which reversed *Millar v. Taylor* to maintain that the statute preempted rights guaranteed by common law. The American corollaries to these two English cases were John Barlow's success in getting the Continental Congress in 1783 to consider securing the author's common law rights to property in their works, and, in the nineteenth century, the famous *Wheaton v. Peters* (1834) decision which held, alternatively, that statutory or republican rights superseded common law property rights.[7]

I want to suggest, however, that the 1790 Federal Copyright Act, like the 1709 Statute of Anne Act in England, really *reflected* (one is even tempted to say mediated or suspended) rather than occasioned what was really an old interpretative crisis over which juridical model was to account for the activity of public writing: a Lockean or utilitarian conception. I say old, since these two conflicting legal accounts, mediated by the ambiguous wording of both the 1709 Statute of Anne and the 1790 Federal Copyright Acts, went back to the very seventeenth- and eighteenth-century origins of the concept of alienable literary activity. But the compromisory wording of the 1790 Federal Copyright Act—which argued ambiguously for absolute property rights for a limited term of time—was not, finally, effective in attenuating the inherent philosophical conflict between Lockean and utilitarian models of authorship. Bracketing the slavery issue, there was perhaps no debate more insistent for writers in antebellum America than the issue of literary "property." More important, the problem of copyright frequently became the site for larger philosophical and economic issues facing a new republic struggling to accommodate largely incompatible republican and liberal ideologies. It is no accident that the debate over literary property, for instance, consistently appropriated the rhetorics of such contested antebellum socioeconomic questions as those of manifest destiny, inheritance, monopoly, nationalism, individualism, agrarianism, and communitarianism.

It is the incompatibility between the two legal accounts of authorship that Irving takes up in "The Art of Bookmaking" and "The Mutability of Literature." I want to argue that by pointing out both the historicity and the incompatibility of these two intractable juridical formulations in the *Sketch Book,* Irving worked to defamiliarize the whole idea of literary property. That is, he hinted at how the communicative activity of public writing—to paraphrase the theorist Bernard Edelman—"caught law in the act" in attempting to rationalize authorship into the predictable workings of the market.[8] The very fact of the tenuous suspension of Lockean and utilitarian formulations in the 1790 Federal Copyright Act exposed, for Irving, at least in an intuitive sense, what I will call here an "incomplete rationalization" of public writing. It revealed not only how authorship came to be defined under the explanatory mechanisms of the market, but how copyright law set out to contain the deep contradictions in American liberalism by allowing the contentious coexistence of two contradictory rationalizations for authorial activity: that is, it made fluid the legal grounds for weighing out the private imperatives of individualism with its attendant ideology of sacrosanct ownership rights (e.g., Locke) with the public need for free commerce and circulation (e.g., Montesquieu). In recent years, these competing imperatives have been seen by political philosophers in terms of a Kantian, or rights-based liberalism on the one hand, and the utilitarianism of Bentham or Mill on the other. Implicit in my argument here—but apparent elsewhere in this study—is that both of these conceptions overwrote civic-republican and Christian humanist traditions which saw authorship in a more communitarian view of situated political activity.[9]

Irving's act of defamiliarization is important in two respects. First, it is clear evidence of an antebellum writer's discomfort with the whole idea of literary property and not just over the statutory formulations. It suggests that despite the fact that most writers in antebellum American argued publicly and vociferously for the relative independence afforded by the Lockean notion of "perpetual" copyright, there was some anxiety over the making over—in law and in public consciousness—of public expression into, alternatively, property or commodity.[10] In other words, even though writers generally endorsed Lockean constructions to protect themselves from the vicissitudes of the market, many also harbored concomitant anxieties about accepting—and, in the case of Irving who may have coauthored a treatise on perpetual copyright, even underwriting—an economic rationale for their rhetorical activity.[11] Second, Irving's two sketches outline rather systematically—albeit belletristically—some of the problems that *both* juridical formulations entailed for public writing in America. That is, while utilitarian formulations reduced writing to "inventions" assembled from the public realm of ideas by commonplace literary "producers," Lockean conceptions rendered authorship the private activity of unique, elite, and therefore antidemocratic personalities who were outside the pressing concerns of society. This gave writers the "false-choice" of being interchangeable agents engaged in the mechanical reproduction of ideas or isolated property owners whose private writing passively reflected rather than actively engaged the people of their age.

To suggest not only that Anglo-American copyright legislation posed obstacles for public writing in America, but also that there were authors like Irving who intuited these obstacles in terms of a "false-choice," is polemical because it is counterintuitive. The development of copyright law traditionally has been accorded a heroic role in literary history, marking a progressive, evolutional step away from, first the tyrannical and arbitrary practices of censorship, then the abominations of plagiarism, bowdlerization, and pirating. But

this role has gained most of its support from the way in which literary historians have projected artificial notions of a mature literary "profession" back in
time into the eighteenth and early nineteenth centuries, suggesting that since
most writers naturally hoped to make a living by their efforts, the legal delineation of literary property was essential for the formation and persistence of
such a thing as the literary career. As William Charvat argued in *The Profession
of Authorship* (1968), "[N]o literary profession was possible until law had given
products of mind the status of property."[12] But the profession of authorship
was as much a response to as it was a cause of the idea of literary property. That
is, copyright engendered—more than it served the aims of—a "profession" of
economically motivated writers of literature.[13]

Along these lines, it is important to remember that while the gradual development of the idea of literary property gave birth to the profession of authorship in America, it did so by collapsing (in social and cultural as well as in
legal terms) a tradition of political and belletristic writing into the nomenclature of the market.[14] Before the emergence of the juridical idea of literary
property, as I have adumbrated in earlier chapters, independent writers often
disseminated the printed word under the binding constraints of a rigorous tradition of censorship. But to say this is to acknowledge that such writers were
circumscribed within a political rather than an economic domain. That is, authorship was regulated by the state because it was a political problem.[15] Public
writing was a potentially dangerous and disruptive activity because it carried
with it the threat of undermining social cohesion and harmony. The development of the construction of "literary property" over the eighteenth century in
America signaled in terms of authorial activity a carving out of the political
domain the separate and autonomous existence of economics.[16] The separation of economics from politics, what Louis Dumont describes as the emergence of an autonomous "economic category," rested on two postulates: inner
consistency oriented to the good of man, and a natural harmony of interests.
The former, expressed so powerfully in Adam Smith's notion of an "invisible
hand," predicated the emancipation of economics from politics because the
surmise of inner consistency made extinct the notion that social order had to
be introduced from the outside by the state. The later postulate, the notion of a
"natural harmony of interests," supported the former in that it both equated
individual economic interest with the general social interest and figured opposed interests (to be worked rationally in a kind of interdependent market
calculus) as the necessary precursor to a peaceful, commercial society.[17]

It was the separation of the economic from the political domain and the
concomitant rewriting of the political legislation of censorship into the eco-

nomic laws of copyright and literary property which allowed the birth of the professional writer.[18] Without this sociopolitical transformation (the reorientation of public writing from a political to an economic activity), there could have been no explosion of the printing trade, no sea change in popular reading habits, and certainly no rise of bourgeois literary individualism—the usual culprits for the emergence of the modern profession of authorship.[19] But the general redefinition of authorship from an externally regulated political activity to an internally organized economic activity was not a rationalization that took place without the nagging questions of whether there was indeed "inner consistency" to "literary economics" and whether individual interest did indeed correspond to the interests of the whole. Nor did it take place without the anxious fear of sociopolitical effacement on the part of writers who worked within a culture which carried in its collective consciousness the neoclassical ideal of the participatory "man of letters" and the memory—especially in the rhetoric (if not substance) of libertarian thinking—of a communicative activity that was, in political terms, urgent and catalytic.[20]

In the pages below, I want to suggest that these nagging questions—and their embodiment in the contradictory Lockean and utilitarian conceptions of literary property—have plagued Anglo-American copyright formulations from the very beginning. That is, the tenuous but persistent coexistence of Lockean and utilitarian formulations replicated in the minutiae of legal discourse the terms of the unsettling macropolitical contests we have come to know as the debates between liberalism and republicanism, possessive individualism and utilitarianism, and agrarianism and laissez-faire. I then want to turn briefly to the current debate over copyright between scholars such as Mark Rose, Martha Woodmansee, Peter Jaszi, David Saunders, and Carla Hesse. These arguments, I will maintain, fall along the very same lines as those of eighteenth- and nineteenth-century proponents and critics of the two traditional "alternatives" in copyright jurisprudence. Finally, I want to return to Washington Irving both to suggest how authorship "caught law in the act" in laying out the ideology of the market, and to intimate some of the problems this ideology posed for a premodern tradition of public writing in America.

■   ■   ■

Like with the 1709 Statute of Anne, the first copyright legislation in the American colonies was initiated by booksellers and printers, not writers. John Usher, a wealthy Boston merchant and bookseller, occasioned the first American copyright statute in 1672 when he persuaded the General Court to grant him exclusive, "perpetual" rights to print a revised edition of *The General Laws and Liberties of the Massachusetts Colony* (interestingly, the 1834 *Wheaton v. Peters* case also addressed the publication of judicial proceedings but was decided in favor of statutory limits on ownership rights). But this measure, as Bruce Bug-bee notes, roughly comparable to the termless Licensing Act in England and based on common law suppositions about property ownership, was qualified less than a year later when the General Court decided in May 1673 to limit Usher's rights to seven years, presumably to check the threat of monopoly.

This juridical uncertainty was a portent of the problem that the activity of authorship was to pose for the rationalizations of both the law and market. When, after the American Revolution, individual states began to pass legislation on literary property, most acknowledged the rights of individual authors to property in their efforts while making certain that such rights did not impede the free commerce thought essential to the public weal. For instance, the 1783 Massachusetts copyright act suggested an unproblematic correspondence between the protection of private property and the commercial interests of the state, asserting that "all books, treatises, and other literary works . . . shall be the sole property of the . . . author or authors [or] their heirs or assigns," but limiting this ownership to twenty-one years. By contrast, Connecticut's 1783 statute, "An Act for the Encouragement of Literature and Genius," did not mention the term "property" at all. Instead, it underwrote the importance of exchange, emphasizing that "every author should be secured in receiving the profits that may arise from the sale of his works" and even allowed another party to reprint a work should the author or proprietor fail to offer it at reasonable prices.[21] Most of the states which passed their own copyright legislation between 1783 and 1786 made some rhetorical gesture to Lockean rights to property in one's labor while giving far more substantive weight to the importance of alienability necessary for free trade. Some, like North Carolina, followed Connecticut's lead by providing a clause to check price fixing; others, like South Carolina's "Act for the Encouragement of Arts and Sciences," made no distinction between the efforts of authors and inventors, considering both to be the invention of useful machines and therefore both subject to the utilitarian interests of the public.

Perhaps the most famous document in early American copyright history, Joel Barlow's 1783 letter to Elias Boudinot, then "President of Congress," urging Federal copyright protection, expresses some of the philosophical merits and consequences of both Lockean and utilitarian conceptions of authorial activity. Barlow empowered his entreaty by condemning a printing industry which freely appropriated the works of writers, noting how the example of the pirating of John Trumbull's *M'Fingal* had forced Timothy Dwight to forego the publication of *The Conquest of Canaan*. Using Trumbull as an example of the plight of writers in America, Barlow noted how Trumbull's reputation, and by extension his livelihood, were compromised by printers who issued cheap editions that contained "typographical errors, a bad paper, a mean letter & an uncouth page." For Barlow, it was authorial sovereignty and intellectual independence, not financial remuneration, which was the pressing concern. This uneasiness was articulated with more precision in an anonymous 1783 essay in the *Connecticut Courant and Weekly Intelligencer*, almost certainly authored by Barlow, in which the writer claimed that

> nothing can be a greater discouragement to a writer of genius, than on the first publication of a work, to see some mean and ungenerous printer, [not having] sufficient taste of learning to understand [it], immediately [stealing] his work out of his hands, reprinting it in so mangled and inelegant a manner, that the author must be ashamed of the edition . . . Such is the situation of an author in this country . . . [and] it is impossible he should be concealed. [The] writer is known and stands forth . . . at which all the arrows of criticism and censure are aimed.

Barlow's anxiety about the vulnerability of writers to printers—and, by extension, to the perception of an anonymous reading public—reminds us that his conception of literary property was an essentially eighteenth-century one. That is, as J. G. A. Pocock has noted, "property" in the eighteenth century was as often a political and juridical term as it was an economic rationale: "it meant that which was properly one's own, that to which one properly had a claim, and . . . it was applied as much to the right as to the thing."[22]

Barlow suggested that as "America has convinced the world of her importance . . . by the wisdom, energy, and ardor for liberty . . . she ought to encourage that variety and independence of genius in which she is not excelled by any nation in Europe." He went on to argue that since America had "few gentlemen of fortune sufficient to enable them to spend a whole life in study, or to endure others to do it by their patronage, it is more necessary in this country than in any other that the rights of authors should be secured by laws." Yet, while Barlow thus challenged the utilitarian rationale for literary activity in his effort to secure property rights for what he called a "new class of authors," he also intimated some of the problems posed by this alternative. Following his reasoning that the proprietary, property-generating author would be more self-reliant than his European counterpart, Barlow expressed anxiety that this independence would result in a decline in the quality of public writing, an embarrassment, he noted, "natural to every free government." Having been liberated from a position of public prominence based on patronage, sinecure, and political favor, modern authors were relegated to the realm of the private and economic, and thus increasingly dependent on the mystical workings of a market governed by "popularity." For instance, while Barlow noted that in modern and commercial European nations "the historian, the philosopher, the poet, and the prater have not only been considered among the first ornaments of the age and country which produced them . . . but have been secured in the profits arising from their labors," this state of affairs guaranteed that they "received discouragement in some proportion to their merit in advancing the principles of mankind." Anticipating Tocqueville, Barlow concluded by intimating how property rights in literature, necessary to protect writers from the perils of the marketplace, might also compromise the "excellence" of a national literature by introducing what Tocqueville was to later call a nefarious "trading spirit into . . . literature" at the same time it infused a virtuous "taste for letters among the trading classes."

I should note briefly that Barlow was not alone in making the radical intimation that the civil freedom afforded by the rise of a market economy did not necessarily translate into unfettered intellectual independence. Charles Jared Ingersoll, a Philadelphia lawyer, member of Congress, political economist, and author of drama, poetry, and an anonymous novel, wrote in 1823 that "the English newspaper press, much less free by law than the American, is in practice more licentious." Attempting to defend the free press in America as "the palladium of liberty," Ingersoll suggested, nevertheless, that writing in America was "regulated by a public tact much truer and stronger than such ordeals [as state prosecutions in Europe]." He argued that "irreligious, obscene, and seditious publications [were] infinitely more common from the English than the American press: scurrilous and libelous newspapers exist[ed] to be sure, but they [were] the lowest and most obscure of the vocation; whereas in England, some of the most elevated and best patronized, [were] some of the most scandalous." While, on balance, Ingersoll considered such ideological constraints on public expression to be offset by the social advantages of intellectual "temperance," he could not help but argue that American institutions, "partaking of the nature of [their] government, [had] a levelling tendency [on the intellect] . . . [assuring that] in the literature of the imagination, [America's] standard [was] considerably below that of England, France, Germany, and perhaps Italy."[23] Reading Ingersoll, one is reminded of Immanuel Kant's discussion of the relationship between civic and intellectual independence in "An Answer to the Question: 'What is Enlightenment?'":

This reveals to us a strange and unexpected pattern in human affairs . . . A high degree of civil freedom seems advantageous to a people's *intellectual* freedom, yet it also sets up insuperable barriers to it. Conversely, a lesser degree of civil freedom gives intellectual freedom enough room to expand to its fullest extent. Thus once the germ on which nature has lavished most care—man's inclination and vocation to *think freely*—has developed within this hard shell, it gradually reacts upon the mentality of the people, who thus gradually become increasingly able to act freely.[24]

While most writers in republican America who addressed the copyright issue followed Barlow's lead in deploying a Lockean model for rationalizing literary activity (usually by arguing for extended or perpetual property rights in literature as a means of guaranteeing authorial control), some, also like Barlow, fretted over the logical implications of circumscribing the activity of authorship within a juridical system of extended property rights.[25] This was especially the case well into the nineteenth century when the contentious debate over the lack of international copyright laws repeatedly exposed the philosophical and juridical inconsistencies of Anglo-American formulations of literary property, and when publishers like Henry Charles Carey went so far as to echo Proudhon's motto that "property is robbery" in their efforts to expand the public domain in literary works.[26] Such debates tended to divide authors and publishers along these lines. For instance, while Noah Webster argued that "no right or title to a thing can be so perfect as that which is created by a man's own labor . . . a man's right to his own productions in writing is as perfect as to the productions of his farm or shop," publisher George Merriam, who later acquired the rights to Webster's *An American Dictionary* (1828), qualified this autonomy by suggesting that "when [a writer] publishes, he parts with his exclusive ownership, and gives it to the public."[27] Such antimony between authors and publishers tended to encourage writers to take as strong a position as possible with respect to authorial sovereignty. This meant that writers were increasingly forced to let go of the ambiguous eighteenth-century notion of property as a set of rights in favor of the more tangible nineteenth-century conception of property as a corporeal, possessible thing. That is, authors increasingly turned to the Lockean strains in American thought—adopting the "common sense" notion of man as a property-seeking individual who existed prior to a society which existed solely to confirm rights to such property—to take as strong a position as possible in a culture that understood and valued property rights more than, to quote the title of Thomas Skidmore's famous 1829 book on the problems of "fixed" property, *The Rights of Man to Property!*[28]

Despite the fact that it sacrificed the concerns of the public to those of the individual, committing authors, at least philosophically, to the everyday task of producing private property, it is easy to see why—aside from economic reasons—writers subscribed to the Lockean rather than to the utilitarian notion of literary activity. The latter was based on the abstract, macrocosmic principles of political economy, and it considered public writing in terms of its place in a national market in intellectual commodities. It was a conception which valued the production, to paraphrase the provision for copyright in the United States Constitution, of "useful knowledge," and it tended to reduce authorship to the mechanical activity of arranging or appropriating preexisting materials in some inventive way. Moreover, it subordinated the communicative and intentional activity of public writing to the commercial demands of the public, demands which made themselves apparent through the "self-regulating" principle of supply and demand. As a strong defender of the utilitarian position wrote in an 1825 *Atlantic Monthly* essay entitled "Intellectual Economy":

> In a free country, where there exist no privileged orders nor unequally protected institutions, it will generally happen that the value of every branch of human knowledge, as far as concerns such a community, will be very nearly indicated by the quantity of intellectual capital, to use the language of political economists, naturally determined to its cultivation. An analogous principle is now acknowledged to be true, with regard to the relative value of the various branches of mere material industry; and we see no reason why the doctrine may not be excluded to the finer and less palpable fabrics of the intellect. The supply of literature and science will be in proportion to their demand, and their demand in proportion to their usefulness. The elements of *really* valuable information, the principles of serviceable, practical, and necessary knowledge, will receive the largest share of cultivation, because they will be most in request.

The author of the article concluded by noting that "in Europe, this self-adjusting principle, is seldom or never left to operate . . . [and that] nothing is considered [there] as well done, which is not done by the externally intruding interference of the law . . . a system engendered in tyranny and bigotry and folly . . . sustained by fraud and prejudice and pride . . . [and] a monument of the barbarous policy and stupendous folly of an age."[29] In this respect, the essayist took up themes common to defenders of statutory rights. That is, he saw the workings of the market as an effective, democratic antidote to the elitism

of privilege, the despotism of monopoly, the degenerative influences of im-
practical cultivation, and the threat to public access. As publisher George Curtis reasoned in his 1847 defense of utilitarian rights, "[E]xclusive possession or
appropriation, intellectually, of ideas . . . becomes impossible, as soon as [an
author] imparts [them] to others . . . if I am permitted to read the ideas and sentiments which another has written, they become part of my intellectual possessions, as far as I can retain them in my memory, and no rule can be
established which would deprive me of the opportunity to use them for my
own enjoyment, or to impart a knowledge of them by speech to others."[30]

Perhaps the greatest advocate of the utilitarian position in America was
publisher Henry Charles Carey, whose *Letters on International Copyright,* first
published in 1854, inflamed the literary world. Citing a long list of authors, including Harriet Beecher Stowe, who had been paid well in comparison to
prominent political figures, and calling into account nonmonetary benefits
such as political sinecures and the currency of reputation, Carey denied the
whole idea of authorial property. "Examine Mr. Macaulay's *History of England*
and you will find that the body is composed of what is common property," he
argued. "The great work of Chancellor Kent," he followed, "is, to use the
words of Judge Story [who from 1839 to 1845 argued for authorship as inven-
tion] 'but a new combination and arrangement of old materials, in which the
skill and judgment of the author in the selection and exposition . . . constitute
the basis of his reputation.'" He concluded by examining the "producers of
works of fiction," asserting that "Sir Walter Scott had carefully studied Scottish
and Border history, and thus had filled his mind with facts preserved, and ideas
produced, by others, which he reproduced in a different form." Likewise, Carey
maintained, "our own very successful Washington Irving . . . made no contribution to knowledge . . . He drew largely upon the common stock of ideas, and
dressed them up in a new, and what has proved to be a most attractive form."

The advocates of utilitarian conceptions of writing repeatedly turned to
the catalytic metadiscourses of nineteenth-century American democratic exceptionalism to rally support for their formulations. Carey, for instance, linked
the activity of authorship to what many producers of American staples saw as
the parasitic industry of European manufacturing. He asserted that "the world
at large is the owner of all the facts that have been collected . . . and its right in
them is precisely the same that the planter has in a bale of cotton . . . When the
planter hands his cotton to the spinner and the weaver he does not say 'take this
and convert it to cloth, and keep the cloth.'" In this sense, the debate over how
to formulate the nature and purpose of literary activity in legal discourse was
often seen as a microcosm of the debate over how to figure the character and
destiny of America in mythic terms. As we have seen in Irving's fictional ac-

count of utilitarian authorship, one of the most common tropes that supporters of the utilitarian position deployed against the "common sense" notion of rights to property in labor was the metaphor of Manifest Destiny.[31] In this configuration, the common "fields" of the intellect were open, free of rent to firstcomers, who, after fencing in an enclosure and reaping the harvests for a fixed period of time, were bound to return the land to the public. Carey demonstrated the power of such a metaphor, claiming that

> we have extensive fields in which hundreds of thousands of [writers] have labored for many centuries. They were at first wild lands, as wild as those of the neighborhood of the Rocky Mountains, but this vast body of laborers has felled the trees and drained the swamps, and has thus removed nearly all the difficulties that stood opposed to profitable cultivation. They have also opened mines of incalculable richness; mines of gold, silver, lead, copper, iron, and other metals, and all of these are common property . . . We invite you, gentlemen, to come and cultivate these lands and work these mines. They are free to all. During the long period of forty-two years [extent of copyright protection in 1854] you shall have the whole product of your labor, and all we shall ask of you, at the close of that period, will be that you leave behind the common property of which we are now possessed, increased by the addition of the machinery as you may yourselves have made. The corn that you have extracted, and the gold and silver that you may have mined during that long period, will be the property of yourselves, your wives, and your children. We charge no rent for the use of the lands . . . Not satisfied with this, however, the persons who work these rich fields and mines claim to be absolute owners, not only of all the gold and silver they extract, but of all the machinery they construct out of the common property.

Just as John L. O'Sullivan had coined the phrase "Manifest Destiny," in two 1845 issues of the *United States Magazine and Democratic Review,* to provide the catalytic terminology for American geographic expansionism, proponents of utilitarian conceptions of copyright sought to appropriate such powerful rhetoric to promote what they saw were the necessary conditions for American intellectual expansionism. But this empire for genius, in contrast to Jackson, Polk, and Tyler's plans for enlarging America's "empire for liberty" westward, looked eastward to the educated in Europe. As an anonymous essay in the *United States Magazine and Democratic Review* claimed, as the American "people have multiplied and become physically great, the national mind has become developed, and its reflex is now working powerfully upon public opinion in the Old World, changing the whole character of its literature, as our political progress is hastening the downfall of its aristocracy . . . Every vessel which leaves the United States," the essay concluded, "carries with it innumerable letters, to scatter through every British county. These letters are revolutionizing the English mind, and the people are becoming aware of the abuses of their government, as well as the excellencies of this."[32]

Not to be outdone, advocates of perpetual copyright often questioned the applicability of such tropes. An 1812 article on D'Israeli's *Calamities of Authors,* for instance, reprinted in an American edition of the London *Quarterly Review,* attacked "the verbal and tasteless lawyers" who claimed nothing could "be an object of property, but what has a corporeal substance." To prove that "there existed no property" in literature, the essay claimed, lawyers "found an analogy in the gathering of acorns, or in seizing a vacant piece of ground . . . [concluding] that literary property was purely ideal; phantoms which . . . their author could neither grasp nor confine to himself." The lawyer most attacked for engendering such refined abstractions was Lord Camden, who wrote the opinion in the 1774 case of *Donaldson v. Becket.* "Never in the annals . . . of legislation and jurisprudence . . . was a more dishonest and insolent sentence uttered," a writer in the *North American Review* wrote, "than that of Lord Camden . . . in the case of Donaldson versus Beckett . . . who denied [the author] the fruit of his labor . . . confiscating it for the public use."[33] Such abstract notions as these, another writer in *Southern Quarterly Review* argued, were "too metaphysical and refined for the common sense of mankind . . . there is such a thing as literary property, as clearly distinguishable as houses and lands, gold and silver coin, or bank bills, or any other kind of property, real or personal, moveable or immovable."[34]

If advocates of statutory rights criticized perpetual copyright as a return to privilege, monopoly, and a degenerate lack of social utility, defenders of perpetual rights assailed utilitarian notions as elaborate fictions undermining the sanctity of property rights and promoting "agrarianism" and an effete species of cheap literature. For if Lockean formulations threatened the democratic social ideals of unrestricted access to—and free and wide circulation of—ideas within the public realm, utilitarian conceptions threatened what many, raised on the popular ideas of Locke, saw as the very constitutive basis of a public realm itself. An anonymous writer of an 1838 essay on literary property in an issue of the *Democratic Review* expressed this thinking in succinct terms.

The Principle of PROPERTY is the key-stone of the arch of society. It is the first, deepest, and most sacred, of the principles of social order and law . . . It is a natural and original principle, and not a mere artificial creation of law, as is erroneously pretended by some few writers. The right of property in the creations of original individual effort—inviolable and perpetual, and transmissible by the will of the owner—is unquestionably a natural moral right, antecedent and superior to legislation; being the object of social union, rather than its effect and consequence. The tiller of the earth moistens the ground with the sweat of his brow; and with the fatigue of his whole frame, and the devotion of the pleasant hours of life . . . calls forth an existence out of the dull clod healthful food for the sustenance of man's body—will any one question his original and perfect right to the exclusive possession and enjoyment of the fruits of his industry? And shall we deny the right of ownership, equally perfect and absolute, of the author to the creations of his intellectual labor—by which he calls forth into tangible existence and visible presence before the eyes of all men, out of the illimitable domain of unexplored truth and unexpressed thought, that spiritual food which is not less necessary to the mental, than the former is to the physical constitution of man.[35]

Looking not to the macrocosmic concerns of nationalism and public utility but to the microcosmic concerns of individualism and private sovereignty, such thinkers pointed out some of the inconsistencies of utilitarian thinking by countering the rhetoric of Manifest Destiny and literary nationalism with the sanctity of individual rights and the indissolubility of a Lockean notion of property: a pair of ideas which formed two of the foundations for modern, rights-based liberalism. As one advocate noted, "Among the objects for establishing social institutions, one is, the guaranty, to each member of the community, of his private, individual rights . . . But not so of the author. He, it seems, is an exception to the rule; and joins society, not as a party to the general bond, but as an outlaw, who is among us, but not of us."[36] Another assailed the connection in utilitarian thinking between authorship and invention, arguing that the deposit clause in English copyright law—requiring authors to submit thirteen copies to various libraries—was analogous to inventors submitting thirteen steamboats to the public in advance of their first sale.[37]

What was at stake for advocates of the Lockean conception was, then, no less than one of the philosophical underpinnings of American liberalism, what C. B. Macpherson described as the doctrine of "possessive individualism." This set of assumptions suggested that the enlightenment project of freeing the individual from dependence predicated the possession of property, and that society emerged in this context as a means of protecting possession.[38] Along these lines, Francis Lieber, one of the most famous of the nineteenth-century proponents of perpetual copyright, suggested that "individual property is absolutely necessary to society, peace, and civilization; and to some one it must belong. Property is so direct an effect of man's nature, that it precedes government." In the midst of the 1837 Depression, Lieber attacked the arguments of essayists like Orestes Brownson and George Ripley, suggesting that the claim that things "unappropriated by any individual or by society, belong . . . to all was erroneous . . . These things belong to no one; but not, therefore, to all. They are not yet property . . . property is the reflex of man's all-important individuality in the material world around him."[39] Cornelius Mathews, another well-known defender of perpetual copyright, echoed Lieber's fear. "If I may throw open literary property to all the world," he disclaimed, "why not all other property? If there may be an allowable agrarianism of ideas, why not of acres and tenements as well? What would be the result if all the farms and estates in America were, to-morrow, made common?"[40] Again and again, nineteenth-century supporters of perpetual copyright suggested that the notion that an author had only temporary right to exclusive property in his or her own creation was a philosophical aberration. As one writer noted, for the United States government to "carry this doctrine of prerogative and supereminent dominion into the intellectual world, and set up an exclusive right of the public to one tenth, or five tenths, more or less, of the profits or benefits of . . . literary compositions . . . is really a transcendent stretch of arbitrary pretension."[41]

Critics of utilitarian thinking turned as often to the character of American writing as to the character of American democracy. The anonymous *A Plea for Authors and the Rights of Literary Property* (1838), perhaps coauthored by Washington Irving and Grenville A. Sackett, asserted that the nation "must have a literature formed upon the principles of our political policy; a literature that respects the people; a literature that trusts in the moral dignity of man and despises, as it ought, the mere artificial honours by which power has too long sought to elevate itself." If American writers, the essay continued, "composed a class of mere idle and dreaming visionaries, whose labours were productive of no practical effect," there would be some reason for restricting their rights to property. But, the argument went on, history has taught man "of the immense importance of an elevated, fearless and honest literature." Such a literature was impossible, the essay concluded, in a country that figured popularity, as American statutory conceptions of authorship did, as the determining factor of pecuniary and nonpecuniary rewards:

> Hence while the flatter of existing follies, the advocate of existing institutions, the panegyrist of living great men, is almost sure of his reward, the fearless, honest, and uncompromising advocate of the truth, must ex-

pect for a while to see his labours reviled, his abilities denied, and his very name a by-word and reproach . . . It is the characteristic of great minds to be far-seeing. They precede the mass, and are never duly appreciated until society [has] come up with them. The present law of copy-right is essentially unwise. It offers a premium to flatters, to the superficial, to the truckling. It creates a mass of light and ephemeral literature, which is manufactured for a particular time, and a particular market. What a premium perpetuity of copyright could offer to the honest and strenuous exertion of talent![42]

If advocates of statutory laws expounded on the virtues of an unfettered public print sphere free from the constraints of exclusive ownership, proponents of perpetual copyright countered that such freedom was sure to engender a commercial literature which merely followed the shallow and promiscuous concerns of public opinion rather than engendering an independent and thus virtuous civic discourse. Such a line of argument almost invariably turned to the problem of what a famous essay by Edward Duyckinck in the *Southern Literary Messenger* called "Cheap Literature." Contrasting a residual state of affairs when "books were so valuable . . . as to be chained like criminals to the desks of libraries" to a situation in which "men do not seek books . . . but are happy to escape from the venders of them," Duyckinck fretted over "the creation of literature which level[ed] downwards and not upwards . . . [bringing] thought down to a level with the narrow views, crude notions, and blind instincts of the multitude."[43] This was a common theme among defenders of perpetual copyright who argued that the American reading public, inundated by cheap books and ushered to a "feast of letters . . . suffer[ed] all the evils of an intellectual dyspepsia."[44]

I should add parenthetically that such questions over the nature and character of the corporeal aspect of literary activity increased over the course of the nineteenth century, and they reflected how the shift in legal thinking from political accounts of the *activity* of authorship to economic formulations of the *materiality* of authorship was one that was uneven. That is, in their efforts to rationalize public writing in terms of simultaneously possessible and exchangeable products, and in terms of coextensively private and public property, legal theorists and essayists went to absurd lengths to pin down the materiality of authorship. Such thinkers repeatedly suppressed the political issues concerning the act of public writing in favor of some tortured rationalizations about the corporeality of literature. The extent to which the debate over copyright was increasingly preoccupied with the object—rather than on the act of—public writing is made apparent in a typically convoluted paragraph from the *Southern Literary Messenger:*

Whether authors have any property at all in the productions of their own minds, has been a question. It has been urged that nothing can be property which has not a corporeal existence, and inasmuch as the ideas of an author are incorporeal, that therefore nothing can be held in them. Ideas have no substantial form. They are spiritual and immaterial in their very nature. They are not perceptible to sense. They cannot be handled or transferred from one individual to another, like goods and chattels, so as to become, in fact, the ideas of other persons. They cannot be wounded or bruised like a man's body. They are imperishable and indestructible . . . But [while] it is true that ideas of the mind are imperceptible to sense, and that the mere fact of transferring them from the mind of the writer to the paper on which he writes, does not change the nature of ideas so as to make what was spiritual and intellectual before, a material, tangible substance . . . the author is thus able to put a mark upon his thoughts, by which they may be known and discriminated as *his* thoughts . . . Now it is this capacity of things to be distinguished and separated from other things of the same kind, and of different kinds, which makes them capable of being held as property.[45]

Tortured thinking such as this was necessary, one might argue, in a philosophical outlook that presupposed the activity of authorship as productive rather than, say, communicative or participatory. This is to say that while nineteenth-century essayists struggled to determine—one is tempted to say to overdetermine—whether the materials of authorship were corporeal and hence capable of occupation and appropriation, and thus distinguishable as property, they collapsed the intentional and communicative aspects of publication into an understanding of authorship that was no different than any other productive activity. That is, writers, like owners or laborers, sent things to the market. It was this focus on the *materiality* rather than the *activity* of authorship which made Anglo-American copyright formulations so very different from those made on the Continent, particularly in Germany and France, where extended and perpetual rights of authors and their heirs were formulated more in the political and statist terms of a "protected personality" than the commercial nomenclature of "literary property."[46]

■ ■ ■

If the argument I have been suggesting is true, that the development of Anglo-American copyright, reflecting a more general separation of economics from politics in America, effected an incomplete rationalization of the activity of public writing, then there is reason to suspect that some of the recent arguments concerning copyright are misplaced, at least in their application to the American case. Mark Rose, for instance, has suggested in a powerful argument that the distinguishing characteristic of the modern author is that he is constituted by the author-work relation in copyright law as a "proprietor." But he focuses solely on Anglo-American jurisprudence following *Donaldson v. Becket* (1774), ignoring in his teleological movement toward proprietorship both the earlier history of vacillation between proprietary and utilitarian figurations of authorship and a whole host of English and American writers who actively resisted this categorization. Deliberating on the gap between poststructuralism's "death of the author" and copyright law's birth of the proprietary writer, Rose's important argument tends to loose its historical force to theory.[47] Going to the other pole, Trevor Ross has argued that the idea of intellectual property changes after 1774, when an older, static conception of literary property as the fruit of an author's labor was modified by a liberal emphasis on how property acquires value through exchange and circulation. Ignoring an earlier, statutory tradition, and glossing over a gradual movement over the course of the nineteenth century toward proprietorship, Ross ties the restrictions on proprietorship to an awareness of English literature as a tradition whose artistic vitality could only be maintained by reigning in author's rights.[48]

Ironically, given her geographical focus, Carla Hesse has come closest, I think, to suggesting the persistent tension between utilitarian and Lockean formulations of Anglo-American copyright, replacing Rose's dependence on Foucault's theoretical account of the privatization of knowledge with some solid historical spadework on author's rights in Revolutionary France. Looking to the discourse of civic virtue, Hesse suggests that legislation on authors' rights, in 1791 and 1793 laws, conceived of writers as public servants rather than property-owning individuals. But her wonderful research on the origins of the French *les droits moraux* is not as effective in evidencing her arguments when she collapses the differences between the statism of France with the commercialism of England and America to argue with Rose. The French understanding of authorship and copyright, it seems, was very different than that in England and America. Finally, David Saunders has followed Hesse with some rigorous cross-cultural scholarship on copyright to interrogate the Foucauldian mode in literary criticism of "subject formation"; that is, how writers came to have personhood through the constructions of the law. Like Hesse, Saunders attempts to complicate Rose's legal birth of the proprietary author by positing three other areas in which writers could be said to be constituted as subjects: legal rights and liabilities, ethical inwardness, and aesthetic standing.

But Saunders's account, in demonstrating that "there is no *necessary* equivalence between a writer's aesthetic or ethical personality and the elements of legal personality that the writer (amongst other individuals) may acquire through the process of publication," glosses the connections between, say, the concomitant historical development of aesthetic theory and copyright law, and the tensions between an author's ethical personality and the legal personality attributed to him or her by the law.[49]

It is this last point, what I am delineating here as the problem of copyright for authorship in America, to which I would like to return in conclusion. Any reader who spends any time in the periodical literature of early America knows that the problem of what D'Israeli called the "Calamities of Authors" was of great concern to journalists and readers from the Revolution to the Civil War. American journals and newspapers were filled with speculations on "the miseries of authorship" and on "the profession and perils of an author." When John Murray published D'Israeli's book in 1812, nearly every well-known American journal printed or reprinted a review, many lamenting the plight of those engaged in such an unprofitable profession which had not existed "before the invention of printing. . . [but which] "as soon as books could be rapidly and easily multiplied . . . became a trade." One essayist wondered how it was that "literature . . . like every thing else which may be made a means of emolument . . . a trade or profession" even if unprofitable, could be the cause for such calamities. After all, "in the regular progress of society, it [was] . . . natural that the author should live by the pen."[50] Yet most essayists, like one in an 1823 edition of the New York *Minerva,* claimed, as English writers had about Grub Street, that "no encouragement whatsoever is given to the unfortunate author. The votary of the Muses, the instructor and improver of mankind, is permitted to saunter around the streets with his elbows peeping out of a more than thread-bare coat."[51]

This is not to suggest that the public response to "the calamities of authors" was uniformly sympathetic; almost as many essayists attacked what they saw as the "vanities of authors." Many writers noted with approbation that the disinterested workings of the marketplace countered the vain ambitions of authors toward immortality. But such comments, too, bespeak of a change in the cultural understanding of the activity of public writing. Whereas in authorship from ancient Greece to the Renaissance, as D'Israeli noted, there had always been "a latent love of fame that prompt[ed] . . . strong devotion to labour," such ambitions toward distinction and immortality were seen sympathetically as a public good. That is, the efforts of writers to transcend their historical moment and to populate a public realm which defied the coming and going of generations was thought to be a vital activity for the preservation of the human community. It was only when such striving toward immortality and civic distinction was redefined as the private vice of vanity that the pursuit of fame was suspect. As Hannah Arendt noted, "There is perhaps no clearer testimony to the loss of the public realm in the modern age than the almost complete loss of authentic concern with immortality . . . testified to by the current classification of striving for immortality with the private vice of vanity." Arendt demonstrated this redefinition at work in a passage from Adam Smith's *Wealth of Nations*—concerning "that unprosperous race of men commonly called men of letters [for whom] . . . public admiration makes always a part of their reward"—where public admiration and monetary reward are equated.[52] Many essayists who sympathized with the "calamities of authors" and who favored the residual concern with authorial immortality had a difficult time defending such a pursuit in an era that tended to collapse all social ends into a Lockean calculus of personal gain, and which viewed the prominent public display of such ends as individual vanity.

It is interesting that the litanies over the "calamities of authors" often had as much to do with concerns over authorial disempowerment as they did over writers' economic decline. In an age when authorship was being redefined as an economic activity underwritten by the purchasing habits of an anonymous reading public, essayists wondered what would separate the independent thoughts of authors from the tastes of their readers. As one writer claimed, nothing could "be more difficult than the business of an *Author*. . . [since] people do not reflect that books are written to correct the heart and the judgment; they rather suppose [books] are meant to confirm everyone in their opinions."[53] Another worried that "as the state of society [became] more refined [and] eccentricity of character [wore] away, . . . a writer . . . of the present age, who aim[ed] to give amusing pictures of the humors of the times, [found] nature less favorable . . . [than] to those who resorted to her, for like purposes, a century or two ago."[54] Still another, in an essay entitled "The Miseries of Authorship," worried about the leveling effect of a mass reading public on the writer, sketching out a parable concerning an artist who wished to ascertain the disposition of his public:

> He placed in as exposed a situation as possible, a picture which he had just completed, with a note attached thereto requesting every spectator to cancel such defects or blemishes as they might perceive in it. Accordingly every one found something disagreeable; one did not admire the chin; another preferred a blue to a black eye; and many lest they should be

thought to know nothing of the matter, or lack of judgment or taste, crossed off any feature which happened to be most convenient. When the artist returned he was extremely mortified to find every stroke of his pencil disapproved of.[55]

As Irving's *Sketch Book* suggests, such anxieties about palimpsestical texts and authorial erasure, apprehensions which must have seemed strikingly paradoxical in an exploding print culture equipped with the fixity of mechanical reproduction and the publicity of wide circulation, found expression throughout the writing of what we now recognize as the contested realm of the American literary canon. And it is in this sense that Kenneth Dauber may have been on to something when he claimed some years back that "American literature is a literature whose primary concern has always been its own nature . . . To the poets and novelists of the classic period of American letters, the object of their work, inevitably, was its own process."[56] But I disagree with Dauber's intention in promoting an extreme kind of ahistorical self-reflexivity. On the contrary, as I hope I have demonstrated here, the "nature" and "process" of public writing have always been historically determined. Irving, after all, like many of the writers in antebellum America who adumbrated on bibliographical whales, scarlet typography, and purloined letters, did not grapple with the abstract, transcendent, Derridean problematics of ecriture. Rather, he wrestled with a historically situated post-Revolutionary culture that was redefining the very nature of authorial activity, a society that was collapsing the sociopolitical ideal of the participatory man of letters into the very different nomenclature of the antebellum marketplace.

PART II

THE
AESTHETIC
RESPONSE

FIVE

Crèvecoeur and Strategies
of Accommodation

One would be hard-pressed to come up with a more palimpsestical narrative in the field of early American literature than Crèvecoeur's 1782 *Letters from an American Farmer.* Beginning with contemporaneous reviews and extending down to current literary anthologies, readers have excerpted and decontextualized individual letters of Crèvecoeur's complex fictional narrative, particularly Letter 3, "What Is an American," in an attempt to provide "empirical" evidence for claims about the fact or ideology of American economic exceptionalism. Such a interpretative mode of excerpting and recontextualizing has neutralized the sociopolitical critique that underwrites Crévecoeur's narrative, and the history of the reception of *Letters* is in some sense the story of the persistent effort of postenlightenment audiences to efface the constitutive role of rhetoric underpinning Crèvecoeur's written observations in order to render discrete decontextualized passages, even overtly fictional ones, as putatively mimetic or descriptive.

Given that *Letters* foregrounds and interrogates this very readerly or cognitive disposition to derive the whole from the part, to read metonymically from the particular to the general, it has to be one of the greatest ironies of American literary history that what is probably the most thoroughgoing critique of the cognitive scaffolding of economic liberalism in eighteenth-century American letters has been seen as a manifesto for the *homo economicus* of American exceptionalism. A close rhetorical reading of the whole of *Letters* does not reveal an ambiguous descriptive account of the colonies, as it is still often read; rather, it suggests the fictional story of a self-professed "man of letters" who reveals at the end of his narrative that his innovative and optimistic focus on the exceptional microeconomic aspects of American labor has blinded him to far more sinister macroeconomic social realities—namely the persistence and expansion of the exploitative relationships of slavery and wage capitalism.[1] As scholarship has gradually come to recognize, *Letters from an American Farmer* is less an account of facts than it is of knowing, less an assessment of the economic conditions of late eighteenth-century America than it is a critique of the way in which writers go about accounting for and validating those conditions through observation and theory. Dennis Moore's recent publication of the darker and more satirical letters left out of the 1782 English edition only promises to accelerate this critical volte-face on Crèvecoeur begun by Henri Bourdin, Ralph Gabriel, and Stanley Williams when they published Crèvecoeur's overtly skeptical *Sketches of Eighteenth-Century America* in 1927.[2]

I want to argue below that the history of the reception of *Letters* is as important as the manuscript itself in revealing an intractable challenge facing those who would produce descriptive accounts of early American social conditions which were critical or analytical in nature. This difficulty has been the tendency of audiences to efface the constitutive role of rhetoric underpinning literary renderings of the American social landscape and to read descriptions, even overtly fictional descriptions, as empirical, scientific observations of "natural" phenomenon. For historians and political philosophers, this tendency has found expression in the imperative to categorize *Letters* as a representative part of the whole of the early American experience, a stubborn transhistorical desire to see in Crèvecoeur's writing the embodiment of American exceptionalism. As a result, Crèvecoeur's narrative has been read almost exclusively in terms of an often excerpted and anthologized chapter entitled "What Is an American," a reading that has consistently yielded an encouraging and apparently timeless celebration of liberal individualism.

But the whole of *Letters* is not the sum of one of its parts. Far from an empirical account of early America, Crèvecoeur's *Letters* is, on careful reading, a literary adaptation of the political philosophy of the French intellectual Abbé Raynal, a rendering that satirizes a would-be political theorist who eschews Raynal's teleological ideas of historical necessity in favor of an empirical methodology which seeks to derive the course of history from the minutiae of observable hard facts. Critiquing the late eighteenth-century rejection of metaphysical and cyclical interpretations of history in favor of a political philosophy which was emerging from the Enlightenment fascination with the natural and physical sciences, Crèvecoeur's narrative is a second rather than a first-order inquiry, a text which endeavors to call attention to the procedures and categories used by observers instead of documenting actual states of affairs or actual sequences of events.

In this chapter I make the following series of arguments. First, I focus on the formal and structural rather than the biographical and histrionic aspects of Crèvecoeur's work, putting James's story alongside Raynal's theory of class exploitation and civilizational decline. In the second part of this chapter I speculate that *Letters* is best read as an intermediary literary genre somewhere between philosophical argument and narrative fiction, a mixed genre which emerged as the product of Crèvecoeur's desire to make Raynal's sociopolitical criticism available and meaningful to a large reading public. Crèvecoeur considered narrative fiction as a means by which a relatively unknown former French aristocrat, living under an assumed identity in the America colonies, could participate in a transatlantic "republic of letters," engaging in an ongoing philosophical discussion with European men of letters at the same time reaching for a wider audience and greater political efficacy. Crèvecoeur says as much as this in his dedication to Raynal, claiming "there is, no doubt, a secret communion among good men throughout the world; a mental affinity connecting them by a similitude of sentiments: then why, though an American, should not I be permitted to share in that extensive intellectual consanquinity?" In Part Three I examine the reception of *Letters* and Crèvecoeur's subsequent exploitation of the ambiguity of his literary creation. I suggest here that Crèvecoeur's narrativization of Raynal's critique in the form of circulating literary artifact subsequently allowed the writer an extraordinary degree of authorial latitude in a dangerous age of political upheaval and revolution.

Much of the confusion over *Letters,* I will suggest, has stemmed from these last two interrelated imperatives: Crèvecoeur's desire to mute the didacticism of Raynal's theories in an effort to reach a popular reading audience; and his apparently well-founded fear that unambiguous political commitments, while appropriate for a "man of letters" in an abstract "res publica," made a displaced French aristocrat who had fought with Louis Montcalm in the French and Indian Wars, and who was residing in Revolutionary British America under the assumed name J. Hector St. John, vulnerable to rapidly shifting political affiliations. I conclude with the claim that the ambiguity of *Letters* not only provided Crèvecoeur the means by which he could participate in a public sphere of discourse without suffering political consequences when existing political arrangements were upended; it enabled Crèveceoeur to rewrite the work when new political circumstances demanded new sentiments, something he accomplished with his subsequent French "translations." That is, I make the sociological assertion that the commodity form of his critique afforded Crèvecoeur a unique mode of protection from what his character James terms the "jarring contradictory parties" which rose and fell in the Atlantic world of the late eighteenth century. James's conclusion that "he who governs himself according to what he calls his principles may be punished either by one party or the other for those very principles," that "any kind of opposition to . . . now prevailing sentiments immediately begets hatred," and that "extremes appear equally dangerous to a person of so little weight and consequence" speaks volumes, I think, to the pressing framing conditions of Crèvecoeur's sociopolitical narrative (203–205).

■ ■ ■

A hint at the structural design which underpins the English edition of *Letters* comes from a narrative which distinguishes Crèvecoeur's intentions from those of his persona James: the text's dedicatory letter to Abbé Raynal, whose 1770 *Histoire Philosophique et Politique des etablissemens et du commerce des Europeens dans les deux Indes* declared that the scarcely born liberty in Europe was buried in the development of American slavery. Here Crèvecoeur recalls reading *Histoire des deux Indes* and reflecting "on the relative state of nations."[3] Proclaiming Raynal's "genius to be at the head of my study," Crèvecoeur admits that he "prosecutes" his labors "under its invisible but powerful guidance" and expresses his wish to "sanctify *[Letters]* under the auspices of [Raynal's] name." *Letters,* in J. Hector St. John's own words, constituted a study of the American scene within the matrix of Raynal's theories on slavery and civilizational degeneracy.

Much of the confusion about *Letters from an American Farmer* has stemmed from a failure to take into account Crèvecoeur's dedication to Abbé Raynal. Raynal's *Histoire des deux Indes* went through countless editions and consistently made the list of the top five most sought-after forbidden best-sellers in pre-Revolutionary France.[4] Historian Robert Darnton quotes one bookseller as claiming in 1774 that the market was so saturated with editions of the *Histoire des deux Indes* that "one can consider its sales potential as destroyed," a situation that was rectified after 1781 when the public hangman burned the book in front of the Parliament of Paris.[5] Raynal's history was so popular that writers like the Abbé Roubaud and the philosopher Hornot plagiarized from it freely, and one historian claims that up to 1789 "hardly a year went by but an imitation of Raynal appeared."[6]

The concept of Raynal's book was one that was self-consciously original: he claimed that he was breaking from histories which sought to chronicle the singular outcomes of battles and the idiosyncratic actions of kings in order to theorize how economic considerations dominated nations. Raynal's materialistic thesis, reflected in the very title of the book, allowed him to critique the course of European nation-building for nearly three centuries, and it afforded him the opportunity to use the settlement of the New World as a backdrop to continue on in the *philosophes'* attack against intolerance and servitude. In the tradition of the great French historian Bossuet, Raynal sought above all to reach truths of a general nature, and he saw the meticulous accumulation of discreet and accurate details as relatively unimportant to a thinker who possessed the key to the mysteries of the world: a philosophic soul. Thus when he was confronted with the myriad of factual errors in his *Philosophical and Political History,* Raynal often responded to critics that the lessons and predictions of his survey more than made up for any factual inaccuracies.

Raynal's history of colonial America was, in theory, a history of humanist agrarianism gone awry. The self-sufficient agrarian in the humanist paradigm was the model citizen because his property protected him—and his ethical and religious principles—from unsettling market forces. Yet the agrarian was both vulnerable to climatic determinants and the pressure of commercial forces which, in the guise of free enterprise, relied on the exploitation of labor to create margins of profit. Such commercialization undermined the public ideals of agrarian individualism and made inevitable the rise of the forces of human tyranny. Because in Raynal's view the New World was, unlike the nations of Europe, founded on the humanist promise of agrarian self-sufficiency, signs of the continent's indigenous climatic decay and the colonies' degenerative slip into commercial free enterprise were particularly disturbing.

Following up on an antediluvian cosmology he first established in Book 17 of *Histoire des deux Indes,* Raynal noted in *The Revolution of America* that European immigrants "who shall go with the projects of cultivation will not have all the satisfaction 'which' they promise themselves, because they will find the good land, even the middling, all occupied; and there will be nothing to be offered them but barren lands, unhealthy marshes, or steep mountains" (179).[7] What Raynal called "the imperfection . . . of nature in America," consisting of "a damper air and a more marshy ground," was left from the biblical flood and yielded a land "almost throughout, bad, or of a middling quality." Offering a rather pessimistic outline of the New World's agricultural resources, a survey that foreshadowed Buffon and Volney, Raynal anticipated Crèvecoeur's topographic survey of the colonies in *Letters.* He argued that

scarcely any thing but maize grows in the four most northern colonies . . . the only resource of their inhabitants is fishery . . . the soil [in New York, New Jersey, and Pennsylvania] is so rapidly become worse than it was that an acre, which formerly yielded full sixty bushels of wheat, now produces but very rarely above twenty . . . though the soil of Maryland

and Virginia is much superior to all the rest, it cannot be said to be very fruitful . . . North Carolina produces some corn, but of a quality so inferior that it is sold for five and twenty, or thirty percent less than the other, in all the markets . . . The excessive rains which fall [in South Carolina and Georgia] finding no means of discharge, form numerous marshes or lakes, in which rice is cultivated, to the great detriment of the slaves and freemen occupied in this labour. (179–180)

Raynal's survey, like James's travels in *Letters,* charted a north-south topography on which the French intellectual contrasted the austere but self-determined fishing enterprises of New England with the mass cultivation of staple crops in the South, all the while relegating the ideals of pastoral self-sufficiency, American plenitude, and social equality to an as of yet unrealized hope.

More disturbing to Raynal than America's environmental degeneracy, however, was its turn from agrarianism to the more impersonal world of commerce brought about both through environmental decline and through the mercantilist forces of colonization and empire. Since in Raynal's definition commerce produced "nothing of itself for it is not of a plastic nature . . . its business consists in exchanges," he considered agricultural production, particularly by the means of independent husbandmen, as the benchmark of a nation's wealth. As Raynal generalized in an odd catachresis, "if the lands be not cultivated, all commerce is precarious . . . nations that are only maritime, or commercial, enjoy, it is true, the fruits of commerce; but the tree of it belongs to those people who cultivate it. Agriculture is therefore the first and real opulence of a state" (8:216–217). Invoking an analogous course of civilization in the Roman Empire, Raynal suggested that the ubiquity of civilizational decline in history was linked to an insidious distancing of the means and modes of agricultural production. Through avarice and sloth, he noted, citizens of Rome "contracted the habit of trusting the care of their subsistence to their slaves," and "proud of the spoils of the universe, [they] held in contempt the rural occupations of [their] founders." Raynal concluded that "the contempt which Romans had for agriculture, in the intoxication of those conquests which had given them the whole world without cultivating it," brought the empire to starvation and finally "to ruin, destroyed rather by its internal vices, than by the barbarians who tore it to pieces."

Raynal's history of the New World up to the American Revolution followed the same trajectory as his history of republican Rome. In the original founding of settlements in the New World, victims of the intolerance and despotism of Europe sought asylum in an environment where they could flourish by subsistence farming. Since, as Raynal acknowledged, taking up on Locke, the "chief basis of a society for cultivation or commerce is property," early agrarians had relatively easy access to both the means and modes of production. As population increased to the point where the enervated landscape could no longer provide enough arable property, inevitable class divisions surfaced to subvert the agrarian ideal of equality (7:281–282).[8] In order to produce agricultural products in an environment with rapidly diminishing returns due to population increases, poor climate, and increasing demands on the land for exports to Europe, planters not unwillingly forfeited their ideal of subsistence and turned to bound wage labor and slaves. The former Raynal saw as a nefarious trade whereby "America acquires its supplies of men for husbandry, as princes do for war, by [artifice]. They are set forth on by 'raptures the delights of the New World' and are inveigled away" (7:408–415). The introduction and persistence of the latter—slavery—Raynal condemned as the harbinger of the fall of the New World, evidence that the corruption of Europe had indeed undermined the ideal of an agrarian asylum.

■ ■ ■

If for Raynal, as it was to be for Marx, the history of all hitherto existing society was the history of class struggle, Crèvecoeur creates in his literary adaptation of Raynal an aspiring philosophical writer who attempts to free himself from such overarching theories of historical necessity by an epistemological method we might call, borrowing from Mary Poovey, "scientific rationality."[9] In the first epistle of *Letters,* where James gives an account of his rationale for writing, a local minister explains why in America a humble farmer, with little knowledge of world history or political philosophy, could aspire to account for the American experience:

> In [Europe], all the objects of contemplation . . . Must have a reference to ancient generations and to very distant periods, clouded with the mist of ages . . . [In America a writer's] imagination, instead of submitting to the painful and useless retrospect of revolutions, desolations, and plagues would, on the contrary, wisely spring forward to the anticipated fields of future cultivation and improvement . . . [In Europe] the half-ruined amphitheaters and the putrid fevers of the Campania must fill the mind with the most melancholy reflections whilst he is seeking for the origin and the intention of those structures with which he is surrounded and the cause for so great a decay. Here he might contemplate the very beginnings and outlines of human society. (42–43)

In this formulation, empirical description of the part (or of the representative individual) takes precedence over knowledge of the whole at the same time that an individualistic concern with process and procedure supplants that of collective concern with common history.[10] James, too, celebrates the limited nature and scope of his experience, turning to a Lockean celebration of microeconomic potentialities. "I [have] ceased to ramble in imagination through the wide world," he asserts at one point. "My excursions since have not exceeded the bounds of my farm, and all my principle pleasures are now centered within its scanty limits. The instant I enter on my own land, the bright idea of property, of exclusive right, of independence, exalts my mind" (54).

It should come as no surprise that such a self-satisfied James, a would-be theorist of the micropolitical and microeconomic, has little interest in confronting either the needs of collective government or the plight of others less fortunate, except when they serve to validate or accommodate his own view of the world. He asserts at one point, "Why should I not find myself happy? Where is that situation which can confer more . . . felicity than that of an American farmer, possessing freedom of action, freedom of thoughts, [and] ruled by a mode of government which requires little from us? I owe nothing but a pepper corn to my country" (52). At another point, after hearing of the distresses of Russian and Hungarian peasants, James replies, "I am happier now than I thought myself before. It is strange that misery, when viewed in others, should become to us a sort of real good . . . Hard is their fate to be condemned to a slavery worse than our negroes" (52).

Thus, like the institution of American slavery, history and experience drop out of James's "empirical" account of America, largely as a result of the particular metonymic reasoning which underwrites much of James's political philosophy. This is a cognitive disposition which, to paraphrase the linguist George Lakoff, tacitly derives a broader, more integral category—presupposed as an ideal case—from a term understood to be its representation.[11] If Locke had deployed metonymic rhetoric in order to instantiate concepts as broad and abstract as citizens and civil government from the concrete bearer of property, and if Adam Smith had theorized the macrocosmic principle of an "invisible hand" by telescoping the actions of an anonymous pin maker, James hopes to account for America by extrapolating the general from the particular, designating general states of affairs from their microscopic material embodiment.

It is through this form of reasoning that James "naturalizes" his "empirical" observations, since by appealing to no ostensible theoretical apparatus or argument James can claim that his observations are merely reflections or amplifications of a concrete but generalizable state of affairs. Thus he can proclaim his innocent objectivity at the same time that he absolves himself of all responsibility for the outcome of his observations. "Remember that you have laid the foundation of this correspondence," he informs his European correspondent. "You well know that I am neither a philosopher, politician, divine, or naturalist, but a simple farmer. I flatter myself, therefore, that you'll receive my letters as conceived, not according to scientific rules, to which I am a perfect stranger, but agreeable to the spontaneous impressions which each subject may inspire" (49–50). James even goes so far as to place intelligibility in the hands of his reader. "Let him have the trouble of sifting the good from the bad, the useful from the trifling," he says at one point. "Let him select what he may want and reject what may not answer his purpose" (44).

The problem, of course, is James's unexamined point of reference, and the plot of Crèvecoeur's *Letters from an American Farmer* suggests the story of a naive political philosopher whose supposedly atheoretical focus on concrete particulars and more generally on what he terms the underlying "nature" of all industry and labor—that of self-interest—makes him blind to larger historical forces, particularly those relating to the formation of exploitable social classes. Raynal, recognizing that the humanistic philosophy of the Enlightenment was insufficient to convert slaveholders to a system of free labor while exorbitant profits were to be had in the New World, came to the conclusion that slavery was intrinsic to the settling of America, predicting its end only through some cataclysmic upheaval.[12] Similarly, Crèvecoeur's James, passing from naive expectations of New World regeneration to an understanding of colonial America's dark and exploitative economic infrastructure, comes to the conclusion that the New World promise of "middling" self-sufficiency was both temporal and ideological, the result of a cognitive retreat from the political.[13]

To parallel Raynal's paradigm, Crèvecoeur constructs James as an aspiring New World author, a would-be man of letters, who begs his European guide to give him his writing subjects lest he be blamed for "an injudicious choice" (49). The new American writer is to be, according to James's minister, a representative voice of the New World's innocence, "a *tabula rasa*," an author of potential and space rather than a writer of history and time (46). Crèvecoeur contrasts the chronometrical and horological concerns of the European writer of histories to the spatial and empirical imagination of this new American writer who, "instead of submitting to the painful and useless retrospect of revolutions, desolations, and plagues . . . [springs] forward to the anticipated fields of future cultivation and improvement" (43). The American man of letters, in other words, is to be a writer of the local and of the unstudied present and future tenses, a documentarian who *records* rather than interprets experience. As

James notes, "I had rather *admire* the ample barn of one of our opulent farmers . . . than to *study* the dimensions of the temple of Ceres. I had rather *record* the progressive steps of this industrious farmer . . . than *examine* how modern Italian convents can be supported without doing anything but singing and praying" (43; emphasis mine). Beginning with the first letter, James is figured as a writer who is to be defined by his potential for transposing the empirical facts of the world rather than by his facility with contextualizing America in terms of political history and philosophy, an author who sees writing only as "conversation put down in black and white" rather than as an instrument of economic or political analysis (44).

Crèvecoeur contrasts this naive assumption about authorship, where "writing letters is nothing more than talking on paper," a mere exercise in documentary and therefore politically neutral observation, both to the suspicions of James's wife, who understands writing to be by its nature political and therefore best kept "as great a secret as if it was some heinous crime," and to a European tradition of written history which, as James notes, presents nothing "but crimes of the most heinous nature" (48, 173). James censures written history because, as he understands it, the writing of a nation's annals inherently aesthetasized violence and oppression, making it a poor foundational genre for the New World's "happy settlements . . . not founded on intrusion, forcible entries, or blood" (108). James suggests that national histories naturalized the forces of exploitation and tyranny by their logic of dramatizing only events of violence and domination and excluding the more harmonious, peaceful, and egalitarian aspects of civilization. As he tells us, "History perpetually tells us of millions of people abandoned to the caprice of the maddest princes and of whole nations devoted to the blind fury of tyrants" (173).

As a foundational writer, James believes (or is led to believe by his bucolic minister) that he can establish the authorial and generic equivalents to the self-sufficient agrarian by redefining the terms of authorship. James intends to give form to the extensive totality of the American experience and not to write the American experience into a preexisting analytic form. He works to eschew the old "European" genre of history in favor of a new literary form, one appropriate to the character of American experience. Against his wife's convictions that authorship will destroy James's agrarian humility by making him "the subject of public talk," make him idle and unproductive and associate him with the "paper economy" of "bank notes" in England, and distinguish him in socioeconomic status from his peers, James argues that if he decries philosophical and historical approaches to literature and writes according to the "spontaneous impressions which each subject may inspire" and the "genuine dictates of [his] mind," he will be able to fulfill the European correspondent's call for an "accurate" account of the American experience (48–50). Moreover, James believes he can perform this task without either disrupting his agrarian pursuits or lapsing into the European convention of history which "never [speaks] of a hero of mathematics, a hero of knowledge or humanity . . . [only of] the most successful butchers of the world" (174). Wanting to avoid a traditional writerly "design" and to compose an "empirical" account of America where man has "in some measure regained the ancient dignity of [his] species," James attempts to defy what we might call the now conventional constraints of rhetorical or analytic discourse: he vows to subscribe to utter realism, allowing to his reader "the trouble of sifting the good from the bad, the useful from the trifling." He aims to eschew all inclinations toward theory and art, again leaving his reader to apply his or her own "warmth of imagination . . . [and] love [of] description." And he chooses to write in the most practical and least "contrived" mode, the epistle, letting form find its "natural" correlative in description (44).

Following this empiricist logic to the letter, James agrees to write for Mr. F. B. only on the condition that Mr. F. B. provides the organization and subjects for his account.[14] Moreover, this new American author intends to use the limits of the American landscape, not the bounds of literary conventions, to frame his description of the New World. As he notes in the conclusion to the first epistle, "I flatter myself, therefore, that you'll receive my letters as conceived, not according to scientific rules to which I am a perfect stranger, but agreeable to the spontaneous impressions which each subject may inspire. This is the only line I am able to follow, the line which nature has herself traced for me" (49–50).

But, from the start, James's correspondence with his European patron Mr. F. B. is linked to the economic and commercial aspects of writing as well as to the rhetorical conventions of political analysis. In the opening sentences of the first letter, for instance, James, despite his assertion that his correspondence is to be an innocent exchange of "raw" information, associates his conversation with Mr. F. B. with the Old World marriage between writing and accumulating capital. He notes that "the knowledge which I *acquired* from your conversation has amply *repaid* me . . . and I abundantly *profited* by the journey; the contrast therefore proves the *debt* if gratitude to be on my side" (39; emphasis mine). In addition, James's minister's most persuasive argument for James responding to Mr. F. B. is that by doing so James might find Mr. F. B. to be of "some assistance" in securing a post in the Anglican church for one of his sons (44).

But perhaps the most persistent challenge to James's desire to establish a depoliticized and derhetoricalized mode of authorship comes in his growing recognition of the relationship between writing and the profession of law. Although James attempts early on to cleave what he considers his mimetic form of authorship from what he sees as the contentiousness of law, asking rhetorically whether it is "not better to contemplate under these humble roofs the rudiments of future wealth and population than to behold the accumulated bundles of litigious papers in the office of a lawyer," he finds it more and more difficult to separate the two as he sees them emerging in America (87). One reason is clear, at least historically. As Robert Ferguson has argued, there was a "remarkable symbiosis between law and literary aspiration" in the early Republic because the "broad cultural responsibilities of the professional man and the writer's imperatives could be made to appear the same."[15] The lawyer/writer could assert himself as an ideological guardian of sorts by using literature to delineate or justify republican principles and to facilitate cultural consensus.

Yet many also feared the implications of having a population of such elite cultural custodians. Nativist hostility toward common law imported from England became more and more vitriolic in the years following the Revolution, a system that was itself undergoing a kind of revolution as entrepreneurs increasingly demanded law that would facilitate property and contract relationships. As Morton Horwitz, William Nelson, and Charles Sellers have all noted, the evolving "adversary system trained legal advocates to practice and to preach the market's emerging ethic—that the unbridled pursuit of self-interest is in the ultimate interest of all," and in this sense adversary advocacy became a principal, and probably the most effective, purveyor of capitalist ideology.[16] As the mercantilist commercial boom intensified, and as merchants increasingly sought to settle disputes through the courts as opposed to more traditional forms of arbitration, many saw agrarian values of truth and equity being supplanted by an increasingly complex procedural amalgam of Blackstonian and commercial legislation. The complexity of this body of law coupled with the commercial interests of its spokesmen worried agrarians. As Perry Miller noted, hostility was based on the suspicion that "the mystery of the law was a gigantic conspiracy of the learned against [the common man's] helpless integrity" and that the exclusive profession of law would beguile "the nation through some scholastic mystique."[17] Such arguments against the law reveal anxieties that a specialized culture of letters would obtain a "profession" whereby elites could exploit untrained agrarians inasmuch as they revealed nativist fear of a European legal institution being transplanted to America.

But perhaps more important, James's preoccupation with lawyers reflects a widespread suspicion that American discourse was rapidly losing its vernacular potential, becoming hierarchical, institutionalized, and political: in short, becoming indistinguishable from established and institutionalized modes of European discourse. The growth of a legal profession in even the remote villages in America not only threatened agrarian autonomy and communalism. It also revealed the successful transplantation of English juridical and political ideologies and their commercializing potential, subverting the national distinction between New and Old, and undermining the ideal notion of a balanced system of pastoral egalitarianism.

James associates this exclusive culture of the legal word with the rise of literacy and writing as the necessary concomitants to economic expansion. Noting in Letter 7 how "lawyers are so numerous in all our populous towns," James laments how in "provinces where every inhabitant is constantly employed in tilling and cultivating the earth . . . the only members of society who have any knowledge . . . promote litigiousness and amass more wealth without labor than the most opulent farmer with all his toils" (152). It is interesting that in contrast to proponents of print culture, like Benjamin Franklin, who saw literacy as one of the founding principles of egalitarianism, James fears the growth in—and uses of—print because it linked the American farmer to a distinctly European, capitalistic, and legalistic "paper culture," an association which, he fears, could only undermine the wealth of individual farmers while seeding sharp divisions of rank capped by a despotic *intelligentsia*. Although he is suspicious of lawyers from the start (making a prophetic reference to "one single lawyer" who has settled on Nantucket and lamenting how "lawyers are so numerous in all our populous towns"), by the time he gets to Charlestown James begins to recognize the invidious connection between an exploding print culture and the significance of his wife's early suspicion that writing inherently disrupts agrarian individualism (151). He recognizes that although the ideal American farmer is, like his father, a man "of *yea* and *nay*, of few words," the explosion of literacy and the concomitant development of a "paper" economy was emerging to threaten the autonomy of such isolated subjects (48). James is particularly incensed by the despotism of Charlestown lawyers who "have reached the *ne plus ultra* of worldly felicity" and who have ensured that, because of their writing, "no plantation is secured, no title is good, no will is valid, but what they dictate, regulate, and approve" (167).

Just how and why James fails to sustain his atheoretical scientific empiricism over the course of the narrative are central questions to understanding the compositional logic of *Letters*. As many literary historians have pointed out, one reason for the collapse of James's world is that Crèvecoeur, for a variety of reasons, challenges James's acclamatory epistemology with macropolitical realities. In this sense, *Letters from an American Farmer* can be seen as a *bildungsroman* of sorts. Because of the sudden outbreak of the American Revolution, James is finally made aware of the structural socioeconomic realities he has been actively suppressing throughout his descriptive account. For example, although James wants to find on Nantucket a perfect geography of individualism and pastoral timelessness, an island without annals and without "ancient monuments, spacious halls, [or] elegant dwellings," he inadvertently reveals Nantucket to be as emblematic of the mercantilist forces of colonization and empire as Europe's fallen citadels. Not only does he record how the island's native inhabitants were eradicated "in the wars which the Europeans carried on against them," juxtaposing the names of colonial towns with the names of their native-American antecedents, but he manages to demonstrate how the fishing industry, despite its promising integration of labor and capital in an environment of scarcity, has created a stratified society wholly antithetical to his ideal of self-sufficiency (123). Nantucket, the reader comes to realize, is as much a decadent society of idle consumers as it is an enlightened community of hardscrabble egalilitarians, complete with women who take opium to alleviate boredom, aristocrats who import extravagant horse chairs, and a wealthy heiress who saves the settlement from the "emoluments" of the island's lawyer by marrying him.[18]

James continues to eschew macroeconomic interpretations of America, even auguries like Charlestown's exploitative class-based society and the persistence of slavery, by focusing on the microeconomic and the micropolitical. Throughout the text of *Letters,* James's observations are paired with meticulous descriptions of the natural world, rendered so painstakingly objective that their telling metaphorical implications are completely lost on the narrator. James describes a Mandevillian phalanx of bees with the unseeing comment: "I am astounded to see that nothing exists but what has its enemy; one species pursues and lives upon the other" (55). He notes how cheap and plentiful the soon-to-be-extinct carrier pidgeon is at the market. And when he observes how a wren attacks a swallow sitting meekly "like a passive Quaker," he responds innocently with the question "Where did this little bird learn that spirit of injustice? It was not endowed with what we term reason" (63). This is accompanied in the text by a crescendo of aptly timed literary feints, topped by James's complete disappearance from the text after coming face-to-face with the sufferings of a caged slave at the end of Letter 9. James the "neutral" observer and traveler leaves the social world to become James the literary stylist to observe—but not theorize on—two metaphorically rich snakes battle in the tenth letter, and he substitutes his usual encomiums with those of Mr. Iw———n

Al——z, a Russian traveler, in the eleventh letter, punctuating a gradual recession by leaving the narrative entirely. By the time he returns in the twelfth and
final letter in the midst of the Revolution, James admits that he can no longer
sustain his scientific objectivity, even rhetorically, and his literary idealizations
finally collapse under the weight of the historical contingencies of the American Revolution.

With the onslaught of the Revolution in the final epistle, James recognizes
how his empirical writing has, at best, veiled actual socioeconomic relationships; at worst, participated in the introduction of yet another degenerative
historical paradigm: the unbridled optimism of a liberal consensus which has
veiled structural socioeconomic conditions. Having relinquished authorship in
the penultimate letter to the naively optimistic Russian traveler Mr. Iw——n
Al——z, a writerly feint that only underscores the author's loss of radiant poetic faith, James concedes in Letter 12 that his literary world has collapsed.
While James talks in the final letter about the destruction of "the whole chain
of frontiers," and even asserts that his family's "fate cannot be far distant," he is
clearly more preoccupied with the disillusionment such events have engendered. We might say that James's horrors are the psychological horrors of dis-
abusement. He notes plaintively that the accounts of the war, "told in
chimney-corners, swell themselves in our affrighted imaginations into the
most terrific ideas!" and that this "fear amplifies every sound," rendering his
world hostile (202). To counter such demystification, James makes a small but
symbolically important attempt to suppress accounts of the nightmares of his
children, but in vain. In a passage that in some sense paraphrases the design of
the whole of *Letters,* James asserts that "these images of their disturbed imagination, instead of being frivolously looked upon as in the days of our happiness, are on the contrary considered as warnings and sure prognostics of our
future fate. I am not a superstitious man, but since our misfortunes, I am grown
more timid and less disposed to treat the doctrine of omens with contempt"
(203).

Reversing his early and optimistic assertion of American economic exceptionalism, James notes, in a phrase that could have been written by Raynal,
how "the innocent class are always the victim of the few; they are in all countries and at all times the inferior agents, on which the popular phantom is
erected" (204). He condemns the pronouncements of men of letters like Solon
and Montesquieu who, "secure from personal danger," can "expiate freely" and
abstractly on the affairs of English imperialism. He beckons them to stop writing simple celebratory maxims and to "trace on the map the progress of these
desolations . . . Observe, then," James notes, "whether the man will not get the

better of the citizen, whether his political maxims will not vanish! Yes he will cease to glow so warmly with the glory of the metropolis" (206). James decides to relinquish his pen, announcing that he has "ceased to consider [himself] as a member of the ancient state now convulsed, [and he will] willingly descend into an inferior one . . . a state approaching nearer to that of nature" (211). Claiming that the American philosopher, like the American farmer, cannot "live in solitude; he must belong to some community bound by some ties, however imperfect," James will flee the factionalized social terrain of colonial America. "What is man," he asserts plaintively at last, "when no longer connected with society, or when he finds himself surrounded by a convulsed, half-dissolved one?" (201)

By deciding to move west and to live with the native Americans, James claims he will be free from "books [which] tell me so much that they inform me of nothing . . . [and] sophistry, the bane of freemen [which] launches forth in all her deceiving attire" (204). He and his family will revert to a life without writing, "unencumbered either with voluminous laws or contradictory codes" (211). He will eschew letters and the "fictitious society in which [he] lives" for the immanence of "the great Maniton of the woods and plains" (214, 224). Intending to submerge himself and his family in an exclusively *oral* culture, James makes it clear that his children will have "no literary accomplishments," and that "not a word of politics, shall cloud [their] simple conversation" (225). He will go to the bush not, like European travel writers, to "*study* the manner of aborigines" and to publish books; rather, he will "go determined industriously to work among them" and "to *conform* to them" (226; emphasis mine). James, in other words, will disappear from the world of writing altogether, leaving only his letters behind as the corporate reliquary of America's collapsed philosophical ideals. "I resemble," he concludes dramatically, "one of the stones of a ruined arch, still retaining that pristine form which anciently fitted the place I occupied, but the centre is tumbled down; I can be nothing until I am replaced, either in the former circle, or in some stronger one" (211).

If James's escape sounds a lot like a conventional ending to an epistolary novel, it is because James himself refigures his story at the conclusion to take this form. In the final sentences of the twelfth letter, James asks Mr. F. B. to acknowledge the "unreserved manner in which [he] has written" and, in looking over the text, to mourn "with [him] over that load of physical and moral evil with which [they] are all oppressed" (227). Admitting that he has overlooked his "own share" of this evil in his writing, James beckons Mr. F. B. to experience his disillusionment secondhand by means of his text. James asks Mr. F. B., the distant reader, to transform him from his role as author of the text to that of its subject, refiguring in several sentences the entire formal structure of *Letters,* and recasting his epistles to Mr. F. B., not as disconnected observations but as a coherent narrative account of the failure of a naive political philosopher who would eschew the idea of history and historical necessity. James becomes, in one brief paragraph, the protagonist of an emerging literary form wholly compatible with the fledgling nation Daniel Boorstin has called "the disproving ground for utopias": the novel.[19]

■ ■ ■

If the English *Letters* of 1782, based on the sociopolitical criticism of Raynal, constitutes a critique of the cognitive trappings of liberalism in the form of narrative fiction, why has its message been lost on critics, historians, anthologists, and readers? As the progeny of the economic transformation of the eighteenth century, are we vulnerable to the very myopia or "micro-opia" Crèvecoeur satirizes in his protagonist James? Or was a designing Crèvecoeur himself responsible for the problems of interpretation? While there is plenty of evidence to suggest that both of these factors have played a part in the confusion over *Letters,* perhaps much of the responsiblity lies in the structural problematics of an emerging commercial print culture, particulary with respect to the problems of objectification. As eighteenth-century critics of "republican print ideology" noted, the occulting of the "I" behind public discourse removed the subjective, designing author from his medium, creating objectivity where none was intrinsically merited. Thus freed from authorial responsibility, misleading texts could conceal their author's pretenses, manipulations, and ambitions. They became commodities divorced from their origins, free to circulate among audiences without a clear authorial source. Divorced from its author and its rhetorical context, the republican text derived its authority from its cultural reputation, its typographical appearance, and its style. Whereas the classical man of letters confirmed his identity in letters, the republican writer fashioned his.

It was precisely such relativity that worried critics of "republican print ideology" who envisioned social instability resulting from a consumer rather than author-based identity for texts. Many saw the transfer of written authority from the patron to the public as more than a simple threat to an elite preserve; they understood such a transit as a displacement of ultimate intelligibility from the province of educated elite to the roar of the marketplace. A text's meaning as it was figured in "republican print ideology," critics argued, was, like a tool or widget, produced out of sight, packaged, marketed, and consumed under a wide spectrum of circumstances with often conflicting intentions and results. Furthermore, because such meaning (unlike that derived from oral discourse or established systems of privilege and patronage which could be tangibly linked to an individual author or authors) was reified textually, it could be easily coopted for a wide range of unintended, delusory, or subversive uses. It could be attributed to (or plagiarized by) persons other than the author; it could be represented as either fact or fiction by the circumstances in which it found an audience; or it could be deployed by persons other than the author (the publisher, the state, designing individuals or factions) to achieve political or economic objectives or to negotiate expediencies. In short, the republican text was disturbingly plastic.

Ironically, the history of the reception of *Letters* seems to substantiate this fear of indeterminacy. In the two years after its English publication in 1782, *Letters* had been read by European critics as, variously, a portrayal of the exotic, a benign literary hoax, a contribution to the English literary canon, a colonial panegyric, an invective against the Revolution, a Tory panegyric, an immigration tract, a French Catholic deceit, a Rousseauistic conceit, and a true documentary account of the Americas. By the end of the eighteenth century, public perception of Crèvecoeur's *Letters* in America had become so divorced from the text's darker origins in Raynal that the author became something of an American icon in his own right. He was made an honorary citizen of both New Haven and Hartford and voted into the American Philosophical Society. Patriot Ethan Allen even went so far as to affix his assumed English name to the American landscape at St. Johnsbury, Vermont.

How is it possible for the author of a collection of essays described in 1779 by British General James Pattison as "a sort of irregular journal of America . . . [favoring] the side of the [British] Government . . . [and throwing] odium on the proceedings of the opposite party [American Patriots] and upon the tyranny of their popular government" to become a representative of the American character?[20] How is it plausible for a text which announces itself as patterned after Raynal's theories of American class formation, which presents a European audience with a naive farmer who observes but does not *see* ravages to the natural landscape, exploitative labor relations, and impending political crisis until he is prepared to flee to the frontier, to become instantiated as the ur-text of American exceptionalism? Furthermore, how could Crèvecoeur's fictional account become so imbued with documentary legitimacy that politicians, anthologists, literary critics, and historians continue to bracket sections of *Letters* as demonstrative of social conditions in eighteenth-century America?[21]

The answer seems to lie within the assumptions and fallacies of republican print culture. In a protonational period of rapid transformations in publishing technologies, at a time when the Republic's separation from Europe was to some extent only tenuously realized in print, and when definitions of "individual, print, public, and reason were [being] readjusted in a new set of ground rules for [public] discourse," the Atlantic world was unprepared for the rush of authors intent on demonstrating how representations in print could produce, in addition to new nations and new ideologies, *new* individuals and new concomitant social mobility.[22] In short, the triadic relationship in an emerging print culture between authors, publishers, and readers was immersed in an ontological and ideological crisis over who was to publish what and with what intentions.

Crèvecoeur negotiated—indeed exploited—this crisis in republican print culture by writing a fictionalized philosophical account which, as a plastic form ideologically and materially, rendered him a participant in the public sphere while simultaneously helping him to elide potentially dangerous political affiliations in a rapidly nationalizing world. In other words, he took advantage of what Lennard Davis has called the "undifferentiated matrix" between fact and fiction, between news writing and novel writing, at a time when reverberations of the revolution in America, and impending revolutions in France and Haiti, made it clear that unambiguous political or philosophical commitments in writing were disadvantageous. More than providing a flexible vehicle to fit his multiple national selves, however, narrative fiction allowed Crèvecoeur a means to address the plurality of rising national audiences and to mediate the changes in attitudes within and between these audiences. For example, *Letters* carried great appeal for Francophone intellectuals and the *philosophes* who could indulge in a fictional account based on Raynal's theories of civilizational decline; yet the book also catered to the interests of the British working class who were hungry for information on opportunities in America, and to American nationalists who were eager to establish a nativist literature.

But why was engendering such a diverse appeal important to Crèvecoeur? Perhaps it was for the same reason most authors in the early Republic wrote or attempted to write narrative fiction: it was a means of participating in public life and rising in reputation and public stature. Crèvecoeur perhaps supervenes Franklin as the prima facie of the self-made American man of letters. While Franklin may have been the first writer in America to fashion a public identity almost entirely by his productions in print, Crèvecoeur extended this self-fashioning to extraliterary concerns, constructing different surnames, nationalities, political and philosophical affiliations, and private and public roles throughout his life. The biographical work done by Julia Mitchell, Thomas

Philbrick, and Allen and Asselineau bears this out. In these accounts, Crèvecoeur's life is often wholly characterized by his skill at adapting (often simultaneously) to opposing religious, philosophical, political, and national groupings out of neccessity.[23]

But it was his writing which proved to be Crèvecoeur's most effective means of suspending potentially deleterious political commitments while establishing his success as a public figure and a participatory man of letters. The speed by which *Letters* fashioned a public identity for Crèvecoeur is perhaps unprecedented in literary history. The text of *Letters* established the reputation of an essentially unknown declining aristocrat who became a confidant to the court of Louis XVI, authored official accounts of the New World, advised Marshal de Castries on American geography, and accepted the French consulship to New York, all by 1784.

Yet Crèvecoeur was not without his critics. Because the ambiguous espistolary composition of the English *Letters* invited a baffling array of readings, and because Crèvecoeur, careful to negotiate the "undifferentiated matrix" between fact and fiction for political and economic expediencies, did not make an overt effort to label his work as fiction, either at first or later in his life, national critics took an active but contradictory role in deciding how their constituents were to read Crèvecoeur's work. These critics, by publishing carefully selected extracts and establishing ideological pretexts, formed "interpretative communities" which appear to have greatly influenced the reception of *Letters.* The first reviewers, for instance, writing as early as April 1782, applauded Crèvecoeur's anecdotal vividness. While suspecting the authenticity of the book, the reviewer of *The European Magazine and London Review* apparently found such fictionalizing in the tradition of Macpherson and Chatterton, whose works, he notes, became valuable additions to English canon. He went on to publish extracts from the second, third, ninth, and twelfth letters (the often-quoted "American Farmer" and "What Is an American" essays and the melodramatic "Description of Charles Town" and "Distresses of a Frontier Man" letters), seemingly to represent the dramatic unfolding of the book. *The Monthly Magazine,* a pro-American journal, took a more political view, praising the book's antimilitarism. Other journals, such as *The Gentleman's Magazine* and *The Westminster Magazine, or the Pantheon of Taste,* reproduced only the ninth letter ("Description of Charles Town"), apparently appropriating Crèvecoeur's description of American slavery in a larger invective on the inconsistency of the ideals of the American Revolution and social realities. Such culling became common in reviewing Crèvecoeur's *Letters,* a practice encouraged by the autonomy of the individual sections. But such extraction also allowed multiple and contradictory readings. Baron Friedrich-Melchior von Grimm, for instance, in *Correspondence litteraire, philosophique et critique,* focusing on the first letters, lauded the author's republican sensibility and a Rousseauistic love of nature and man, proclaiming that "this book, written without method and without art, but with a high degree of sense and sensibility, perfectly fulfills the object that the author seems to have proposed: that of making the reader love America . . . it attracts simple and true pictures, by its expression of an honest soul" (14:88).[24]

By far the most interesting contemporary response to *Letters,* however, attacked its ideological malleability. Contextualizing *Letters* with domestic forgeries of "a Lauder, a Bower, and a Chatterton" and with a "new species of forgery imported from the Continent of America," English critic Samuel Ayscough unveiled Hector St. John as mountebank attempting "to mislead the people [to immigration]" and asserted "that the publication [was] a fraud, artfully disguised, and hostile to the happiness of [Great Britain]." Ayscough suggested that "the pleasing, romantic manner in which the letters, said to be the production of an American farmer, [were] written, [were] calculated to work upon the passions, and [had] gained them a credit in the world, which will be with difficulty effaced by a dry writer of mere facts." Ayscough was particularly concerned that Crèvecoeur's book would like "poison [be] . . . permitted to spread to the gross imposition of the inattentive and credulous," specifically to the poor in a postwar England burdened with debts and taxation. He charged Crèvecoeur with undue artistic license, asserting that "the pen of this writer would make an Irish hut appear a palace most devoutly to be wished; surrounded with a potato garden; their cow flowing with healthful lacteal springs." Barely concealing his concern about English emigration, Ayscough suggested that in Crèvecoeur's artfulness "the wretched inhabitants of the barren islands of Nantucket and Martha's Vineyard become the envy of those who enjoy every blessing which Nature kindly grants." After a lengthy critical exegesis of *Letters,* in which he argued for gross inconsistencies and fabrications in everything from the author's claim to nationality to the snake story in the tenth letter (he argues Crèvecoeur borrowed it from an earlier manuscript), Ayscough recommended censorship. As a romance, Ayscough allowed that *Letters* afforded "some amusement to those idle readers who are the sole support of circulating libraries." But as a free and public document, he saw *Letters* "fraught with a . . . fatal tendency" that urged English subjects to "pursue romantic schemes."

It is interesting that Ayscough condemns *Letters* for the same indeterminate status that critics of "republican print ideology" feared would encourage authorial manipulation to arrogate political power, suggesting the cultural consequences of a public text which, as narrative fiction did, blurred or broke conventional distinctions in emerging genres. This is another face of the same argument opponents of "republican print ideology" leveled on Franklin. If credibility resided not in persons but in print, if objective truth was best preserved as a nonparticular public vision rather than an aligned private authority, the question remained over what to do with designing authors and texts. Ayscough had reason enough to fear the problematic status of *Letters*. Because he discerned what he considered the line between fact and fiction in *Letters* unintelligible to all but the most sophisticated readers, Ayscough anticipated the power Crèvecoeur would have over a nation facing "the weight of accumulated taxes . . . [and] an overflowing of hands to all our manufactories." Ayscough saw the book as designed solely "for the purpose of encouraging foreigners to emigrate and settle in America." And, as Ayscough pointed out, Crèvecoeur's dedication in *Letters* seemed to affirm this purpose, since Crèvecoeur invoked Raynal's praise of the "asylum of freedom," "the cradle of future," and "the refuge of distressed Europeans" without making explicit the conditionality of Raynal's optimism.

A suggestion of the difficulty of interpreting *Letters* for the average eighteenth-century reader, an effort compounded by the popularity of Ayscough's critique in England, survives in the marginalia left in a first edition of the English *Letters* deposited at Houghton Library. On the leaf opposite the title page, one late eighteenth-century English owner was stirred enough to write:

> It must be evident to every reader at first view, [that the] Author could note *[sic]* be a mere farmer, as he pretends. The Gent. Mag. for Dec. 1783 speaks of the pamphlet lately published entitled *Remarks on [the] Letters from an American Farmer.* The Remarker insists [that] St. John is an imposter; that he is a French man born in Normandy; that his residence was chiefly at New York where he was looked upon as no true friend to England; that many which he asserts, are false; many old stories, if not old women's stories calculated to excite wonder. He exposes many of them as absurd and romantic; and clearly shows [that the] design of the book, was principally to encourage Foreigners to emigrate and settle in America. It appeared soon after in [the] public papers [that] Hector St. John was appointed Comis of the packets passing between France and America.

The bitter irony of the last sentence suggests the degree to which Ayscough's challenge demystified the contents of *Letters* for this reader, leaving in the place of a descriptive account of New World agrarianism an invidious immigration tract designed by a feigning Frenchman to rise in public life. Although this is scant evidence on which to base eighteenth-century reader response to *Letters,* the annotation suggests the malleability of Crèvecoeur's fictional narrative given the alternative interpretative framework provided by Ayscough.

There is also evidence to suggest that critics of different nationalities— and, perhaps, readers of different nationalities—embraced Crèvecoeur's work with varying assumptions and predispositions, making one wonder if there were structural differences in the sociological conditions of the print cultures of European nations. In his study of the reception of Crèvecoeur in German-speaking Europe (selections from the Nantucket sequence were translated into German as early as 1783), David Eisermann has discovered that eighteenth-century German critics, editors, and translators had a different understanding of the fictional aspects of *Letters* than what Ayscough imagined his readership to have had. He notes that individuals "in the German-speaking countries who had actually read Crèvecoeur, his contemporary critics, editors, and transla-tors, can be shown to have had a far more developed understanding of the fic-tional overtones in his work than might have been expected."[25] But Eisermann's findings raise more questions than they answer, since critics in Germany, unlike those in England, applied the term "fiction" to all of Crève-coeur's books, providing yet another interpretative frame by which readers gauged their readings. English readers of the 1782 edition had no such com-mentary linking *Letters* with fiction. The fact that Irish publishers hurried to print at least two editions by 1783 in the midst of a weak economy suggests the extent to which Ayscough's critique was prophetic. Furthermore, what Stan-ley Kunitz and Howard Haycraft briefly document as the "unfortunate effect" of "so laudatory and idyllic a picture of American farm life" on more than 500 families who apparently left France to settle on the Ohio River—where most perished from hunger and malaria—provides an anecdote to suggest that some readers, left to the ambiguities of the text, interpreted Crèvecoeur with con-clusions very different than those offered by Ayscough.[26]

If the reception of Crèvecoeur's *Letters* varied according to the predispo-sitions of national critics and their audiences, the publication in 1784 of the two-volume French *Les lettres d'un cultivateur Américain* only hopelessly com-pounded the malleability of Crèvecoeur's narrative. Announcing itself as a translation of the English edition—but leaving the space for the translator's name blank—*Les lettres* was an entirely new text materially (it was nearly twice the size of the English edition) and ideologically. Crèvecoeur replaced the English edition's dedication to Abbé Raynal with a letter to Marquis de

Lafayette, going on to describe punishments he suffered at the hands of the British in New York while at the same time tabulating atrocities committed by the English and their allies and condemning English imperialism taking place in places as far-flung as Bengal. Terming loyalists "monarchists" and the revolutionaries as "Republicans," Crèvecoeur did not use the persona of James regularly in *Les lettres.* Rather, he proclaimed his satisfaction with America's newly won independence, suggesting that the "fruits of victory will heal wounds of war."[27]

Crèvecoeur apparently undertook philosophical as well as political revisions, since he realigned *Les lettres* to cater to the Parisian *philosophes,* going so far as to avoid "God" (Dieu), which to the *philosophes* seemed papist superstition, in favor of "l'Etre Supreme" (the Supreme Being) or "le Tout-Puissant" (the Almighty).[28] The French "translation" of *Letters* was so different from the English edition that Crèvecoeur had difficulty securing a license for publication, it being perceived as an exhaltation of American political and religious freedom too dangerous for pre-Revolutionary France. Yet the book, perhaps because of its sensational defense of American democracy and its tailoring of *philosophes'* doctrine, was a phenomenal success. If *Letters* had fashioned Crèvecoeur as the dubious documentarian of agrarian America, *Les lettres* reinvented Crèvecoeur as the French champion of American democratic idealism.

Les lettres was followed, three years later, by yet another edition, this time comprised of three volumes. As Everett Emerson has demonstrated in a fascinating comparative study of the various French texts, this edition further solidified Crèvecoeur's disposition as a democratic idealist. The new edition began with Crèvecoeur's departure from New York, his concern for his family at Pine Hill, and narrated with pathos his return three years later. Describing Americans "as long-term victims of calamities produced by fanaticism, tyranny, and feudal oppression, people who now seek liberty and quiet," Crèvecoeur provided an account of the development of the new nation, augmenting the optimistic first letters of the 1782 English edition.[29] He concluded by asserting, panegyrically, that the American, founded on the most favorable principles, was "destined to cultivate an immense continent," all but burying the critical and analytical nature of the first edition of *Letters* beneath nationalist ideology.[30]

Interestingly, what was originally a need to see in Crèvecoeur's *Letters* a genuine documentary voice of agrarian America was, beginning in the nineteenth century, supplanted by a desire to find an emotional and pastoral corrective to Franklin's urbane wit and to solidify this voice in American history.

Consequently, the adoption of *Letters* continued, William Hazlitt, Percy Shelley, and Samuel Coleridge all praising what D. H. Lawrence called, sarcastically, the "world of the Noble Savage and Pristine Nature and Paradisal Simplicity and all that gorgeousness that [flowed] out of [Crèvecoeur's] unsullied fount" (34). With the republication of *Letters* by Lewisohn in 1904, Crèvecoeur experienced something of a renaissance in the early twentieth century. Yet even with the publication of the darker and more skeptical *Sketches* in 1925, Crèvecoeur continued to be figured in readings as a thinly veiled James in the exultory first three letters. Marcus Cunliffe, for instance, cites a list of mid twentieth-century literary critics and historians, including Henry S. Commager, William J. Chute, and Richard B. Morris, who, on the basis of the third letter, anthologized Crèvecoeur as representative of "the new spirit of nationalism which pervaded the Revolutionary movement . . . an idyllic concept of America as a land of opportunity" (129n.1c). Vernon Parrington, while conscious of the "firm fabric of economic fact" beneath *Letters,* identified the narrator with Crèvecoeur, arguing he "was an embodiment of the generous spirit of French revolutionary thought, a man whom Jefferson would have liked for a neighbor" (147). Similarly, Spiller, Thorp, Johnson, and Canby's *Literary History of the United States* (1948) proclaimed Crèvecoeur to be "one of our most sympathetic immigrants" (I:xiii). Moreover, despite several articles in the last decade which have focused on the literary and economic aspects of *Letters,* even as recent a synopsis as Peter Conn's *Literature in America* (1989) could still assert that Crèvecoeur's "America is a haven, a refuge for the dispossessed of Europe . . . [And] *Letters from an American Farmer* codified the celebratory elements of America's public discourse" (95–96).

Perhaps Lawrence came closest to overturning the persistent tendency to nationalize *Letters* away from its analytical and critical origins when he exclaimed, rhetorically, "Hector St. John, you have lied to me" (34). But even Lawrence had difficulty separating the designing Crèvecoeur from his fictional character James, constructing instead a psychological division between Frenchman's passion for the wild in nature—what Lawrence calls "blood knowledge"—and his enthusiasm for a more aestheticized nature in the abstract. The identification of Crèvecoeur with his fictionalized narrator continues to beg the questions "What then is this Crèvecoeur?" "What then is this American Text?" As Marcus Cunliffe suggests and then disavows, Crèvecoeur seems to be a Vicar of Bray, "one of those trimmers of chameleon-like adaptability who modified their attitudes according to circumstance."[31] We might go so far as to call him an opportunist, if the term was not now linked solely and pejoratively with the marketplace. Crèvecoeur was not a transcendent figure but a series of provisional identities geared toward the production of a transcendent public self in rapidly changing social conditions. Crèvecoeur's *Letters from an American Farmer* is a bit easier to compass. Like most of the fiction which constitutes the early American literary canon, *Letters* is a cultural artifact and transcendent icon in its own right, both a historically specific rhetorical performance and a continually yawning vault for ideologues.

SIX

Brackenridge and the Resistance
to Textual Authority

As the two best works of criticism to date on Hugh Henry Brackenridge's self-proclaimed "opus magnum" make clear, *Modern Chivalry* is a commentary on the struggle of the writer in American culture.[1] But *Modern Chivalry* reflects Brackenridge's performative as well as evaluative intentions. Assuming the role of a republican "man of letters" and borrowing from Cervantes's *Don Quixote,* Brackenridge drew on a tradition of discursive public writing to revolt against emerging literary conventions, claiming that chivalric romances lulled readers into a sense of unreality and into an avoidance of their own authenticity, that histories distorted truth with the "romance of the human mind," and that didactic genres failed to engage an adequate popular audience.[2] Continually confronting readers with what they did not expect from fiction, Brackenridge was proleptic in his skeptical assessment of some of the technological and sociological problems of an expanding print sphere. He worked in *Modern Chivalry* to shock his audience into an awareness not only of their social predicament as citizens in a fledgling republic but also of their vulnerability to the structural limitations of a print culture constituted by mass-produced and widely disseminated texts. Moreover, by refusing to settle into any one mode of literary production and by choosing to publish his penumbral "work" in at least six volumes over a period of thirteen years by (depending how one tabulates it) at least three different publishers in three different locations, Brackenridge went further than simply thematizing the problematic relationships between authors, texts, readers, and publishers in post-Revolutionary America: his career as an author embodied them.[3]

One might claim that this is an ambitious list of assertions about a text which has usually been ignored because of its bibliographical and formal complexity and length or deprecated as another example of derivative, tiresome, and generally elitist literature of the early Republic. But it is my contention here that critics have applied to *Modern Chivalry* the very standards and conventions of print culture that Brackenridge attempted to undermine in his effort to inculcate a skeptical attitude toward cultural assumptions about textual authority. Not surprisingly, within such interpretive frameworks, Brackenridge comes up short. But from a critical perspective which approaches *Modern Chivalry* in terms of the sociology of texts in early America, Brackenridge's narrative is as important as Crèvecoeur's in thematizing its intermediary status as participatory communication and circulating commodity. Both writers adopted vexing transitional authorial postures between civic commentary on the one hand and literary production on the other. What makes Brackenridge stand out in dramatic opposition to Crèvecoeur, however, was his refusal to exploit the sociological conditions of a consolidating commercial print trade and his fear that a new morphology of literacy, governed by a logic of objectification and homogenization, threatened to render the idealized critical participant of classical political theory anachronistic.

I want to argue that in *Modern Chivalry* Brackenridge worked for two interrelated ends. First, he attempted to destabilize and desacralize what recent critics have described as the disciplinary apparatus of "republican print ideology," a body of beliefs about the rationality of print which engendered such immutable texts as the Declaration of Independence, the Constitution, and the Bill of Rights.[4] This desacralization had, in turn, two rhetorical components: to warn the public against the manipulative power of print, and to chastise it for its gullibility and blind appetite for sensationalism. Second, Brackenridge cautioned his readership about the conventionalizing power of an emerging print culture industry (an industry fueled by economic forces as well as the imperatives of "republican print ideology") and attempted to disrupt its persuasive and pervasive logic of material, formal, and ideological uniformity.

While I am reluctant to invoke through my use of "print culture industry" the ardor and pessimism of Theodor Adorno's theory of technological hegemony, I *do* think *Modern Chivalry* explores the very tension Adorno suggested was inherent in democratic-capitalistic societies between artistic meaning and the textual or extratextual signs which conveyed that meaning, between the work of art as a source of "transcendent" meaning and its signs, which, in addition to carrying content, were leveled in the process of mass reproduction and made to advertise "the pleasure about to be derived from the product, so that the work of art sinks to the level of consumer goods in general."[5] In this sense,

Brackenridge may well be our first critic of the phenomenon Adorno was to term, in a slightly different context, the "culture industry," that technologically based apparatus which, he claimed, through the "achievement of standardization and mass production," evacuated the liberal subject from the public realm by destroying the capacity for critical thinking. Although in *Modern Chivalry* Brackenridge came at the problem from the historical perspective of the revolution in eighteenth-century printing rather than the twentieth-century communications revolution, we might, for the sake of argument, say that he shared Adorno's fear of technology and its capacity to reify society and individual consciousness, where the two were made to seem homologous, and both appeared given and unchanging.[6] Brackenridge's concern, however, was ultimately more local, in that his anxieties were specific to the glorification of printing technologies in the new Republic. Namely he feared the power of a democratic print culture (founded in, and guided by, texts, textual production, and textual interpretation) to consolidate a coercive public opinion and was anxious that such a consensus would stifle the critical individualism that made a liberal republic philosophically if not practically viable. This hegemony, Brackenridge reflected, would ultimately encourage an unarticulated but uniform intolerance.

Of course, we do not have to turn to a twentieth-century critical theorist to find a critique of the hegemonic potential of public opinion made possible by the geographic and demographic reach of print. Theories of a democratic culture industry have a discernible genealogy going back at least to the first four decades of the nineteenth century. In *Democracy in America,* for instance, Alexis de Tocqueville asserted that

> the nearer men are to a common level of uniformity, the less are they inclined to believe blindly in any man or in any class. But they are readier to trust the mass, and public opinion becomes more and more mistress of the world . . . Public opinion has a strange power . . . It uses no persuasion to forward its beliefs, but by some mighty pressure of the mind of all upon the intelligence of each it imposes its ideas and makes them penetrate men's very souls. The majority in the United States takes over the business of supplying the individual with a quantity of ready-made opinions and so relieves him of the necessity of forming his own. (435)[7]

Expanding on the way in which public opinion in America "surrounds, directs, and oppresses the individual," Tocqueville concluded *Democracy in America* with a rather bleak account of "an immense, protective power" which worked for the material happiness of individuals, but which "daily [made] the exercise of free choice less useful, . . . [restricted] the activity of free will within a narrower compass, and little by little [robbed] each citizen of the proper use of his own faculties" (643, 692).[8]

While Tocqueville may have been the first observer to have rendered such a rigorous account of the displacement of the individual by the expansion of a mass print culture in America, he was certainly not the first spokesman who qualified or rebuked the progressivist euphoria of "republican print ideology." In an 1801 essay, Fisher Ames argued that it seemed as if "newspaper wares were made to suit a market" rather than to inform the public. "Pray tell us, men of ink," he proclaimed, "if our free presses are to diffuse information, and we, the poor ignorant people, can get it no other way than by newspapers, what knowledge we are to glean from the blundering lies, or the tiresome truths about thunderstorms." Complaining about how gazettes "will not long allow room to any thing that is not loathsome or shocking," Ames envisioned a readership so saturated by journalistic sensationalism that it was incapable of thinking critically. "Every horrid story in a newspaper produces a shock," he concluded, "but after some time, this shock lessens . . . The increasing fashion for printing wonderful tales of crimes and accidents . . . corrupts both public taste and morals . . . [It] makes shocking things familiar; while it withdraws all popular attention from familiar truth, because it is not shocking."[9]

Even before Ames's comments, in the same month that a 1787 issue of *The Worcester Magazine* was declaring on its front page that print was "the greatest gift from heaven," rhapsodizing about the potential for the "glorious art" and "offspring of heaven" to overturn political tyranny and "immortalize . . . the genius of humanity," a writer in the *New Haven Gazette and Connecticut Magazine* was criticizing "the design of newspapers as entirely perverted," excoriating the printer of the *New Haven Gazette* for undermining one of his communications with "a multitude of typographical blunders" and unauthorized additions. Having lost authorial control of his original piece, this same writer faced the double injustice of the newspaper's refusal to print either an errata or a retraction. He concluded by declaring, "I wish to know how far that boasted prerogative [freedom of the press] extends; whether to a right of altering, adding to, or clipping from every essay presented for publication."[10] Nor was this an isolated case. In the years leading up to the publication of the first volumes of *Modern Chivalry,* there was an outpouring of articles and publications in the popular press questioning the national glorification of the printing trade, warning in newspapers, pamphlets, and books how the medium was indeed becoming the message.[11]

Literary figures were also suspicious of the extravagant claims for a free press engendered by "republican print ideology." Charles Brockden Brown's account of his first contribution to a periodical is a *locus classicus* of a canonical writer's authorial anxiety about the print sphere. Ironically, the piece, written by a man whom many consider America's first professional author, was a poem dedicated to the father of colonial print culture, Benjamin Franklin. Brown recorded in his journal that "the blundering printer, from zeal or ignorance, or perhaps from both, substituted the name of Washington. Washington, therefore stands arrayed in awkward colors . . . The printer by his blundering ingenuity made the subject ridiculous. Every word of this clumsy panegyric was a direct slander upon Washington, and so it was regarded at the time."[12] If, as Benjamin Franklin suggested in *The Autobiography*, the close relationship between print and reason emerged as an enlightened alternative to the tyranny of an oral-based tradition, Brown's journal entry reveals the extent to which both authors and readers also were subject to manipulation, error, and misprision. While proponents of "republican print ideology" lauded the ethical principles of a free press and held up productions in print as "vehicles of discussion in which the principles of government, the interests of nations, the spirit and tendency of public measures, and the public and private characters of individuals are all arraigned, tried, and decided," a surprising number of writers worried about the implications of a government seemingly basing its effective operation on a public print sphere.[13]

Brackenridge takes up some of these popular concerns in *Modern Chivalry*. What makes his critique of the tyranny of a print consensus different from those of contemporaneous newspaper and pamphlet accounts, and from Ames's, Tocqueville's, or Adorno's, is the way in which he deploys the mixed didacticism and sensationalism of prose fiction in an effort to scrutinize and demystify the nation's seemingly uncritical faith in print. Hence, Brackenridge was probably not only the early Republic's most prescient critic of the way in which a dangerous spirit of consolidation found its origins and authority in the Founder's idealization of print; he also might have been the only early American writer with enough sensitivity to this threat to devise deliberate strategies to extricate his social criticism from an exploding print culture's insistent logic of objectification and equivalency. The supreme irony of the reception of *Modern Chivalry* is that, in the years following his death, Brackenridge's painstakingly discontinuous narrative was transformed into the very objectified and commodified literary "work" he sought to challenge in the first place.

■ ■ ■

Modern Chivalry was not Brackenridge's first attempt to foster a more critical readership. His initial public literary enterprise was to found in 1779 *The*

United States Magazine, a publication that would "contain a library and be the literary coffee house of public conversation."[14] His intentions in this undertaking appear to have been broadly republican and shaped by an awareness of the practical problems of fulfilling the ideals of representative government. Acknowledging that in a republic "the mechanic of the city, or the husbandman who ploughs his farm by the river's bank, has it in his power to become, one day, the first magistrate of his respective commonwealth, or to fill a seat in the Continental Congress," and recognizing that such a citizen could not get "knowledge from the first source, that is from the best writers, or the conversation of men of reading and experience," Brackenridge offered an anthology of sorts. In possession of such a "library" of printed works, ranging from the "reasonings of the politician" to the "observations of the curious traveller," the common citizen, Brackenridge hoped, would obtain the requisite literary experiences to become a critical participant in a liberal republic.

Brackenridge made the aesthetic strategy and sociological function of his magazine clear in the introduction to the first issue:

> Instruction will appear in every shape of essays, sketches, schemes, tracts, and dissertations. Amusement will disport, in every form of letters, tales, dreams, scraps, and anecdotes. The first of these will brace the mind, and make it capable to judge in matters of the highest moment. The last will pleasurably unbend it from what may border upon study and severer application. The honest husbandman who reads this publication will improve in every kind of knowledge. He will be shortly capable to arbitrate the differences that arise amongst his neighbors. He will be qualified to be a magistrate . . . He will be capable of any office to which the gale of popularity amongst his countrymen may raise him.

Brackenridge's civic enthusiasm, however, was tempered by the suspicion that few of his countrymen had the means, access, or discipline to indulge in the prolonged study necessary to make informed decisions in the public realm. Nevertheless, Brackenridge apparently had faith that such an obstacle could be overcome by two by-products of the printing revolution: the development of new aesthetic strategies and literary forms which might make education entertaining rather than laborious, and the technological transformations which made possible the wide reproduction and distribution of cheaply printed materials.

Brackenridge's design here is important because it is the same one that was to underpin many of the representations of Farrago and Teague in *Modern Chivalry.* While he acknowledged public criticism of literature that was divert-

ing because it made "the path to knowledge easy . . . more swiftly traveled over
. . . and [not] so accurately examined, as when [a] student [faced the] long and
heavy reading of the authors that are found in libraries," Brackenridge was also
conscious of the fact that not everyone was interested in or capable of acquiring such a rigorous education. Brackenridge saw a realistic compromise in
offering *some* literary competence to a mass readership, and he questioned
rhetorically in a kind of utilitarian calculus, "Is it not more eligible that the
greater part be moderately instructed, than that a few should be unrivaled in
the commonwealth of letters?"

However, despite Brackenridge's optimism in *The United States Magazine*
about the potential for popular and widely disseminated literary forms to
"raise the credit of the age," the preface to the inaugural issue revealed
prophetic fears that "the public [would] not sufficiently attend to the expenses
of the press . . . [and would] complain that [the] publication [was] too highly
rated." The phrase "too highly rated" suggests Brackenridge's perception of the
public's association of *belles lettres* with the dangers of pre-Revolutionary social
hierarchies and reveals that Brackenridge worried that his magazine, a hard sell
anyway in a climate of scarce currency, would suffer from the popular condemnation of anything that hinted at aristocratic privilege. His suspicions
seem to have been confirmed. When *The United States Magazine* folded eleven
months later, Brackenridge, while blaming the war for depreciating currency
and making the enterprise untenable, assailed those who would cheer the magazine's passing, those "people who inhabit[ed] the region of stupidity, and
[could not] bear to have the tranquility of their repose disturbed by the villain-
ous jargon of a book." "Sleep on, and take your rest," Brackenridge taunted. "It
is but ceasing to blow our flutes for a while, and the beasts will retire to their
coverts, and be happy in the brown shades of their own hills."[15]

Disillusioned by the failure of *The United States Magazine* to sustain a readership and musing about the difficulty in winning over an audience to whom
reading was "the worst of all torments," Brackenridge sought solace in those
few "pleasant swains to whom our flutes were agreeable . . . every month calling for a new song." Yet in his last editorial for *The United States Magazine,*
Brackenridge asserted that he no longer believed that most Americans, freed
from England's rule, had the wherewithal to govern themselves. He feared that
such a lack of literary discernment did not bode well for a government based
on principles of representation.

Brackenridge's doubts regarding the educational potential of literary anthologies did not dissuade him from beginning, within a decade, a similar enterprise, this time in a mixed form based loosely on the quixotic adventures of

a Captain Farrago and his Irish servant Teague. Yet Brackenridge, perhaps having seen his former attempts at public expression fail because of what he perceived to be the apathy, antielitism, and anti-intellectualism of the American reading public, developed new expectations about his readership. He apparently recognized that he could not easily persuade readers, raised on the ideological formulations of Revolutionary Whigs (who had aligned the public good with the oppositional ideology of English antiparlimentarians and attacked anything tainted by association with aristocratic privilege), to indulge in something as suspect as *belles lettres* solely on the basis of his paternalistic pronouncements.[16] Hence, Brackenridge turned to an entertaining serial narrative which fused formal aspects of the novel, *belles lettres,* public commentary, and political pamphlets.

Nevertheless, Brackenridge apparently still believed that he could create through education a more discriminating reading electorate, an audience with the capacity to evaluate representations in print and, by extension, representations in politics. Such readerly skills, Brackenridge believed, could be acquired through exposure to—and the study of—a wide range of textual representations. Given the popular ideological formulations which made the print trade a synecdoche for the nation as a whole and an educated readership a synecdoche for the electorate, it is easy to grasp Brackenridge's reasoning. Poor readers meant a poor electorate. A poor electorate meant a weak nation.

All this is not to suggest that Brackenridge's literary ambitions were divorced from the political and economic opportunities opened up by an expanding print culture. Like many post-Revolutionary men of privilege who hoped to rise in power and prestige, Brackenridge considered the public realm of print an ideal arena in which to make his influence felt nationally. But I think it is a mistake to align Brackenridge, a lawyer whose career as a justice of the Supreme Court of Pennsylvania was seemingly little affected by his literary successes and failures, with an aristocratic counterrevolution or to characterize *Modern Chivalry* as the writing of a member of a displaced elite seeking a return to the social hierarchies of the *ancien régime. Modern Chivalry* is too concerned about articulating and resolving—if provisionally—some of the problems of representative government to be seen, as it often has been, as an aristocrat's satirical invective against the weaknesses of a nascent democracy. Rather, *Modern Chivalry* represents Brackenridge's most ambitious and sophisticated attempt to expose the logic, workings, and contrivances of a democratic print culture. I say sophisticated, since in *Modern Chivalry* Brackenridge cleverly redefined the paternalistic relationship between writer and audience he unsuccessfully attempted to establish in *The United States Magazine* in order to meet the sociological conditions of the post-Revolutionary literary marketplace.

Brackenridge begins the first volume, printed by Philadelphia bookseller John McCulloch in February 1792, with the assertion that his text reproduces only the "stile" of "learned men" in an attempt to fix the English language "before the eyes" of his reader. Just as musicians "pay no attention to the words that are set to music . . . but take the most unmeaning phrases," his narrator will "pay no regard to the idea; for it is not in the power of human ingenuity to attain two things at once" (3). Brackenridge's method combines the attractiveness of novelty built by irony and hyperbole with a subtle message about the sociology of texts, namely their potential to arrogate uncritical consent. Emory Elliott has observed that Brackenridge's strategy "is that of the philosopher employing parables. While he declares that he merely has a tale to tell, which will neither offend nor teach, he slyly hints to alert readers that he will subtly intrude morals into the minds of the less sophisticated readers . . . Like Shakespeare whose lines *spoke* differently to the groundlings than to nobles, Brackenridge entertains and instructs different readers with different facets of his craft."[17] This strikes me as a persuasive reading, but I would add that unlike Shakespeare's plays, which were acted out on stage, Brackenridge's narrative cannot depend on the physical presence of performers. Knowing that his text was to be consumed by an anonymous and silent readership who, like the audiences of Shakespeare, would come to the text for the diversion of representative voices, but who, unlike those audiences, could not rely on ocular and aural clues to discriminate among such voices, let alone the motives behind them, Brackenridge works to foreground the problem of—and demystify the claims for—textual authority.

This demystification works on two levels in the first volume: Brackenridge dramatizes the pragmatic nature of literary production, and he points to the danger of omniscient narration characteristic of a bibliophilic republic which had produced such paradigmatic disembodied texts as the Federalist papers (Publius) and the Constitution ("We the People"). Brackenridge's narrator declares, for instance, that he writes a postscript to the volume only because the printer had space to fill, inviting the printer to add a paragraph of his own, and asserting that he will publish further material only if the book sells enough to defray the costs of printing. Irreverently revealing the nitty-gritty practices of book production and literary economics to an audience weaned on such spiritual and thus sacralized texts as the Bible, the *New England Primer,* and *Pilgrim's Progress,* Brackenridge's narrator secularizes the printed word.[18] He invites his audience to view texts not as instruments of immeasurable and immanent authority—a readerly habit developed by the exegetical disposition of early America—but as rhetorical productions devised to solicit consent.[19]

Brackenridge not only undermines the credibility of his text by having his narrator assert that good language and good sense are mutually exclusive, he also brings the very notion of narrative authority under scrutiny by hiding behind three radically different (but all potentially reliable) representatives. Whether the moralizing Brackenridge lies behind the aristocratic Farrago, the bog-trotting Teague, or the unidentified narrator—who claims at one point to be making the whole story up, at another to be transcribing journals given to him by Farrago—is made laboriously unclear in the text. Indeed, it is *the* stumbling point for readers. Emory Elliott has attempted to circumvent this problem by asserting that "basically then, there are two ways to read this work: with the main character Captain Farrago as the hero or with the narrator-author as the hero."[20] But even a cursory survey of the almost two centuries of commentary on *Modern Chivalry* reveals that there are more than two ways to read Brackenridge's narrative. The moral center of the "work" has been variously located in the voices of Farrago, Teague, Brackenridge's narrator, and in Elliott's hyphenated narrator-author.

Confronted with such uncertain narration, one might be tempted to dismiss the confusion (as many critics have done) as a fault in Brackenridge's prose, if Brackenridge did not go to such great lengths to foreground this narrative ambiguity. Most of the adventures that confront Farrago and Teague in the first volume involve issues of representation, misrepresentation, and authority. Moreover, most of these incidents focus on elevated, specialized, and stylized discourses and their capacity to suspend the critical judgment of their audiences. From a surgeon who uses abstruse medical language in an attempt to fleece Farrago for a barely perceptible injury, to the elite jargon of the American Philosophical Society which validates absurd discoveries and gives seemingly arbitrary credence to the claims of an illiterate slave, to a treaty maker who takes advantage of Indian commissioners who cannot discriminate between Welsh, Dutch, or Low Irish and the native tongue of the Kikapoos, Brackenridge demonstrates the power unfamiliar discourses have over an uncritical audience.

But even vernacular discourses in print are questioned in the text. The extent to which Brackenridge considers the printed product as an open rather than a sacred or authoritative device, an instrument given its shape by its extra-textual circumstances and/or designs, is suggested by a hermeneutic crisis posed in the first volume, when the illiterate Teague, observing a traveler bearing the eagle of the Society of Cincinnati on his clothing, proclaims it to be a goose. This, it turns out, is not the first misreading of the image, since the traveler goes on to tell of a clergyman who has interpreted it as a graven image. Both Teague and the clergyman err by overinterpreting "nothing more than a hieroglyph" (70). They are unable to distinguish the native eagle and its political and social significance from a common fowl or a graven image because of an exclusive reliance on their own illiberal and totalizing preconceptions: Teague's insatiable appetite for all things of the body and the clergyman's authoritative decalogue.

Not coincidentally, this incident also illustrates Brackenridge's awareness of the synecdochic relationship between printed and political representation, since Teague's mistake occasions a lengthy condemnation of partial representative bodies—textual as well as social—which "cut men from the common mass, and alienate their affections from the whole, concentrating their attachments to a particular point and interest" (71). When Farrago argues that "a circumstance of this kind is unfavorable to general philanthropy, giving a temporary and artificial credit to those who are of the body . . . and individuals do not stand on the natural basis of their own merit," one cannot help wondering whether he is also talking about the body of texts, since Brackenridge goes on to reproduce the Cincinnati Society speech *written* like oratory to "persuade the judgment, or affect the passions," yet textually calculated for America "for here so wide a canvas is spread that it is difficult to fill it up, and to take a particular part could seem to be a dereliction of the rest" (72).

In the second volume, published by McCulloch five months later in July 1792, Brackenridge continues to critique the complex nature of textual discourse. This time, however, he reveals the power of the desire to represent one's self a certain way in print to determine real world actions. Having not yet assumed the romantic role of a knight-errant, riding "about the world relieving fair damsels," Farrago asks Teague if they might sleep outside. "It will make a good chapter in our journal," Farrago argues, "to describe you lying at the foot of an oak tree" (91). When Teague demurs, suggesting that it would be easier to just "write down the chapter in the journal than lie under the trees to beget it," Brackenridge, whose narrator has already admitted in the first volume that he is merely transposing Farrago's journal, indicts the truth claims of all texts by revealing their fictionality and homogenizing conventionality. As Farrago admits, "[M]any navigators and travellers make many a fiction; and those who have been in battle have killed many, that were killed by others, or have not been killed at all."[21]

Other episodes in the second volume are variations on these same themes. Two Irishmen, one a legitimate clergyman, the other a interloper, battle for a set of written credentials which confers the title of minister. Here Brackenridge dramatizes the epistemological crisis brought on by a shift in social relations from a hierarchical political system based on performative utterances (in which figures were already invested with authority and merely exercised that authority ritually before the people) to a democratic system based on solicitation (where figures petitioned the public to legitimate their authority). Farrago has the two Irishmen each give their own best discourse. "Let the two men preach," he asserts, "and the best sermon take the purse" (99). While the legitimate clergymen presents a traditional exegesis of a passage from the Proverbs, "dividing [the excerpt] up under several heads, and splitting each head into branches," the mountebank decides "to take no text at all" and instead, like a storyteller, preaches "up and down the scripture" (102–103). Farrago, on the basis of these performances, decides to confer legitimacy on both men, asserting that since both have "considerable gifts"—the genuine clergyman appealing to an older and more sophisticated audience while the impostor pleasing the less educated—both should be allowed to preach (104).

But the egalitarian idealism of Farrago's decision to let the "popular" interloping minister preach is undercut two chapters later when Brackenridge's narrator criticizes a celebrated Universalist who "had made a great noise" preaching about universal salvation and fornication (119). Taking an already muddled passage about the millennium, the Universalist argues that the text speaks of a "period when, as the sea shall give up her dead, so hell shall give up her dammed" (119). A Scotch "gentleman" named M'Donald, representing Brackenridge's undiscriminating public, proclaims that "I dinna muckle care if there were na' hell ava . . . If ye could make that out, I wad rather hear it, than o' being smoked with two' or three thousand years in the devil's nuke, or singed wi' his burnt limestone, even if we should get out afterwards" (120). With M'Donald, Brackenridge underscores the vulnerability of an unlearned audience to the prejudices established both by the will of others and the manipulable influence of their own desires.[22] Confronted with such scenes, one cannot help suspecting Brackenridge's fear that men of standing, in order to establish and maintain their power, would merely cater to the popular tastes of a mass reading public.

In the third and fourth volumes of *Modern Chivalry* (published in 1793 by John Scull in Pittsburgh and in 1797 by McCulloch in Philadelphia), Brackenridge continues to desacralize the profession of authorship, expose the instability of print as a medium for communication, reveal the coercive function of narrative conventions, foreground the problem of the disappearance of writers in printed discourse, and chastise a mass reading public for their appetite for the novel and sensational. After asserting at the beginning of volume 3 that all writing is a kind of conceit, Brackenridge sets about demonstrating this claim by using his narrative authority, first to introduce a spurious magazine review which facetiously lauds Brackenridge as the "restorer of all that is correct and beautiful in writing," and then to reprint a phony manuscript (supposedly found in a dead writer's garret in Philadelphia) attacking the Society of Cincinnati (164).[23] As if to make clear to his readers that he is catering to their preconceptions about—and the conventional tropes of—print culture (e.g., that printed endorsements from reviewers are legitimating and sanctifying, and that old and unrecognized manuscripts contain true statements), Brackenridge reveals the underlying nature of authorial power when he suggests things are legitimate because they appear in print. As a tongue-in-cheek narrator claims,

> I know it will be immediately surmised . . . that I myself have written [the manuscript], and that the story of any author . . . is an invention to make it the more interesting to the reader, and to keep myself out of sight and behind the curtain . . . as Cervantes, in his Don Quixotte, pretends that his history is a translation from a Moorish writer . . . and the author of the Adventures of a Guinea tells us of his tracing the work to its repository in manuscript from a single sheet which he found . . . Many writers of fictitious works, in order to give them an air of truth and reality . . . invent tales of finding shreds and scraps of compositions, and thence tracing to the source . . . I may be suspected of adopting a common mode of introducing what I myself have written; but the fact is as I have stated. (173)

If the first section of the third volume works to defamiliarize texts and to educate readers to be more discerning about productions in print, the remainder and much of the fourth volume set out to dramatize the dangerous effects of an emerging consumer print culture. For instance, Teague is dressed up—complete in the "stile" of Monsieur Douperie—in much the same way a text is prepared for publication, and he is set loose in the public realm as a kind of synecdoche for designing texts. Because he appears to be what his democratic audiences want him to be, and says what they want him to say (he is humble and speaks unpretentiously), Teague finds he can gain entry into the confidences of wealthy and attractive women, into political discussions, and even into a presidential levee. Teague, in essence, becomes both a political fiction and a representation of the seductive power of narratives; the dressed-up Teague moves in the public realm as republican critics said novels circulated.[24] What Brackenridge's narrator calls "Teagueomania" is not only linked with the captivating power of fiction; it is also associated with the consequences of the "undifferentiated matrix" between news and novel discourses.[25] Brackenridge's narrator proclaims of the stylized and designing Teague, "[H]ere was a new object, unknown as to its origin, and high as to its pretensions; and what is *novel,* and not fully comprehended, and lofty in its nature, has a supereminent dominion over the human mind" (229). This too bears a striking resemblance to contemporary criticisms of the novel which, as one writer noted, mixed good sentiments with "seducing arguments" and therefore required "more discernment" than was apt to be found in most readers.[26]

Brackenridge takes up the issue of the seductive power of fiction and a mass reading public's appetite for the new and the sensational in the first volume of Part Two, printed by Loudon in Carlisle, Pennsylvania, in 1804. In this volume, however, Brackenridge goes after blackguard journalism in an attempt to delineate the limits of the constitutional guarantee of a free press, merging his fictional narrative with the "real" fictional identity of journalist William Cobbett. In the narrative, Farrago and Teague enter a village where an editor who calls himself Peter Porcupine has recently set up an office to satirize local citizens. A debate ensues in which a victim, fighting the popular assumption that the "press is the palladium of liberty," stubbornly insists that it is a medium of "oppressive" violence (337). "If the ink cast into black letter, and carrying with it pain and pungency from ideas communicated is tolerated," he claims, "much more the volatile alkali . . . [is] to be born" (338).

Brackenridge makes clear the sociological and political issues surrounding the idea of a free press. "It is the right of the tongue transferred to the hand: it ought to be as free as the air that we breath," argues an advocate concerned about restricting rights of expression, while another raises the issue of paternalism, elitism, and the potential tyranny of an aristocratic monopoly on print culture. "Is it only men of polished education that have a right to express their sentiments?" he asks rhetorically. "Let them write down in magazines, or make books, or have gazettes of their own, but not restrict the right that people of a more uncultivated understanding have to amuse themselves and others by their lucubrations" (339–340). A third suggests that the popular press may contribute to "a man's knowledge and serve to correct foibles that he would not otherwise have been conscious of, or amended. Men will hear from the buffoon or the jester, things they would not take from a friend, and scarcely from a confessor" (340).

Reading through a series of debates which takes up over five chapters, one gets the sense that Brackenridge weighs the advantages and disadvantages of a free press in a democratic society while exposing its features and characteristics to his readers. But he offers no solution to the antagonistic—and seemingly mutually exclusive—relationship between elite and popular forms of literature other than his claim that his own aesthetic strategy—using his colorful tale of a wandering captain as a vehicle for making moralisms—offends less "the self-love of men than what has the appearance of immediate and direct instruction" (350). Nor are such issues resolved within the story. Porcupine departs the town after the captain spreads rumors that Teague is going to open a competing press and begin a paper war. But the larger concerns of the role of the public writer and the function of print culture in a democracy are left unresolved. The same townspeople who argue over whether or not their town should allow Porcupine to print his paper ultimately decide first to burn down their college and then their church because they suspect that "all learning is a nuisance," and want to emancipate themselves from the textual "shackles" of a minister who uses Bibles with foreign rather than domestic commentaries (370).

Interspersed among these episodes, the pronouncements of Brackenridge's narrator become more and more didactic and more exclusively focused on the condition of the public writer and the status of *belles lettres* in an expanding, consumer-orientated print culture. He makes short arguments that men of letters are naturally aligned with the democratic interest in a commonwealth because they are seldom men of wealth and that despite fears of vain learning states should rival each other in producing men of letters in an effort to raise the character of the republic. He even speculates on whether the multitude invent art or whether art is invented by individuals among them. He repeatedly justifies his use of drama, arguing that "it is so extremely difficult to engage attention to any thing serious, that one must enliven with something singular to be read" and that "there is nothing so difficult as to manage the public mind. It must be done by the lever, or the screw, or other mechanical power; to speak figuratively, and not by direct force" (470, 602). At one point he goes so far as to remind his readers he is writing for the common people, every "Tom, Dick, and Harry, in the woods" and not for public officials, as if to claim, and thus win, a popular reading audience (471).

Brackenridge's turn to even more didactic pronouncements persists into the final volume of Part Two, published by Loudon in 1805. Here Brackenridge's narrator reasserts the need for a diverse literature, and he supports this need with cynical characterizations of both the popular press and a national reading public. On the one hand, Brackenridge continues to advocate *belles lettres* as a guarantor of representative government because its cacophony of voices and mixture of literary forms worked to diffuse the arrogation of centralized power, kept a disinterested and watchful eye over the public realm, and functioned to educate a participatory electorate; on the other, he seems to fear more and more the commodification, conventionalization, and factionalization of print culture brought about by an exploding printing trade, a growing emphasis on mass production and consumption, and a public contempt for intellectual rigor left over from the ideological rhetoric of the Revolution.[27] He contrasts the oratory of Greece and Rome with the press in America and France, claiming that "in the ancient republics, founded like ours, on reason and the laws, the power of speech was the greatest means of keeping people together . . . With us the press is a great pulley, by which the public mind is hoisted up, or let down to any sentiment. It is a wonderful block and tackle, so to speak, on board the state ship" (559). This sinister vision of a society subject to the sway of the popularizing logic of the press is, moreover, linked by Brackenridge to the specter of the French Revolutionary press. He notes reproachfully that "an uninformed inflammatory print is a corruptress of public opinion. It is the torch that sets Troy on fire. There is no Marat, amongst us, at the head of a journal; but there may come to be" (416).

It is against this threat of a politically and aesthetically homogenized public print sphere that Brackenridge apparently consignes his last volumes to the public. In the seventh and final installment, published ten years after Loudon's 1805 second volume of Part Two (vol. 4 in Johnson and Warner's 1815 edition of the whole), Brackenridge reiterates the tendency of writers, this time historians, to give "too much sensitivity to public opinion [and] too great a fear of wearying the reader" (674). He again champions *belles lettres* as the essential literary form of a republic because the genre tended to be dialogic and local rather than ideologic and abstract, going so far as to stress the belletristic quality of the Bible. At the same time, one is left with the suspicion that Brackenridge was skeptical about the likelihood that *belles lettres* would become a prevalent literary form in the commercial atmosphere of the new nation. One wonders if Brackenbridge was disenchanted by his avocation, his readership, and the status of writing in America, or if Brackenridge saw himself in a lawyer who claims morosely at one point in the text that "in all the lovers of the arts . . . there is a neglect of riches, the mind is carried off from the love of money, and placed on the art itself. The main chance is overlooked; and it is only late in life that the folly is discovered by the person himself, though others have been remarking it all his life long" (362).

As he had in the introduction to his first volume, Brackenridge concludes the penultimate chapter to the last volume with the premonition that *Modern Chivalry* would be conventionalized—and thus made "famous"—by the industries of print culture, attributing his text's lack of popularity to his refusal to cater to the desires of a popular audience. Noting how there are few men in an age that "could write such a book," Brackenridge reveals his surprise that his narrative "has not got up in the world as [he thinks] it ought to have." But, he concedes, "a great deal depends upon having a felicitous introduction. When it comes to be published with drawings, or what are called cuts, it will look quite another thing to a grown gentlemen; and will come into vogue, and be a stock book" (803).

■ ■ ■

True to Brackenridge's uncanny predictions, American editors set about altering *Modern Chivalry* soon after his death, turning what appears to have been a sustained critique of republican print culture into a representative American "novel." By contriving elaborate textual apparatuses from advertisements to critical introductions to biographical sketches to explanatory footnotes, the publishers who reprinted the texts of *Modern Chivalry* worked to contain both the size (by abridgement) and the ambiguity (by critical introductions, footnotes, and omissions) of the text in an attempt to figure Brackenridge as a sacrosanct and thus marketable American author.

For the editors of the Patterson and Lambdin edition, published in 1819 and advertised as a two-volume edition of the whole with the last corrections and additions of the author, placing Brackenridge in the nation's collective literary biography even meant disposing of the corpse of the first edition. The frontispiece, as if confirming Brackenridge's suspicions about the ability of the print culture industry to distort or create new meanings, advertised that it, not the first edition volumes, was authoritative.

> This is the first edition of Modern Chivalry published since the death of the author. Those which previously appeared, were imperfect, particularly in typographical accuracy, as the judicial avocations of the author prevented that minute attention to the proof sheets which is always so necessary in the publication of an original work. Hence almost every page had become disfigured with inaccuracies . . . Some chapters have been transposed, and a few excluded, as these were not intended to constitute a permanent portion of the work.

The complex publishing history and the difficult form of *Modern Chivalry* gave American editors a great deal of latitude in their reconstructions of the text; the numerous sites of publication and the periods of time between Brackenridge's various writings apparently had little effect in destabilizing the commodification of his efforts into a unified literary work. While most subsequent editions were abridged versions of Part One, usually containing volumes 1 and

2, even the reprintings which advertised themselves as complete editions of the "original work" were, like Patterson and Lambdin's edition, substantively altered to make them more manageable for readers and publishers.

After Johnson and Warner's four-volume compilation of the original six volumes was published in 1815 (the fourth volume was entirely new material added by Brackenridge), there were three separate efforts to publish comprehensive editions. Patterson and Lambdin's "revised" two-volume edition of the whole in 1819 gave the author of the work as an authoritatively conservative "H. H. Brackenridge, late a judge of the Supreme Court of Pennsylvania" and obviously targeted the text for a sophisticated readership. Carey and Hart followed with their two-volume abridgment of *Modern Chivalry* in 1846, using the text of Patterson and Lambdin's 1819 edition and making the book part of their "Carey and Hart's Library of Humorous American Works" series. Carey and Hart seem to have intended their reprint to reach a more varied audience. Priced modestly at fifty cents a volume and richly illustrated with etchings by Darley, the title pages advertised the book as "the second edition since the author's death," and the book came complete with a critical disquisition on the work, a reprint of a biographical sketch on Brackenridge originally published in the *Southern Literary Messenger,* and explanatory footnotes.[28] The title page bore an excerpt from the *Saturday Courier* which announced the text as "a book of maxims and sayings under the guise of pleasantry, with a very strong satirical undercurrent that gives the work a pungency and raciness rarely met with," while the introduction claimed that "a thousand original expressions, thoughts, and allusions derived from it, are in daily use, forming a surprising proportion of the national stock of ideas, and of which few readers are aware." But these comments stressing both the utilitarian and belletristic quality of *Modern Chivalry* are uncharacteristic of other editions, and were apparently part of Carey and Hart's attempt to appeal to both elite and popular audiences. Claude Newlin's 1937 American Book Company edition was the only other attempt at a comprehensive printing of *Modern Chivalry.*

Most of the other nineteenth-century editions, including at least ten reprints that published only parts of the original six volumes (and sometimes parts of the seventh included in Johnson and Warner's 1815 edition), stress in some way—usually by various operations of typography—the theatricality of Farrago and Teague. Many, like T. B. Peterson's 1853 edition, set Teague O'Regan's name on the title page in a typeface as large as the title. Others, like George Metz's 1815 edition, published only the first two volumes, which, of the whole, are the most theatrical. Beginning in 1856, T. B. Peterson began publishing his versions of Carey and Hart's 1846 edition, first under the title of

The Adventures of Captain Farrago (1856) and then *The Adventures of Major O'Regan* (1856–1858).

The production of similar "works" with similar editorial apparatuses has extended into twentieth-century reprints. Ernest Bennecke introduces the Rogue's Bookshelf edition (Greenberg 1926) as an unpolished imitation of *Lazarillo de Tormes* and includes only heavily edited versions of Part One complete with his own chapter headnotes. Even Lewis Leary's attempt to make *Modern Chivalry* available in a 1963 paperback frames the text in its introduction as the adventures of an embattled Jeffersonian aristocrat named Farrago. This, too, is an abridged version of Part One, and a "Note on the Text" justifies its omissions by deprecating Part Two as adding little to the "essential matter of the narrative." "In fact," the note goes on, the chapters of Part Two "often become tedious or spoiled with second thoughts and evasive, politely phrased rewritings."

Even this cursory look at the conventionalization and literary and nationalistic co-optation of *Modern Chivalry* by nineteenth- and twentieth-century publishing concerns suggests that Brackenridge's anxiety about the workings of a commercial print culture were uncommonly prescient. After all, despite his efforts to wake common readers from the anesthetizing power of print, *Modern Chivalry,* like *The United States Magazine,* attracted surprisingly little attention.[29] Just as his ironic command in *The United States Magazine* to his readers to "sleep on, and take [their] rest" seems to have fallen on deaf ears, so his admonishments at the conclusion of the third volume seem to have had little effect, despite their candor. Here Brackenridge exclaims,

> I wish I could get this work to make a little more noise. Will nobody attack it and prove that it is insipid, libelous, treasonable, immoral, and irreligious? If [not] . . . do something else, praise it, call it excellent, say it contains wit, erudition, genius, and the Lord knows what! Will no body speak? What? Ho! Are ye all asleep in the hold down at Philadelphia? (250)

Such cries reveal more than an alienated author. They suggest the frustration of a public writer who clung tenaciously to the ideal of an educated republic, who saw the free dialogue facilitated by *belles lettres* as essential to a liberal state, but who apparently witnessed the failure of his efforts to surmount the conventionalizing power of a print culture industry and the hegemonic ideology of his readership. Moreover, they suggest how rapidly an expanding and consumer-oriented print trade worked to render the eighteenth-century political writer powerless and anachronistic at the same time that they elevated a nineteenth-century notion of literary artist to new prominence.

PART III

THE
RHETORIC
OF
FICTION

SEVEN

Authorial Coquetry and the
Early American Novel

Over thirty years before the publication of what is now widely considered the first American novel, William Hill Brown's *Power of Sympathy* (1789), an anonymous writer in *The New England Magazine,* in an essay entitled "Of the Duty of Authors," adumbrated on what he considered an essential transformation in the conditions of authorship in the American colonies. Lamenting how "moral good and evil" were becoming relative in the age of Enlightenment, so that they varied "according to the turn of mind, temper and manners of the inhabitants, to the form of government . . . [and] to the nature of its religion and laws," the essay called for a radical change in a more traditional, directly civic mode of authorship. In doing so, I want to argue in the pages below, it intimates a structural account of the rise of the novel in America.

To bring an expanding and increasingly heterogeneous readership to a nostalgic "due sense . . . of virtue again," the essayist suggested that authors should turn from a political to a more private, social mode of public discourse. He noted that

> it is expected of us [authors], that we should keep a watchful eye over the Administration; that we should from time to time make the strictest inquiries into their conduct, and lay it before our worthy patrons and readers . . . and therefore it would be beneath even the meanest of us to write dull and heavy lectures of morality (for everything of that kind must be so) which no body would read; or if any did, which would be more becoming Pedants than *politicians* to give. I will further allow that it might tend in good measure to spoil *the sale of our works,* the *first* and *most immediate concern* of an Author, and afford a favorable opportunity for some

new writer to sit up; who by pursuing the contrary scheme, might get
the start of us in the esteem of the town, and live and flourish upon our
ruin! And yet methinks notwithstanding all these difficulties that lie in
our way, we ought to employ the good opinion that our readers and ad-
mirers have of us to their own advantage, and try if we cannot with as
much ease make them honest men, as we have made them deep politicians; if we cannot as well teach them their own duty, as that of Princes
and Ministers of State; if they will not as readily learn to manage their
own families at home, as to settle the affairs of the Nation.[1]

In reorienting the purpose of virtuous public writing from a residual notion of
civic criticism to an emerging formulation of moral reform, the essayist suggested a series of authorial reconfigurations which are now familiar to students
of the emergence of the novel in America: the move in what Hans Robert
Jauss has called the "horizon of expectations" on the part of writers from an
elite to a popular audience, the recasting of the site of critical pressure from the
public and the political to the private and the domestic realm, and the change
in critical focus from that in which political functionaries were made account-
able for their actions in public roles to one in which private individuals were
presented with fictional representations of ordinary life (e.g., those of domestic production and reproduction).

   What is interesting about this prescription is what the essayist considered
as a complicated set of impediments to such a transition. He notes that the prescriptive role of the domestic moralist, unlike that of the sensational exposer of
political corruption, promised to alienate and bore readers; and in so doing, it
threatened to make formerly esteemed political writers contemptuous peda-
gogues. Moreover, this loss of a wide readership burdened the public writer
with economic failure, and hence the loss of self-sufficiency; and it virtually
guaranteed that polemical—and hence more popular—writers would carry
the day, to the detriment of both "virtuous" writers and the reading public at
large. In short, the obstacles to a moralistic and domestic mode of writing, apparently unlike those of the political polemicist, were the vicissitudes of a developing literary marketplace: not persecution, but the erosion of authorial
control, the threat of privatization, the problems of literary competition, and
the tyranny of public opinion.

   We are not used to thinking about political and domestic writing in these
terms. The alignment of a tradition of civic authorship with popularity and
sensation, and that of social moralist with obscurity and pedantry strikes the
modern reader—used to comparing the cerebral writing of eighteenth-cen-

tury political theorists with a domestic writing which not only addressed the concerns of the common individual but often did so in the salacious context of incest, seduction, and coquetry—as a strange inversion. In fact, the "origins" of American domestic fiction have traditionally been attributed to the separation of the language of interpersonal domestic relations (usually sexual) from that of politics, alongside the development of both the means and the market for mass entertainment. That is, critics have argued, the rise of domestic fiction was a positive function of liberalism: both in terms of an explosion in commercial printing which both generated and capitalized on an expanding market for diverting entertainment, and in terms of a society that was increasingly preoccupied with the private concerns of the bourgeois individual (say, working through the limits of individual rights) rather than those of the collective (say, formulating a consensus of the public good).

In this story, the question the literary historian has usually asked is not how the political activist of classical thinking overcame the new and challenging obstacles of an evolving literary marketplace but, rather, how a new group of private, secular, and sensational writers, bent on profit, or on personal or factional political interest, and accompanied by a voracious and heterogeneous reading public, overcame opposition to their efforts by traditional moralists and ethicists.[2] Outlining such a heroic account of the liberal writer, Nancy Armstrong, for instance, argues that the emergence of the domestic novel signaled the birth of the modern individual: the private, desiring, and sexual woman. In other words, the novel allowed women to "seize the authority to say what was female . . . to contest the reigning notion of kinship relations that attached most power and privilege to certain [feudal] family lines." In Armstrong's account, these writers struggled against an entrenched group of cultural authorities critical of domestic fiction, a residual faction who "adopted a rhetoric that earlier reformers had used to level charges . . . against the old aristocracy . . . [placing] themselves in an old tradition of radical Protestant dissent, which argued that political authority should be based on moral authority."[3]

Like Armstrong, most theorists of the novel have considered the genre as the literary offspring of liberalism, suggesting that the novel form emerged over the course of the eighteenth century to mediate the social changes wrought by the new emphasis on "ordinary life" that emerged alongside capitalism.[4] As one recent critic claims, "[M]odern theorists who agree on little else concur that the novel was a powerful expression of ascending bourgeois culture in early modern western life . . . in an era of consolidating liberal capitalism, the novel seemed to express the instincts of a new society struggling for maturity."[5] Ian Watt paved the way for this understanding of the novel with his classic study of the rise of the English middle class and the concurrent emergence in literature of what he described as "formal realism." In Watt's account, by its valuation of singular individuals, its promotion of secularization, and its defiance of social authority, the novel was the logical vehicle for the relations of modern capitalism.[6] Revising Ian Watt's causal juxtaposition of "formal realism" and the rise of an individualistic middle class, Michael McKeon has given the most recent comprehensive account of the rise of the novel. McKeon argues that the novel—a loose narrative form continually in flux— emerged to "explain" a set of problems that came into existence in the Early Modern Era, problems he typologizes as two kinds of categorical instability. One form, what McKeon terms the "generic," was epistemological. He asserts that in the years between 1600 and 1740 there was a major transition in contemporary attitudes about how to tell the truth in narrative. The other form of categorical instability concerned a change in how the external social order was perceived in relation to the internal, moral state of its members. He calls this category the "social," and he claims that this ethical crisis was consolidated into "questions of virtue." McKeon's study traces how the novel came into existence to mediate the instability of these two categories. And in this sense, he, like Armstrong, assigns a positive cultural role to the genre of the novel. He argues that "genres fill a need for which no adequate alternative method exists. And when they change, it is part of a challenge both in the need they exist to fill, and in the means that exist for that fulfillment."[7]

But such accounts, while rich in their delineation of the ways in which the "democratization of the printed word" allowed previously marginalized groups a public voice, and in the ways the novel emerged to accommodate the ideological demands of liberal capitalism, may hide the extent to which the emergence of the novel was as much a symptom of a dramatic transformation in authorship as it was an agent for profound socioeconomic changes. Which is to say that, at least in the American context, such accounts tend to project an artificially mature and historically static notion of the productive, creative writer of nineteenth-century romanticism back into the eighteenth century, and to demarcate the extent to which this figure was given economic and political freedom by the explosion of a free press and the rise of a heterogeneous reading public. Such a model reifies a modern notion of artisanal or productive authorship as historically transcendent. This protoliberal writer has been dressed in a variety of different producer-guises, but most frequently in that of the premodern artisan, what Raymond Williams has considered in his typology of artistic production "the independent producer [who] . . . offers his work for direct sale."[8] In literary histories, this figure has been situated along a reductive register of social status or "class" and usually appears in one of two suits: the marginalized "street writer" who took advantage of the transformations wrought by print capitalism to carve out a place for his or her "radical" notions, and the cultivated man of letters who performed the high cultural artisanal work of *translatio studii* in Augustan verse.[9] With respect to the former, Cathy Davidson argues that novelists in America emerged from the producers of street literature, "crime confessions, captivity narratives, and picaresque tales," and she goes on to suggest that this clandestine literature allowed writers on the periphery not only to "coexist with elite literature, but to replace it . . . by addressing those unprivileged in the emerging society." She concludes that "no wonder the novel was derided by those who profited from the status quo and strove to perpetuate it."[10] With respect to the latter, Lawrence Buell summarizes a long tradition in American literary historiography when he claims that "during the early national years . . . [public writing] was dominated by an ethic of genteel amateurism that encouraged sublimation of literary impulses into the socially acceptable forms of cultural patriotism and a bourgeois version of the Old World aristocratic ideal of refined accomplishment."[11]

Depending on the perspective, literary historians have tended to insist that the novelist in America has emerged from one of these two sources, or a combination of both. Either he or she has been cast, heroically, in the Revolutionary role of unseating an authoritarian high culture by reformulating a popular, commercial literature which could serve as "the literary equivalent of a Daniel Shays"; or, alternatively, he or she has been seen as an anachronistic champion of national culture, struggling to maintain an elite literary refuge from a bourgeois marketplace economy which threatened to destroy an Augustan tradition of polite letters.[12] In other words, the novelist has been seen as the archetypal figure of the private realm in one of two ways: either the producer of commercial entertainment which, however ambiguous politically, sought to reach a mass readership through mass production and distribution; or the artisan of high culture, the wordsmith who, in the isolation obtained by leisure, crafted literary artifacts for a cultivated audience.

But, in addition to reducing literary forms to the expressions of the interests of social groups artificially polarized according to gender or class, such conceptions also privilege an interest in material production over issues of participation and communication.[13] America, unlike England, had no real native tradition of vocational arts (e.g., playwrights, patronage writers, romancers) from which such a modern literary artist could emerge.[14] And notwithstanding a long tradition of broadside and chapbook literature, the literary critic has to come to terms with the fact that nearly *all* of the fifty or so works of popular prose fiction written before 1800 were authored by members of a rather prominent cast: lawyers, Supreme Court justices, professors, clergymen, schoolteachers, prosperous merchants, and even the wife of a United States senator. While the explosion of print in America certainly allowed previously disenfranchised writers a new voice in public affairs, once in print most of these writers expressed sentiments very similar to the spokesmen of the dominant classes. Thus, on the one hand, we have to acknowledge that disenfranchised figures who were given a new voice in the public realm overwhelmingly tended to aspire to the supposedly conservative ends of their supposed "betters." And on the other, we have to recognize that much of the prose fiction written by so-called elites, ambiguous stories of passion, seduction, coquetry, and death, would hardly seem to be translatable into the thinly veiled ideological maneuvers of conservatives perpetuating the status quo.

In saying this, I do not mean to suggest that the issue of gender is collapsible into that of class and that we should abrogate such questions in theorizing on the rise of the novel. By no means do I want to gloss the fact that most of the novels written in republican America were for, by, and about women. Quite the contrary, I hope to explore some of the reasons why this was, in terms of history, suddenly so. Nor do I wish to deny that contemporaries saw the novel as a feminine form. Indeed, as I hope to suggest below, the novel in republican America took on the deportment of a "coquette," a woman who flirts with men to win their admiration and affection, in order to engage a changing reading public. Long excluded from expressing their thinking in public documents, republican women found that the novel allowed them a new means to speak to civic questions. Although in my focus on the novel as a communicative mode of indirection (in contrast to an earlier rhetorical heritage) I do not focus on the conditions whereby woman writers *had* to assume the oblique posture of the coquette to speak in public, the issue is obviously an important one and deserves attention elsewhere. But I agree with Caroll Smith-Rosenberg's claim that too often critics have imported nineteenth-century notions of consolidated gender opposition into their readings of eighteenth-century novels, and I'd like to suggest, alternatively, that the rise of the female seduction novel was continuous with what I've been calling a transformation in political writing.

In contrast to that in Europe, as I have suggested in earlier chapters, a tradition of public writing in America found its origins in civic rather than economic or artisanal imperatives—a heritage of public writing, moreover, that spawned from an intellectual tradition of classical republicanism and from a long history in America of Protestant political dissent. Together with the explosion of a catalytic pamphlet literature in the years leading up to the American revolution, a popular genre Bernard Bailyn has gone so far as to tie to the formation of a unique Revolutionary consensus in his *Ideological Origins of the American Revolution,* a strong philosophical tradition of civic writing survived intact well into the nineteenth century. This was true to such an extent that Charles Brockden Brown could write in 1799 that eighteenth-century American readers were the inheritors of a different literary tradition than their English contemporaries. "There is one kind of authorship to which Americans have shown a stronger propensity than any other," Brown argued, "and that is, the composition of political invectives . . . those diurnal sheets are, perhaps, more widely diffused and read here, than in any other part of the world." Brown went further than making this observation on literary sociology in America; he argued that foreknowledge of this sociology was requisite to effective public writing. "Such [political writing] appears to me to have hitherto been the literary harvest of America," he concluded, "and this is the harvest which critics must superintend."[15]

In this vein, critics have recently turned to the sources of the overt republicanism (rather than the intimations of liberalism) that inhere in most of the novels published in America through the early years of the nineteenth century. In her powerful study of the rise of the novel in America, Cathy Davidson has pointed out the extraordinary fact that *all* early American novels, without exception, contain a discussion of the theory of public education.[16] She also observes the astounding fact that nearly every American novel carried with it a preface which painstakingly sought to articulate the civic rather than the private benefits of domestic fiction, regardless of the ambiguities of its more dramatic and often salacious predicate. In his meticulous account of the way in which the association of the novel with individualism and the middle class "exaggerates the novel's collusion in the coming order," Michael Gilmore argues that the early American novel "was often more in sympathy with republicanism than with the liberal and private values of the nineteenth century."[17] And, in perhaps the most political reading of the early American novel to date, Caroll Smith-Rosenberg has suggested that the principle question for the early American novelist may not have been that of forming the modern bourgeois subject but that of resolving how "independence and individual happiness be made compatible with social order." Admonishing critics who have projected a reified notion of post-Victorian gender relations back into the early modern novel, Smith-Rosenberg argues convincingly that "whig theorists and republican mothers belonged to the same class, read in front of the same fires, often from the same texts." "Too often we have read the class identities and the sexual attitudes of the Enlightenment conditioned by Victorian texts," Smith-Rosenberg concludes. "Sexual and class identities were more hesitant and ambivalent in the years when both were taking form. The rigidities of the later period—and its new potentials for subversion and revolt—cannot be projected backward."[18]

But even such convincing attempts to restore early fiction to a more nuanced historical context have tended to focus on the material text in isolation from the vexing conditions of authorship in post-Revolutionary America. The story they tell is one of a frustratingly malleable literary form caught between the residual imperatives of classical republicanism and the emergent dictates of liberal capitalism. This textual emphasis has led one recent scholar, struggling against the legacy of Ian Watt and the cult of the novelist/seer, to go so far as to suggest that the novel was essentially a "script" for "a republican paradigm of public virtue." In Michael Warner's provocative account, modern readers have assimilated the early American novel to "a liberal aesthetic of authorial craft" which privileges works that seem to be "indirect, artful, and privately anchored." But in making his argument, Warner seems to go from one pole to the other; that is, from the novel as a product of liberalism to that of republicanism. No longer a sacralized liberal artifact, the novel becomes something of a transparent outline for a totalizing discourse. Warner's study concludes that "the republican paradigm had such widespread influence in official discourses of and about print that early national American society developed no coherent alternative model for letters . . . as a publication, the early American novel strives for the performative virtue of republican textuality."[19] Given the unsettling implications of such an account—namely that the early American novel was merely coextensive with a hegemonic republican discourse of publicity—it seems clear why recent critics have retreated to a middle ground, arguing, as Steven Watts has, for a more inclusive—but equally less forceful—model. Watts concludes in this manner that "the novel itself, as a fresh genre that helped define cultural discourse in this transformative age, uniquely explored and articulated the fluid new market relationships of a liberalizing society . . . The fact that it incorporated elements of accommodation and resistance . . . reveals the complexity, at times even ambiguity, of the process itself."[20]

But what if, by focusing on the challenges a liberalizing society posed to both a practical and intellectual tradition of civic-republican authorship, we look at early American novels, not in terms of the way they "expressed" the unique sociopolitical conditions of the early Republic but as literary "markers" or "signatures" of the attempts by post-Revolutionary writers to persist in a residual, civic-participatory mode—this despite the profound changes in literary sociology wrought by the commercialization of publishing. In other words, instead of applying the romantic notion of the transcendent artistic "seer" to post-Revolutionary print culture to argue that a relatively unchanging tradition of authorship found a new literary mode to mediate profound social changes, we could consider the novel as a textual by-product of sorts, what we might term a "rhetorical effect" of a tradition of civic writing attempting to persist in an age of print capitalism. And by this means, by focusing on the embattled civic ends of writers rather than the republicanism of their texts, we might also avoid the critical misprision of collapsing the novel into republican discourse which saw textuality as the unproblematic extension of publicity.

In the following pages, I want to argue that the anonymous "Of the Duties of Authors" (1758), cited above, prognosticated the terms of both the emergence and the ascendancy of the novel in America. In contrast to popular theories of the novel which tend to view it as a literary form in isolation from its authorial context, a form which emerged from older literary forms to *explain* or to *translate* the increasingly unstable categories of genre and those encompassing the individual's relationship to society, I want to suggest that the novel in the American context arose, at least in part, as the literary means of last resort for a tradition of civic authorship facing the vicissitudes posed by the dawning of the age of economic liberalism and mechanical reproduction. I want to explore the extent to which the novel in America was the "generic," textual result of a residual, civic mode of authorship battling with the new and vexing complications of accessing the public realm in post-Revolutionary America. These were not simply the problems of negotiating an increasingly complicated nexus of publishing, distribution, and reading spheres ushered in by the development of mass publication for a mass reading audience. They were also the problems of writing in a culture that was redefining the very notions of "authorship," "print," and "texts," enfolding them into the nomenclature of the market as a rights-based politics and a liberal jurisprudence attempted to rationalize all cultural activity in terms of private material production. Whereas authorship and books had for centuries been defined in political terms as public "actions," they were, in the last years of the eighteenth century, increasingly considered in economic terms autonomously as private "things," or property. As a result, I would maintain, the twinned tales of virtue and seduction, fidelity and coquetry, what Cathy Davidson has called "a novel divided against itself," may not necessarily reflect the translation, mediation, or explanation of abstract sociopolitical changes; rather, they may remain as symptomatic artifacts attesting to a very real loss of political agency as a tradition of civic authorship was reconfigured by the new demands of a market society.

■ ■ ■

"A novel never can succeed, in which the fable merely serves as a vehicle for tedious disquisitions on theoretical ethicks," one essayist wrote in 1818. "Novel readers insist on being amused, in the first place, and merely submit to be instructed in the second . . . the moral must be the *invisible power,* which directs the events of the story."[21] This mandate for an invisible moral directive in fiction, coming on the heels of Adam Smith's famous metaphorical formulation of an "invisible hand" by which a beneficial society emerged as the incidental consequence of the sum of the self-interested actions of individuals, suggests the extent to which the imperatives of popular sovereignty, coupled with the expansion, diversification, and privatization of a mass reading public, confronted a tradition of public writing with striking new challenges. Whereas the idealized writer of classical republicanism appealed to the virtue of identifiable members of elite political classes (considered "free" individuals in a political sense because their position in a hierarchical society liberated them from the dictates of economic dependency), the rise in political importance of an anonymous bourgeois reading public (seen as "free" in the different, economic sense, as at liberty to pursue individual wants and needs) meant that authors had increasingly to address an audience that, in the nomenclature of classical republicanism, was neither wholly political nor wholly economic, a public that was utterly free in one sense but thoroughly dependent in another.[22]

Republican essayists tended to figure the simultaneous liberty and dependence of the bourgeois individual in terms of the free choice of his or her reading—an activity which was perceived by many as one of the few remaining in which an increasingly privatized citizen entered into public discourse. While, on the one hand, this freedom of choice was seen in virtuous terms as a perquisite to the *res publica,* on the other, it was considered in terms of dependency, since the isolated reader, limited in reading experiences, unfamiliar with the conceits of public affairs, and drawn, after a long day's labor, to entertainment and diversion, was thought to be predisposed to selecting a certain kind of reading and perusing it with a certain mode of literacy. As one journalist noted, literature popular with the economic classes such as novels were generally "read for mere amusement, to prevent vacancy, and to relieve fatigue . . . [consequently] the mind is usually passive under the impression of their sentiments."[23] To republican theorists, the problem of negotiating such a private and anonymous bourgeois reading public reflected much larger philosophical questions over the incommensurability of economic and political freedom. The concern over novel-reading was not just the fear on the part of cultural authorities fretting over the transfer of the interpretative powers of religious, pedagogical, and political authorities to the individual reader, as has often been argued.[24] It was also the suspicion on the part of writers and essayists that the freedom of bourgeois readers to chose literature according to their "natural" interests—and the freedom of a literary market which, more and more, existed as a function of those interests—did not necessarily lead to the political freedom which was necessary for a participatory democracy.

Rhetorically, the most effective embodiment of the simultaneously free and un-free bourgeois reader proved to be the republican daughter, who, not coincidentally, also has been seen, in sociological terms, as the most assiduous reader of prose fiction in post-Revolutionary America. As Caroll Smith-Rosenberg has suggested, it was the plight of the republican daughter—both the implied reader of novels and a familialized and sexualized metaphor for the gentry's concern over whether private, "commercial men," living in the fantastical, passionate, and unreal world of paper money, stocks, and credit, could achieve civic virtue—which most clearly articulated the "ideological battle between classical republicanism and the rhetoric of economic and political laissez-faire." That the social problems associated with the emergence of "economic man" should appear in the feminine guise of the Columbian daughter, and explored in the private context of the republican domestic realm, is not as incredible as it may seem to modern readers. As J. G. A. Pocock has argued,

> [E]conomic man as a masculine conquering hero is a fantasy of nineteenth-century industrialization. His eighteenth-century predecessor was seen as on the whole a feminized, even effeminate being, still wrestling with interior and exterior forces let loose by his fantasies and appetites, and symbolized by such archetypically female goddesses of disorder as Fortune, Luxury, and most recently credit herself . . . to pursue passions and be victimized by them was traditionally seen as a female role, or as one which subjected masculine virtue to feminine fortuna . . . [and] the new speculative image of economic man was opposed to the essentially paternal and Roman figure of the citizen patriot. Therefore, in the eighteenth-century. . . relations of polity to economy, production and exchange are regularly equated with the ascendancy of the passions and the female principle.[25]

While the connection between the female quixotes/coquettes of the early American seduction novel and the threat economic liberalism posed to republican conceptions of the sociopolitical order was seldom articulated in such precise terms in the prose fiction of the early Republic, there is, nevertheless, concrete evidence that contemporaries saw the problem of the individual's private passions in classical political terms. For instance, in J. Horatio Nichols 1802 dramatic adaptation of Hannah Foster's famous novel, *The Coquette* (1797), Eliza Wharton's confidante Lucy begs her coquettish friend to "revolutionize that ill-constructed government of habit in your temper, establish a republic, let its legislation be quite elective, let passion be the most inferior branch, while philosophy and reason sway the power, executive supreme."[26] And in Nichols's play, Eliza herself sees her vulnerability to her passions in the political and economic terms of slavery. "I am the slave of disappointed love," she declares at one point, "and as the bloody despot props his throne from sinking, by making vassalage a habit, so sorrow, my tyrannic task master, sways in my heart, and will sway me to the tomb."[27]

While one could certainly read the plots of quixotism, coquetry, and seduction in such novels as *The Power of Sympathy* (1789), *Charlotte Temple* (1794), *The Coquette* (1797), or *Female Quixotism* (1801) in like terms—that is, as microcosmic explorations into the political problems of a society composed, theoretically, of unrestrained individuals all seeking individual ends—this kind of analysis tends to render prose fiction historically inert. It places a post-Romantic emphasis on the text as a transcendent artifact at the expense of that as a historically situated intentional or communicative activity. It is important to remember in this context that republican texts, often by their authors' own admissions, were not written as static "explorations" or "explanations" of complex social and political issues; they were authored out of a belief that individual writers could participate in, and even guide, their society's negotiation of such concerns. This is rendered most demonstrable by the fact that early American novels were, almost without exception, ostensibly written *for* republican daughters—addressed, like the anonymous *History of Constantius and Pulchera* (1796), "to the young ladies of Columbia"—at the same time they were *about* them. And one does not have to spend much time thumbing through the marginalia in first editions of early American fiction before realizing that they apparently found their intended audience.[28]

But why Columbian daughters? And why the new focus on ordinary life, on the everyday concerns of production and reproduction: vocation and marriage, work and the family? Although rich symbolically, especially in the way they embodied the perdurable threat of human passions, young women seem to have been an extremely unlikely implied audience for what I am arguing was a tradition of civic writing in America. And certainly the focus on the everyday affairs of the household rather than the extraordinary concerns of the public realm seems an odd choice for what I am arguing was a heritage of authorial participation in political matters. Nevertheless, I want to suggest here that as a tradition of civic authorship—mediated more and more by the impersonal relations of a commercial print culture—was increasingly rendered powerless to engage the state in any direct and meaningful way, for reasons I have suggested in earlier chapters, writers were forced to adopt a social rather than political role in their efforts to leverage cultural authority.

Along these lines, we might consider the possibility that the development of domestic prose fiction in America in the years following the Revolution was not simply a function of—or a response to—an emerging trade in bourgeois entertainment. Perhaps the market for such literature was created by post-Revolutionary authors inasmuch as it was accommodated by them. As writers were increasingly forced by social, political, and economic changes to address the problems of maintaining civic virtue by the indirect means of inculcating domestic or private virtue, they no doubt turned to the audience through whom they felt they could still effect significant cultural changes— changes on the scale of what was formerly possible, as demonstrated in the political writing which had marshaled the colonists to independence. In doing so, they turned to the site where the disposition toward virtue was thought to be instilled—the republican household—and addressed the audience on whom their writing could make the biggest difference—the impressionable Columbian daughter.[29]

With respect to the new focus on everyday life, we might see the morally ambiguous emphasis on the actions of "ordinary" protagonists in the similar terms of a structural reorientation of public writing. This boils down to how a tradition of civic authorship was to engage an anonymous and heterogeneous reading public which, although surprisingly literate, was saturated with an unprecedented volume of competing printed material (usually imported from Europe), capable of affording few books, and inclined to reading material which was seen as diverting and entertaining. More important, this was a question over how writers were to influence—in some meaningful way—an audience predisposed to considering letters as nefariously elite or paternalistic, and which was beginning to view writers in the less political and more economic terms of either mechanical producers of useful knowledge or as isolated creators of artistic property. In short, how was the classical writer to negotiate a post-Revolutionary culture which increasingly saw the age-old ambitions of public acclaim, fame, and immortality as private vanity, and which viewed the activity of authorship in terms of material production (defined by copyright as the production of textual artifacts or intellectual property)?

We might consider these the problems of maintaining communicative efficacy and rhetorical power in a liberalizing society attempting to forsake hierarchical visions of the good—in classical thinking the province of the virtuous public writer—for the common principles, injunctions, or standards which, it was thought, ought to guide individual action. This concern with the procedural rather than the substantive aspect of the good of society, what was to engender both modern utilitarianism and the now predominant rights-based liberalism of Kant, was tied to a widespread cultural celebration of ordinary life. Charles Taylor has argued that "the modern, naturalist-utilitarian hostility to 'higher' goods and defense of ordinary, sensuous happiness, emerge from . . . the affirmation of ordinary life, which in early modern times brought about a similar repudiation of supposedly 'higher' modes of activity in favor of the everyday existence of marriage and [vocation]." This shift in focus also worked to redefine the activity of authorship into the terms of occupation and labor—that is, homogeneous material production for public consumption—not only because of a need to see public writing in terms of the ordinary and the private but also because the idea of a "naturally" ordered society based on the stratified existence of the free and the un-free—so familiar to classical theorists—was deemed intellectually regressive and morally sinister in a post-Revolutionary climate which had cast off the hierarchical trappings necessary for an articulation of an ethical "good life" in favor of the egalitarian ones necessary for the widespread pursuit of material happiness.[30]

Thus, while it is now commonplace in the practice of American literary history to consider the activity of republican authorship as a function of this new cultural emphasis on "the ordinary," it is also possible to think of it in terms of a complex rhetorical response to a mass reading audience which was increasingly antagonistic to proponents of hierarchical conceptions of the good. For if, as it was maintained in the rhetoric of liberalism, each individual in society was the best judge of his or her own happiness, the very idea of the prescriptive author was suspect. This was so to such a startling extent, I would hazard to guess, that it was only when a far more ambiguous version of the authorial spokesperson was reasserted in the guise of the "artist-seer" of antebellum romanticism—a figure which could only reappear in public by being willfully inarticulate on important moral and ethical questions—that the visage of the civic author would seem to regain some of its cultural legitimacy.[31]

To negotiate these and other problems posed by a new kind of audience, writers were increasingly forced to adopt a more cunning mode of public participation and persuasion. This is not only reflected in the persistent injunction leveled by essayists that modern writers had to transform their social and political prescriptions into an "invisible power," but also in the prefaces of early American novels where writers repeatedly—if subtly—argued that readers had to be deceived, enticed into acknowledging virtue by the indirect means of a compelling story. This imperative was usually figured in the sexualized language of courtship and seduction. As Tabitha Tenney proclaimed to the implied readers of *Female Quixotism* (1801), a work, the preface noted, that was about a girl "whose head had been turned by the unrestrained perusal of Novels," "the work, ladies, now courts your attention; and I hope you will be induced to read it." And the search for a mode of public writing, which could not only find a mass readership but could bewitch and captivate it into consciousness or action, found its object in the tantalizing "tales of truth" and the salacious stories of seduction, death, and abandonment which served as the basis for the early American novel. As one American journalist noted in 1791, "[O]f all the artillery which love has made use of to soften hearts and brighten eyes, the most effectual is the modern *novel* . . . there is no resisting it; it is the literary opium that lulls every sense in delicious rapture . . . [the novel] dazzle[s] the multitude."[32]

But the novel as an indirect means of inculcating civic virtue and the novel as seducer of readers were at odds; and nowhere was this contradiction more apparent than in the prose fiction of the early Republic. Noting this division in a recent reading of Hannah Foster's *Coquette* (1797), Michael Gilmore has suggested that because Foster's "anti-individualistic message is at variance with her book's openness to subjectivity and desire . . . the novel as coquette struggles against the novel as teacher."[33] While I would rephrase this opposition to read something like the novel as seducer struggles against the novel as teacher (at the same time that the former is a precondition to the latter), I think the idea of the republican novel as a "coquette" is a powerful insight into the peculiar structure of early American prose fiction. The strategy of the coquette—a young flirt who entices an audience but does not follow through with the promise, who simultaneously surrenders and withdraws herself from the object of her attention, and who, in an indecisive erotic play, leads her partner to an end he cannot fathom—is a wonderful analog to what I am suggesting was the structural nature of the early American novel. The coquette neither consummates the seduction nor wholly repudiates it either; instead, she suspends allure and rejection in one mesmerizing dance. What better trope to describe the efforts of early American authors who found they had to identify with bourgeois readers at the same time they lectured to and chastised them? And what better description of the divided nature of the early American novel, which both wanted to teach, and was compelled to seduce, its readership?

■ ■ ■

One way of getting at some of the reasons why almost all novelists in post-Revolutionary America adopted flirtatious relationships with their readers is to look at how these very same writers thematized the issue of coquetry in their narratives. The image of the coquette was a powerful one in the early national period. Not only was Hannah Foster's *Coquette* immensely popular (stories of Eliza Wharton and her real life source, Elizabeth Whitman, were repeated in newspaper accounts, magazines, and pamphlets), but popular journalists were also preoccupied with the idea of the young woman who used arts to gain the affections of men, not for reciprocal ends but merely out of the passion of vanity or an "irrational" desire for conquest. One essayist, in a humorous piece entitled "Anatomical Description of the Heart of a Coquette," compared the mysterious agitation of "coquette" to the irrationality of the sea.[34] Another, in "A Coquette's Account of Herself," asserted that the coquette, "passionately fond of running into debt . . . [was] happily calculated to break a husband's heart."[35] Poet John Trumbull even put the machinations of the coquette to verse in his 1773 pamphlet, "The Progress of Dullness, Sometimes Called, the Progress of Coquetry, or the Adventures of Miss Harriet Simper."

A clue to why the image of the coquette was so powerful for readers of the early Republic lies in the way she was portrayed in prose fiction. In Hannah Foster's *The Coquette* (1797), Eliza Wharton, a republican daughter disengaged from both paternal authority and her marital fate by the deaths of her father and her future husband, struggles with finding her way in life, having been suddenly "freed" from her "implicit obedience to the will and desires of [her] parents" (5). In this microcosmic exploration into the philosophical consequences of the colonies' independence from England, Wharton espouses a liberal ideology which, in the political sphere, transformed the irrational "passions" of classicism into the rationalized, visible "interests" of modern economic man. This ideology is that of freedom in its negative aspect; that is, the freedom from restraint, the freedom to pursue pleasure without encumbrances, what Wharton herself describes as "all egotism" (6). Warned by her confidants that she has the "wrong ideas of freedom," that her sacrosanct "freedom . . . is [but] a play about words," Wharton responds that she is reluctant to enter into "the marriage state . . . [which refines] by circumscribing our enjoyments" (24). After all, Wharton notes, her outward, self-interested actions corresponded to her nature, and since they proceeded "from an innocent heart, and [were] the effusions of a youthful, and cheerful mind," they were certain to be consistent with her own and the public good (7).

Wharton's rationale for pursuing pleasure over the duties imposed by an institution such as marriage must have been vaguely familiar to a generation raised on the political philosophy of Locke. Where a skeptical Hume had argued that "in contriving any system of government . . . every man ought to be supposed a knave, and to have no other end, in all his actions, than private interest . . . [and] by this interest we must govern him . . . make him, notwithstanding his insatiable avarice and ambition, cooperate to public good," precursors to Adam Smith totally absorbed the citizen into the pursuit of private gain.[36] This new emphasis, one that made the citizen and the self-interested individual wholly commensurable, was to have a profound influence on the founding of the American state. Albert O. Hirschman notes that "the stability and lack of turbulence that were expected to characterize a country where men pursue single-mindedly their material interests were very much on the minds of some of the 'inventors' of America, such as James Madison and Alexander Hamilton." Alexander Hamilton even went so far as to argue that "the safest reliance of every government is on man's interests. This is a principle of human nature, on which all political speculation, to be just, must be founded."[37]

But it is not so much Wharton's unbridled pursuit of her own passions which evokes the consternation of her associates as it is her apparent disinterestedness, her self-professed wish "for no other connection than that of friendship" (6). In other words, it is Wharton's remoteness and her impenetrability which makes her socially opaque, and thus a concern, to her companions. Contrary to what we might otherwise think, however, this apparent passivity does not suggest an indecisiveness on the part of Wharton, who, from the beginning of the novel, clearly prefers the rake Peter Sanford over his more unexceptional competitor, the minister Boyer. Although Wharton frets over the disparagements cast upon Sanford by her acquaintances, she never wavers in taking pleasure from what Mrs. Richman, a virtuous republican matron, calls the "syren voice of flattery" (38). And although Wharton suspects that a union with Sanford would be her ruin, and thus does not *actively* seek him out, she clearly desires "his person, his manners, his situation [which] all combine to charm [her] fancy; and to [her] lively imagination, strew the path of life with flowers" (22). Glimpses of Eliza Wharton's true feelings toward Sanford are made apparent throughout the text. At one point, following a declaration that she does "not intend to give [her] hand to any man at present," Wharton describes Sanford as "an agreeable person [to whom] has [been] superadded, graceful manners, an amiable temper, and a fortune sufficient to ensure the enjoyments of all the pleasing varieties of social life" (52). Speculating that Sanford's roguery was merely the result of a "gay disposition" and a "lax education," Wharton invokes the adage that "a reformed rake makes the best husband" (53). She concludes, "[M]y fancy leads me for happiness to the festive haunts of fashionable life . . . the idea of relinquishing those delightful amusements and flattering attentions, which wealth and equipage bestow, is painful" (53).

Part of Eliza Wharton's coquettishness stems from this odd paradox. She does not pursue the rake Sanford, which would go against social convention, the advice of her friends, and even her own intuition. But neither does she dismiss him. Exploring the new limits of freedom in post-Revolutionary America, Wharton defends herself from the accusations of Mrs. Richman by asserting that she does "not chuse [her] company," suggesting that she follows to the letter the laws of social convention. But Richman counters this, gravely, by asserting "nor [do] . . . you refuse it" (38). In other words, Foster interrogates the new problem of crimes of omission rather than those of commission in a society which was redefining liberty from a "positive" notion of freedom as that of sharing in the power of the state to a "negative" conception of freedom as the right of self-interested individuals to act without undue restraint, provided it was exercised within the prescriptive tenets of custom and the technical provisions of the law.

But Wharton's coquetry also seems to stem from her attempt to exploit the psychological determinant of social and eudaemonistic value in a liberal, exchange economy. Freed—by the death of her father and suitor—from the marital fate imposed by a hierarchical social order, Wharton is given the liberty to enter into an open marriage market. Here disconnected from the binding relations of family and custom, and thrust into an impersonal world of more voluntary and contractual social relations, Wharton conceives of interpersonal relations in the economic terms of exchange. As she notes early on in the novel, substituting the relations of the market for those of heredity, "[F]ortune, indeed, has not been very liberal of her gifts to me; but I presume on a large stock in the bank of friendship" (9). Moreover, it is this "stock" of freely entered into associations which Eliza sees as incompatible with the institution of marriage. "Marriage is the tomb of friendship," she notes at one point, "why do people . . . as soon as they are married, centre all their cares, their concerns, and pleasures in their own families . . . [while] former acquaintances are neglected or forgotten" (24). Wharton is thus something of a champion for the interpersonal relations of a commercial world, a world of perpetual exchange which promised, from the philosophy of the physiocrats to Mill, to keep individuals from disappearing into the insidiously private, egotistical realm of the family.[38]

The story of Eliza Wharton is the tale of what happens to the interpersonal behavior of individuals when human relations begin to take on the characteristics of commodity exchange. In terms of marital relations, Carole Pateman has explored how the rhetoric of the Founding Fathers, drawn from the social contract theory of Locke and Hobbes, worked to transform the institution of marriage, to some extent always a contractual relation, into a "political fiction" of pure exchange, ostensibly in an effort to defeat "the classic form of patriarchy."[39] The failure of this enterprise in philosophical terms, rendered demonstrable by the persistence of what Pateman terms a patriarchal "sexual contract," attests to the problems of modeling social relations on those of exchange. Foremost among these difficulties is dealing with the fact that, in a Lockean universe of self-interested individuals, a party to a contract will always break his obligation if it appears to be in his interest to do so. Another lies in the tenuous assumption among contract theorists that parties are free agents prior to an agreement. And still another—and perhaps the most important for us here—has to do with the mechanism for valuation governing the exchange of marketable items. After all, value is not simply a technical relation but a social relation between people; that is, an item has a psychological exchange value as well as a functional use value in a commercial economy. Value is thus not something wholly intrinsic to a given artifact, but, in large part, something conferred to it by the mechanisms of market exchange.[40]

I want to suggest that it is in having to maneuver in this commercial marriage economy which, in part, predisposes Eliza to adopt the public posture of the coquette. This is because in a credit and exchange economy driven by such psychological forces as pleasure, desire, confidence, and scarcity (the South Sea Bubble credit debacle of 1720, after all, was probably the foremost economic scandal on post-Revolutionary minds), the coquette, perhaps more so than any other deportment, by simultaneously embodying desire and scarcity, possession and loss, could control her own value and thus command her own price.[41] Where the value of a good was increasingly determined less by the concrete determinants of use and labor, which could be directly controlled by the possessor, and more by the collective psychology of the market, which could not, the coquette could still be the authoress of her own worth by creating a market while at the same time providing for scarcity. The coquette enjoyed a position of power by projecting the appearance of consent and refusal at once. For in flirtation, the coquette chronically and ubiquitously foregrounded her power to choose, which remained in force so long as this oscillation remained in an enduring form. Once she decided one way or the other, the coquette lost the power to control her "market value," since she no longer held the symbolic reigns of desire and scarcity.

In these terms, the outward appearance of apathy on the part of the coquette is, as nineteenth-century sociologist Georg Simmel noted in his economic analysis of flirtation, "Die Koketterie," an illusion crafted to manipulate perceptions of her value. Although writing on the phenomenology of the coquette in fin de siècle Germany, Simmel nevertheless touched on some of the dynamics of flirtation which made it such a resonant figure in republican America. He conjectured:

> Inwardly, the flirtatious woman is completely resolved in either one direction or the other. The meaning of the entire situation lies only in the fact that she had to conceal her resolve and that, as regards something that is intrinsically certain, she can place her partner in a state of uncertainty or vacillation which holds true only for *him*. It is this that gives the flirt her power and her superiority: the fact that *she* is resolved and determined within herself, as a result of which an understanding obtains between her and the man that uproots *him* and makes *him* uncertain.

Simmel, always concerned with the problem of objectification, noted that the game of the coquette, precisely because of its unfulfilled promises of desire and risk, ultimately becomes desirable in and of itself. Where the pleasure in the coquette's dance was at some original moment only confined to the physiological pleasure of final consummation, the pleasure "gradually come[s] to include all the earlier moments of the sequence as well." He concluded that "the sequence of experience oriented to a final feeling of happiness radiates a part of its eudaemonistic value onto the moments of the sequence that precede[d] [the] final moment." Flirtation in this regard surrenders up its provisional function as an instrument to enhance worth or pleasure. Instead, it assumes that of an ultimate value or end in itself. To say this is to say that coquetry becomes commensurable with pleasure and value.[42] It is in regard to this capacity for coquetry to assume value in and of itself—the ability of the coquette to derive pleasure from the maneuvers alone—that Eliza Wharton's friends condemn "love," "pleasure," and "desire" as emotions too variable to be the foundation for a long-term union like marriage. This is because these sensations are seen as the unstable product of the idiosyncrasies of interpersonal commerce rather than the affective consequence of usefulness or intrinsic worth. The latter, Wharton's advisors maintain, could only be known in the context of duty and obligation, responsibilities which situated the bearer in a stable, hierarchical world. Thus, to counter Wharton's claims that she would have to forfeit her freedom and would enter the realm of dependency if she married the minister Boyer, Eliza's mother responds that

> with regard to its being a dependent situation, what one is not so? Are we not all links in the great chain of society, some more, some less impor- tant; but each upheld by others, throughout the integrated whole? In whatever situation we are placed, our greater or less degree of happiness must be derived from ourselves. Happiness is in a great measure the result of our own dispositions and actions. Let us conduct uprightly and justly; with propriety and steadiness; not servilely cringing for favor, nor arro- gantly claiming more attention and respect than our due. (41)

While one could certainly read such a passage in ideological terms as a justifi- cation of the status quo—for instance, a vindication of women's subservience to men, or a conservative call for stable social hierarchies—I think such a read- ing, by importing modern assumptions about class and gender antagonisms, occludes the more abstract and universal problem of how a liberalizing society was to reconcile its notion of absolute freedom with the need for social coher- ence. Or, in more specific terms, how republicans were going to accommodate the growing importance of a fluctuating exchange value with their stable, timeless assumptions about the transcendent value of virtue.

With respect to these concerns, the line taken by Foster's novel seems clear. Wharton, having through coquetry suspended her power to choose be- tween consent and refusal until the mature age of thirty-seven, dies abandoned and destitute. She espouses the liberal notion of the freedom of choice to the very end, never acknowledging—despite the advice of her correspondents— that it is precisely this worship of the abstraction of free choice which undoes her. To this end, she asserts, with apparent "common sense," that "as human life has many diseases . . . are we not right in selecting the most agreeable and palat- able . . . why should I refuse the polite attentions of [Sanford] . . . they smooth the rugged path of life, and wonderfully accelerate the lagging wheels of time" (86). The rake Sanford, who, at the outset of the novel, scorns the coquetry of Wharton as "mischief," and vows to "avenge [his] sex," finds himself, through the very same maneuvers, in love with her by the novel's end. This is ironic, be- cause Sanford begins by considering his relationship with Wharton a game of "manoeuvring," and himself a "Proteus [who] . . . can assume any shape that will best answer [his] purpose" (22). But Sanford, repeatedly captivated by the power of Wharton's coquetry, which creates the "glow of jealousy," "the want of success," and the exhilaration of alternating acceptance and banishment, becomes a victim of what he calls "the show" (94). Although he marries another on the basis of wealth, Sanford proclaims that his infatuation is so great that he almost asks Wharton "in marriage, and risk[s] the consequences, rather than to [lose] her" (95). Thus a married but disconsolate Sanford is as much a victim of Wharton's flirtatious behavior as Wharton is, admonishing his confidante at the novel's conclusion to "shun the dangerous paths which [he has] trodden." "Virtue alone," the novel concludes, "independent of the trappings of wealth, the parade of equipage, and the adulation of gallantry, can secure lasting felicity" (168).

. . .

For Hannah Foster, and undoubtedly for most republican Americans, the figure of the coquette was the embodiment of a narcissistic self-reflexivity. Concerned with herself, how her visage, movements, and deportment influenced the behavior of others, the coquette was something of an actress. By calling attention to her own power to choose or rebuke a suitor, and by foregrounding this power by alternatively flattering and chastising, surrendering and vanquishing, the coquette concealed her internal resolve and thus prevented her audience from exercising a dominion over her interiority. In other words, the coquette performed behind a veil of unaccountability and inscrutability in an effort to sustain her social value, freedom, and power.[43]

It was precisely such maneuvering which I would like to suggest characterized the deportment of the early American novel. Not only was the issue of coquetry thematized again and again in the novels of republican America; novelists themselves adopted the posture of the coquette to engage an audience. As writers were forced to adopt new modes of interacting with a changing reading public in their effort to persist in a tradition of public commentary, they found themselves increasingly preoccupied with the performative as well as the communicative aspects of their discourse. This generic self-preoccupation was evident in the way American novelists were obsessed with issues of reception. They wrote belabored prefaces which pointed readers to morals and principles which they knew their subsequent narratives made deliberately unclear. They authored long apologies for the social transgressions—real or imagined—they thought that their novels embodied. At the same time, they titillated readers with promises of "true" scandals, heartless seductions, squandered virtues, and, in the case of Susanna Rowson's novel *Mentoria* (1794), salacious passages cited from other infamous books. They asserted, time and again, that their works were edifying. Far more so than prose fiction in eighteenth-century England, the typical republican novel tended to be, to a surprising degree, formally self-conscious and generically self-reflexive.

Along these lines, most American writers set out in their prefaces to frame their prose fiction as a different sort than that of their English counterparts, arguing self-consciously, as William Hill Brown and Susanna Rowson did, that their novels were substantively different than English "novels which *expose*[d] no particular vice and which recommend[ed] no particular virtue." Addressing herself to "a multiplicity of strangers," Susanna Rowson even repeated Samuel Johnson's claim that "the works of fiction with which the present generation seems more particularly delighted, are such as exhibit life in its true state" in order to assert, in contradistinction, that her *Trials of the Human Heart* (1795) was meant to "awaken . . . a thorough detestation of vice, and a spirited emulation, to embrace and follow the precepts of Piety, Truth, and Virtue." As Cathy Davidson has argued, such prefaces worked to engender the odd morphology of the early Republic's "twinned novel": a prose fiction that was divided against itself, and which identified with popular suspicions about the corrupting influences of novels, especially those imported from England, at the same time it denied this association.

But it was not only in its simultaneous sanctification and repudiation of prose fiction, its catering to and contempt for the desires of its readers, that the early American novel resembled the figure of the coquette. Novelists extended the self-reflexivity of the prefaces into the content of the stories themselves. Many early American novels—and *almost all of the popular ones*—tended to be about novels and novel reading. Taking up on an antinovel tradition in European literature that went back to Cervantes and extended through to Lennox, and, as I've suggested, Brackenridge, republican novels foregrounded, again and again, the power they held over an unsuspecting readership. William Hill Brown's *The Power of Sympathy* (1789), a novel in large part constituted by its discussions of novels and novel reading, concludes with the suicide of the protagonist Harrington alongside a copy of Goethe's *The Sorrows of Werther.* Enos Hitchcock's *Memoirs of the Bloomsgrove Family* (1790) laments the fate of "thousands" who, by "a free use of such books [as novels], corrupted their principles, inflamed their imagination, and vitiated their taste." Tabitha Tenney's *Female Quixotism* (1801), a two-volume, 300-page demonstration of the power of novels and romances over one republican daughter, deplores "the indiscreet writers of that fascinating kind of books, denominated Novels, [which] fill the heads of artless young girls, to their great injury, and sometimes to their utter ruin."

In Brown's *The Power of Sympathy* (1789), the popular story of Eliza Whitman (the real-life source for Hannah Foster's fictional Eliza Wharton in the *Coquette*) occasions a long discussion about novels and novel-reading which suggests that it was the issue of free choice which worried republican novelists. Brown's account describes Whitman as "a great reader of novels and romances, and . . . [who] from those fallacious sources, became vain and coquettish." And in the discussion of prose fiction which follows, the selection of books is presented as homologous to choosing a companion or a partner for marriage. In other words, in a world in which unscrupulous books, like mercenary suitors, vied for favor, Brown foregrounded the idea that his audience would have to develop new skills which would enable them to choose wisely among textual products in a commercial print market. "It is a manner of *more* importance than is generally imagined," the virtuous young confidante Worthy argues, "as much depends on the choice of books, care should be taken . . . We all agree that it is a great matter of virtue and prudence to be circumspect in the selection of our books, as in the choice of our company."

But while early American novelists writing to an anonymous and distant reading public had something to say *about* the issue of free choice, they also recognized that they increasingly had little say *in* it. This was especially so in a culture which was driven more and more by the freedom of the economic realm, a freedom which brought onto the market an unprecedented volume of printed material regulated to a large extent only by the cumulative taste of American readers. "Most of the novels with which our female libraries are overrun are built on a foundation not always placed on morality," interrupts the father of a young republican daughter in *The Power of Sympathy,* suggesting that the problem was not only that of choice but that of the field of possible selection. And given "as most young people read," adds his wife, intimating the fact that the American audience for books was *already* coming to the market in what republican essayists called "a novel-reading age," "what rule can be *hit upon* to make study always terminate to advantage?" Given the desires of a mass reading public, appetites to some extent publicly valorized by the emerging tenets of liberalism, how were writers to compete for a readership and at the same time sway them to purposeful action in a public realm that was increasingly indistinguishable from that of the private?

In this and other passages, *The Power of Sympathy* foregrounds the obstacles a burgeoning mass readership posed for a tradition of civic authorship in America. Foremost among these vicissitudes was the sense that modern writers had lost their ability to communicate with readers, both because, in a saturated marketplace, their efforts competed indistinguishably with countless others, and because, as books were increasingly considered material goods consumed by private individuals, writers had difficulty maintaining their communicative emphasis. As one of Brown's characters asserts at one point, "by immoderate reading, [readers] hoard up opinions and become insensibly attached to them . . . *conversation* only can remedy this dangerous evil, strengthen the judgment, and make reading really useful. They mutually depend upon, and assist each other" (37–38).

But how was a writer to convey such idealized conversation through a medium which was considered, more and more, a fixed artifactual product for consumption? In other words, how was an author to assert the rhetorical power of conversation in something as uniform and autonomous as a mass-produced good like a novel? I would suggest that the popularity of literary forms which mimicked interpersonal communication in republican America—the epistolary novel, the dialogue, the serial, the overheard conversation—stand as a testimony to the efforts of authors to reassert the imperatives of communication and participation in an age which ushered in what N. N. Feltes has called "the commodity text."[44]

The republican novel, I would hasten to add, is also part of this testimony. Nowhere else do we find such a passionate invocation and celebration of the raw rhetorical and communicative power of texts. While critics of the novel in newspapers and magazines certainly catalogued the nefarious consequences wrought by the circulation of fiction, they could hardly compete with the panoply of tyrannical texts and victimized readers presented in the early American novel itself.[45] Novels have power, works like *The Power of Sympathy* and *Female Quixotism* asserted to their readers; they are sensational, illicit, sexy, seductive, and anarchic. They possess the minds of readers and force them to do things they would not otherwise do. For good or for bad, writers like Brown and Tenney proclaimed, novels have the power to transform individuals and their world.

The posture of such a self-conscious literary form speaks, I think, to the odd morphology of the early American novel. In foregrounding its power by dramatizing its psychological and social effects, it enticed an audience and legitimated its existence. Yet, at the same time, it sought to disassociate itself from claims that it, as a form, was responsible for engendering precisely those same effects. And while it catered to the desires of its readers, flattering their vanity with sentimental scenes from "ordinary life," it rebuked those same readers for allowing themselves to be so indulgent.

In short, the novel suspended allure and rejection, flattery and repudiation, in one erotic and apparently indecisive dance. The deportment of the modern author was to be, from the early Republic on, that of the playful but serious coquette, and even Kant's liberal claim about the nature of modern art—that it is "purposiveness without purpose"—would appear to have some of its origins in this sociological dynamic. After all, the republican novel—ambiguous in its emphasis on sentiment, sensation, and anarchy—seemed to have no overt didactic purpose; yet its constitutive parts appeared to be so important and inextricably related that they intimated a moral intent nevertheless. What better precursor for what William Charvat has described as the transformation in critical thought brought about the development of the autonomous category of the "literary" in the early years of the nineteenth century, whereby injunctions that narratives in print be didactic and political gave way to the more individualistic prescriptions for ambiguity and symbolism made by the proponents of romanticism?[46] And what better prehistory for some of the resonating phrases about the vexations of nineteenth-century authorship, such as Emily Dickinson's famous injunction at mid-century to tell all the truth, but tell it slant?

As at least one critic has suggested, it is Holgrave the daguerreotypist of *The House of the Seven Gables* (1851) who most resembles the idealized conception of public writing advanced by the Nathaniel Hawthorne of his prefaces.[1] Like the "citizen of somewhere else . . . the scribbler of bygone days" of the *Scarlet Letter* (1850), and the denizen of remote "precincts" where inhabitants have "a propriety of their own" of the *Blithedale Romance* (1852) and the *Marble Faun* (1860), Holgrave is the epitome of intellectual independence.[2] Having "continually chang[ed] his whereabouts, and therefore, responsible neither to public opinion nor to individuals," Hawthorne notes, "[Holgrave] never violated the innermost man . . . [He] carried his conscience along with him." In contrast to the orthodox Pyncheons, whose identity is sustained, embodied, and ultimately revealed to be imprisoned, by the property—real and titular—known as the House of Seven Gables, "the true value of [Holgrave's] character lay in [his] deep consciousness of inner strength" rather than in the dissenter's proprietary or professional ties. Having been a wanderer, serving as "a political editor of a country newspaper," and having spent "some months in a community of Fourierists," Holgrave's occupation as an artist "was of no more importance . . . nor more likely to be more permanent."

Such disinterested autonomy, such a "lack of reverence for what was fixed," unsettles those around Holgrave, particularly Phoebe Pyncheon, who recognizes that although Holgrave "was ready to do them whatever good he might . . . he never exactly made common cause with them, nor gave any reliable evidence that he loved them better, in proportion as he knew them more." An impartial reformer who "looked upon the world . . . as a tender stripling, capable of being improved into all that it ought to be," and who with a millennialist tenor thinks "that in this age, more than ever before, the moss-grown and rotten Past is to be torn down, and lifeless institutions to be thrust out of *173* the way," Holgrave works to resist what he sees as reified and stultified customs and conventions. He does this not by championing "some practicable cause," and thus taking up a particular factional interest, but by unsettling the present with two kinds of reflections: "hard and stern" daguerreotypes which, because there is "no flattery in [the daguerreotypist's] humble line of art," bring "out the secret character with a truth no painter would ever venture upon"; and loose romance tales which "lay out a street that infringes upon nobody's private rights" yet, by directing people to truths, "produce [an] effective [moral] operation." Certain with a reformer's faith that man is "not doomed to creep on forever in the old, bad way[s]," Holgrave the amateur artist "applies his own little lifespan" to "see the tattered garments of Antiquity exchanged for a new suit, instead of gradually renewing themselves by patchwork."

Along these lines, one could read *The House of the Seven Gables* as the story of how such an idealized intellectual independence is compromised. Early on in the novel, Hawthorne notes that Holgrave's social activism was certain to "be modified by inevitable experience." And, sure enough, Holgrave's radical assertion that "our public edifices—our capitols, statehouses, court-houses, city-halls, and churches . . . should crumble to ruin, once in twenty years . . . as a hint to people to examine into and reform the institutions which they symbolize" is qualified at the novel's end when the death of Pyncheon yields Holgrave and Phoebe a substantial inheritance.[3] When Phoebe observes a corresponding change in Holgrave's social ethics ("why how wonderfully your ideas have changed!" she exclaims), Holgrave responds despondently but unalterably that he had "told [her] how it would be." "You find me a conservative already!" he laments. "[L]ittle did I think ever to become one." Such contrition marks the end of Hawthorne's optimistic identification with Holgrave and dramatizes what Hawthorne undoubtedly saw as the central threat to the independent political conscience at the middle of the nineteenth century: not persecution but the corrupting conservative effects of institutional entrenchment and material success.

Within the fictional world of *The House of the Seven Gables,* it is important that Hawthorne's fictional author-figure is the descendent of a seventeenth-century Salem dissenter executed for witchcraft, a man Hawthorne characterizes as "one of the martyrs to that terrible delusion, which should teach us . . . that the influential classes, and those who take upon themselves to be leaders of the people, are fully liable to all the passionate error that has ever characterized the maddest mob." In the nomenclature of classical republicanism, a political philosophy which interpenetrates both the plot and dialogue of *The House of the Seven Gables,* the Maules suffer because the Pyncheons have failed to identify their private interests—their pursuit of private and particular ends—with the general good of the public.

It is also important—although apparently still unrecognized in the scholarship—that Hawthorne took the name "Maule" from the very same Salem dissenter I began this book with, whose 1696 trial for publishing *Truth Held Forth and Maintained* (1695) probably made him the first successful defendant in a criminal action involving the freedom of the press to be tried in the American colonies (preceding the famous 1735 Zenger case by nearly forty years).[4] In fact, the surviving court records of the plight of Thomas Maule reveal some startling parallels to Hawthorne's author-figure in *The House of the Seven Gables*. Unsettled in vocation, working variously as tailor, shopkeeper, and tradesman, Thomas Maule ultimately became a well-to-do merchant and landowner, and, despite his early predilection for social criticism and civic reform, was appointed to various town offices, eventually even serving as clerk of the Salem market. Moreover, despite the fact that, upon arriving in Salem, Maule was pilloried publicly for announcing that the town minister's "doctrine was of the devil"—two men were fined for the mere "entertaininge of Thomas Maule"—he eventually became a large property holder, getting into several protracted disputes over property rights with both his neighbors and the town.[5]

Such correspondences go on and on, and suggest that there is some urgent revisionary work to be done on readings of *The House of the Seven Gables* in this light. For instance, the famous penny-shop passage where Hepzibah's first youthful customer devours two gingerbread biscuits in the shape of Jim Crow, often read as Hawthorne's faint allusion to a missing "impending crisis," may have a narrower historical source. Maule apparently got into a dispute with a baker named Elizabeth Haskett while serving as the clerk of the Salem market. According to a complaint initiated by the poor of Salem, Haskett was accused of shorting the weight of white bread sold at her shop. Weighing the bread and finding it too light, Maule seized it for the poor, as the law directed, but was hindered from confiscating the "basket of penny biscuit" when Elizabeth Haskett's "negro servant" made off with it.[6] Then there are the names. Maule was whipped in 1675 by a constable named "Clifford" for working on a public fast day. As a counterexample to Hawthorne's fictional account, William Pynchon was the venerable founder of Springfield who in 1650 changed his conservative views, publishing a book on political hypocrisy thought to be heretical by Massachusetts leaders. This prompted Governor Endecott to lament that Pynchon "might have kept his judgment to himself, as it seems he did above thirty years, most of which time [Pynchon] hath lived amongst us with honour, much respect, and love."[7] While not a Salem resident, Pynchon's book was burned in the Salem marketplace, and his conversion, his sudden advocacy of an enlightened rationalism complete with a call for the toleration of diverse Christian opinions, plots a trajectory diametrically opposed to that of the fictional Pyncheon in *The House of the Seven Gables.*[8]

I conclude my argument by demonstrating the connection between Hawthorne's authorial figure of Holgrave with the early dissenting Salem writer Thomas Maule, not to introduce a new reading of *The House of the Seven Gables,* but to call attention to perhaps the most famous antebellum author's invocation of an embattled Puritan tradition of civic authorship in what was probably his most popular book. Hawthorne's gesture to Maule suggests that the memory of a civic mode of public writing survived intact well into the middle decades of the nineteenth century. In casting a fictional descendent of Maule as his archetypal American author-figure, I want to suggest that Hawthorne harkened back, both to an intellectual tradition and to an actual history of public political writing in America. This was a mode of public discourse which campaigned actively against the perdurable threat of a political sphere compromised by private interest. In doing so, Hawthorne not only perceived a line of continuity between himself and early American dissenting writers like Thomas Maule who argued for the importance of a public print sphere in supervising the virtue of the state; he dramatized this historical continuity in *The House of the Seven Gables* (in the transformation of Holgrave from an independent social critic to a conservative bourgeois property holder) as the inevitable erosion of an idealized disinterested social activism in the face of enfranchisement and material success. Entirely dependent on writing in 1851 for income to support himself and his family, Hawthorne was keenly aware that the independence of Holgrave's public conscience was illusive in the commercial world of antebellum America, in an age of individualism where, as Hawthorne argued in the novel, "everything is free to the hand that can grasp it." Hawthorne's invocation of a tradition of effective authorial dissent in *The House of the Seven Gables,* I would argue, was a lament over the world of sociopolitical agency American writers had lost, and suggests that the memory of such a world remained in the collective consciousness of American writers well into the middle of the nineteenth century.[9]

At the same time, the Nathaniel Hawthorne of *The House of the Seven Gables* was keenly aware of the political problems posed by a commercial free press, as well as the paradoxical loss of meaningful civic agency in an age which championed America as a "republic of letters." As his disembodied voice touts in a chapter entitled "Governor Pyncheon," the members of modern *res publica* are practiced politicians, every man of them, *and skilled to adjust those pre-liminary measures which steal from the people, without its knowledge, the power of choosing its own rulers. The popular voice, at the next gubernatorial election, though loud as thunder, will be but an echo of what these gentlemen shall speak, under their breath . . .* This little knot of subtle schemers will control the convention, and, through it, dictate to the party.

Facing an obstruction more menacing to the autonomous civic conscience than that of censorship and persecution—that is, a commercial print culture which threatened to rob the individual of his or her capacity to participate in public affairs and his or her ability to envision a world different than that which was rendered by custom and tradition—Hawthorne found himself endorsing a rather peculiar mode of public writing. That is, he translated the disinterested civic conscience of the classical citizen into the disinterested aesthetic con-science of the modern author, appropriating to his domain of the American "romance" a neutral "street that infringe[d] on nobody's private rights" and which might "connect a by-gone time with the very Present which is flitting away from us." As Brook Thomas has suggested in this light, "to study the lim-its of [Hawthorne's] romance is to study the limits of visions of political re-form." I would add to this the limits imposed by a free press and the rise of a commercial print trade.[10] In a world in which access to the public realm was increasingly mediated by an increasingly co-opted mass print culture, Hawthorne sought in his romances to find a way to reconnect a reading public to what he idealized as "institutions that had grown out of the heart of mankind" rather than to perpetuate those ruled by convention and underwrit-ten by a well-orchestrated public's opinion.[11]

Like a surprising number of other well-known writers of the American Renaissance, Hawthorne longed for a political life which did not compromise his integrity. Having spent much of his life lobbying for political appointments and struggling with publishers, and having himself authored the propagandis-tic campaign biography of Franklin Pierce, Hawthorne must have been keenly aware how his attempt to reintegrate a tradition of independent civic writing into an antebellum print culture threatened to make him "the obscurest man of letters in America." His efforts to negotiate this impasse, to reach and affect an anonymous reading public which demanded convention rather than inno-vation, concord rather than controversy, is, I would argue, the story of *The House of the Seven Gables.* But if Hawthorne found an analog between his ro-mance and a residual mode of disinterested civic authorship, the resolution of the plight of his authorial descendent of the dissenting Maules, the figure of Holgrave, bespoke of some pessimism about his ability to engender the capacity for political reform in public writing. That is, the marriage of the dissenting writer to wealth and public stature foretold of what Hawthorne undoubtedly considered the dim prospects for the viability of the independent dissenting conscience for the new professional literary artist in the world of commercial and material success that was antebellum America.

Introduction

1. Max Weber, *The Protestant Ethic and the Spirit of Capitalism,* 74.

2. Michel Foucault, "What Is an Author?"

3. Michael Warner, *The Letters of the Republic;* Jürgen Habermas, *The Structural Transformation of the Public Sphere.*

4. Jürgen Habermas, *The Theory of Communicative Action,* vol. 1: *Reason and the Rationalization of Society.* Habermas's theory of communicative rationality is in some sense a response to Weber's pessimistic account of "goal rationality" and the Frankfurt School's notion of "instrumental reason." For Habermas, it is not rationalization per se which is a problem but the forms it has taken in history.

5. Jürgen Habermas, *The Structural Transformation of the Public Sphere,* 88.

6. For an account of what one critic has described as the most powerful metaphor in the free speech tradition, see J. Ingber, "The Marketplace of Ideas: A Legitimizing Myth."

7. Joyce Appleby, *Capitalism and a New Social Order;* Albert O. Hirschman, *The Passions and the Interests.*

8. See Isaiah Berlin, "Two Concepts of Liberty."

9. Basil Hall, "Puritanism: The Problem of Definition," 283–296. Hall excludes Separatists on the basis that they were not reformers at all because they rejected the established church as a lost cause and sought to seek a pure church elsewhere. See also Margo Todd's *Christian Humanism and the Puritan Social Order.* Todd follows Hall's lead to derive a working definition of Puritans as "a self-conscious community of protestant zealots committed to purging the Church of England from within of its remaining Romish 'superstitions,' vestments and liturgy . . . They are distinguished not by adherence to a particular form of church government or to predestinarian theology, but by intensity of evangelical concern and vocal commitment to further religious reform within the state church" (14).

10. Michael Walzer, *The Revolution of the Saints.*

11. Miklós Haraszti, *The Velvet Prison,* 7, 8.

12. Ivan Klíma, "An Upheaval for Czech Readers."

One

1. Perry Miller, "The Puritan State and Puritan Society."

2. Christopher Hill, *Intellectual Origins of the English Revolution; Puritanism and Revolution;* and *Society and Puritanism;* Michael Walzer, *The Revolution of the Saints.*

3. Margo Todd, *Christian Humanism.*

4. Perry Miller, *The Puritans,* 192.

5. Margo Todd, *Christian Humanism,* 7, 178.

6. The title of *Areopagitica* was Milton's neoclassical allusion to the Athenian Council of Areopagites, a tribunal originally envisioned by Solon as a means to supervise collective morals, but which had degenerated into a mechanism for arbitrary censorship. See Patrick's discussion of *Areopagitica* in *The Prose of John Milton.*

7. There may also be some connection to Lord Brooke's *The Nature of Truth,* the work of a Commonwealthman who attempted to harmonize Puritan moralism with the humanist exhortation of reason.

8. Thomas Maule, *Truth Held Forth and Maintained.*

9. It is interesting to note that Maule apparently drew much of his defense from the tenets of classical republicanism, suggesting that to live in a commonwealth, like the Greek *polis,* by definition meant that everything was to be decided through words and persuasion rather than by external coercion and violence.

10. Although Maule was probably a Quaker by the time of his trial, there is reason to believe that he had not joined the sect upon arriving in Salem. Matt Bushnell Jones notes that in 1672 the town selectmen contracted him to sweep out the meetinghouse and ring the bell, a perquisite no Quaker would have ordinarily been allowed. As Christopher Hill reminds us for an earlier English context in *The World Turned Upside Down,* "[I]t is perhaps misleading to differentiate too sharply between [the] politics, religion and general skepticism [of various dissenting sects] . . . men moved easily from one group to another," 11–12. See Matt Bushnell Jones, "Thomas Maule, The Salem Quaker," 3.

11. T. H. Breen, *Character of the Good Ruler.*

12. I am grateful to Emory Elliott for pointing out to me that there may have been an almanac printed in Cambridge prior to the 1642 *Freedman's Oath.* See Isaiah Thomas, *The History of Printing in America.*

13. *The Freedman's Oath* (1642); cited in John Child, *New England's Jonas Cast Up in London.*

14. Thomas Maule, *New England Pe[r]secutors Mauled with Their Own Weapons,* 60–61 (emphasis mine).

15. See, e.g., Nathaniel Ward, *The Simple Cobbler of Aggawam;* and Edward Winslow, *The Dangers of Tolerating Levellers in a Civill State.* For an account of the rhetoric of Puritan Nehemiahs, see Sacvan Bercovitch, *The Puritan Origins of the American Self;* and his *The American Jeremiad.*

16. Thomas Maule, *New England Pe[r]secutors Mauled with Their Own Weapons.*

17. Perez Zagorin, *The Court and the Country*, 37, 156.

18. Michael Walzer, *The Revolution of the Saints*, 12.

19. For the former, see J. G. A. Pocock, *The Machiavellian Moment*, 462–552; for the latter, see the chapter titled "The State as an Order of Repression," in Michael Walzer, *The Revolution of the Saints*. For a discussion of how these contradictory ideas played out historically in colonial New England, see T. H. Breen, *Character of the Good Ruler*. For an account of the links between Puritanism and the radical Whigs, see Caroline Robbins, *The Eighteenth-Century Commonwealthman*. For an account of conceptions of Puritan citizenship, see Edward S. Morgan, *Visible Saints*.

20. Perry Miller, *The Puritans*, 192. See also Michael Walzer who argues that Puritan radicalism depended on such republican notions as the separation of politics from the household, the appearance of formally free men, and a rational and pragmatic consideration of political methods (*The Revolution of the Saints*, 13–17).

21. See F. S. Siebert, *Freedom of the Press in England, 1476–1776*, chaps. 5–7; L. W. Hanson, *Government and the Press, 1595–1673*; Donald Thomas, *A Long Time Burning*.

22. Jürgen Habermas argues in *The Structural Transformation of the Public Sphere* that the public sphere was transformed from a state of affairs in which authority embodied in special persons is represented before the people to one in which authority is constituted by a discourse in which people are represented. Applying such thinking to the American context, Larzer Ziff, for instance, argues that it was only into the middle decades of the eighteenth century that "social conduct [e.g., in discourse] was taken as an adequate sign of individual virtue and individual virtue, in turn, taken as an adequate sign of the sanctity of the soul" (*Writing in the New Nation*, 14–15, 55). See also Michael Warner, *The Letters of the Republic*, 8, 34–38.

23. Michael Warner's strenuous efforts to level Puritan conceptions of public writing can be seen most clearly in his refusal to accept as plausible John Adams's 1765 assessment of the links between Puritanism and a tradition of civic humanism, noting that "we are perhaps unaccustomed to seeing the Puritans described as republican classists . . . the success of [Adams's assessment] depends on his ability to revise the meaning of the Puritan's relation to letters." Thus, Warner does not stop with questioning critically the motives behind Adams's observations; he dismisses them altogether, replacing them with his own account. In Warner's Foucauldian history, "ignoring [the] organizing and disciplinary force of sacred exegesis, Adams *must see* the Puritan's literacy as self-reflection for its own sake . . . if he is to regard their westward migration as the beginning of a national history of enlightenment" (*The Letters of the Republic*, 1–3). While there is undoubtedly something to be gained by interrogating the emancipatory teleology of Adams's observation, I would argue that there is enough historical evidence to suggest that there was something to Adams's account.

24. I realize that these statements are disturbingly close to radical formulations of "repressive tolerance" by Marxist critics like Barrington Moore and Hebert Marcuse. In suggesting some of the problems the rise in libertarian thinking posed to a tradition of civic authorship, I am attempting to counter a monolithic critical tradition which has tended to see the emergence of the modern author as coextensive with the freedom of the press. I certainly do not mean to suggest that the rise of a free press was an inherently bad thing, or that it did not give a new voice to the previously disenfranchised.

25. This act stipulated that all printed materials be licensed by two appointees of the state. The General Court amended this act in 1663 but reinstated the 1662 provisions when Marmaduke Johnson attempted in 1665 to set up the first private commercial press. The General Court also reaffirmed its intention of permitting no other press than that already in Cambridge. Some historians have suggested that this act was occasioned by writings of the Quakers and was meant to compensate for the fact that the Press Restriction Acts of the English Parliament did not extend to the colonies. For accounts of some of the other writers in this transatlantic exchange of radical civic criticism, see Clyde Duniway, *The Development of Freedom of the Press in Massachusetts;* Leonard W. Levy, *Legacy of Suppression;* and Philip F. Gura, *A Glimpse of Sion's Glory.*

26. Samuel Gorton, *Simplicities Defense against Seven-Headed Policy.*

27. John Child, *New England's Jonas Cast Up in London.* Much of the account described here is also described in the introduction to a nineteenth-century reprint of *New England's Jonas . . .*

28. John Child, *New England's Jonas Cast Up in London.*

29. See also Roger Williams, *The Bloudy Tenent of Persecution.*

30. See Clyde Duniway, *The Development of Freedom of the Press in Massachusetts;* and Leonard W. Levy, *Legacy of Suppression.*

31. Edward Winslow, *New England's Salamander Discovered by an Irreligious and Scornfull Pamphlet, Called New England's Jonas Cast Up at London.*

32. Cited in a nineteenth-century reprint of John Child's *New England's Jonas . . .* See Sabin collection.

33. Quoted in Philip F. Gura, *A Glimpse of Sion's Glory,* 206.

34. David D. Hall, *Worlds of Wonder, Days of Judgment;* Stephen Greenblatt, "The Word of God in the Age of Mechanical Reproduction." See also essays in Sacvan Bercovitch's collection, *Typology and Early American Literature.*

35. Michel Foucault, "What Is an Author?"

36. Cited in Lewis Simpson, *Men of Letters in Colonial Maryland.*

Two

1. Leonard W. Levy, *Legacy of Suppression,* 24–29.

2. Elizabeth Christine Cook, *Literary Influences in Colonial Newspapers,* 81. For

accounts other than Levy's, see Jeffery Alan Smith, *Printers and Press Freedom*. The classic account is Zechariah Chafee's *Free Speech in the United States.*

3. Clinton Rossiter, *Seedtime of the Republic,* 141.

4. See Mary Patterson Clarke, *Parliamentary Privilege in the American Colonies,* 117.

5. Leonard W. Levy, *Freedom of the Press from Zenger to Jefferson,* xxxvi.

6. Ibid.; Arthur M. Schlesinger, *Prelude to Independence,* 189. Levy's classic study of American libertarianism, while having been revised and heavily qualified by him in his 1985 *Emergence of a Free Press,* is still the most detailed work on the rise of a free press in early America. For a critique of Levy's overall argument that the persistence of the doctrine of seditious libel precluded a true understanding of libertarianism by the end of the eighteenth century, see David M. Rabban's churlish "The Ahistorical Historian," 795–856.

7. For an account of the arbitrary political use of seditious libel in the form of the Alien and Sedition Acts by both Federalists and Jeffersonians, see James Morton Smith, *Freedom's Fetters.*

8. See Bernard Bailyn, *Ideological Origins of the American Revolution.*

9. I am borrowing this, of course, from Max Weber's famous rhetorical question in *The Protestant Ethic and the Spirit of Capitalism.* As Albert O. Hirschman has rephrased it, "[H]ow did commerce, banking, and similar money-making pursuits become honorable at some point in the modern age after having stood condemned or despised as greed, love of lucre, and avarice for centuries." To my mind, the two questions are inseparable.

10. Cited in Albert O. Hirschman, *The Passions and the Interests.*

11. I am speaking here of the oft-cited *ideal* of the individual's critical self-consciousness in classical political writing; I am not arguing here for the possibility of this self- consciousness on philosophical grounds. For a recent critique of this project, see Stanley Fish, "Critical Self-Consciousness, or Can We Know What We're Doing."

12. Along these lines, it is no accident that the newspapers and journals of colonial America, while frequently championed as the "palladium of liberty," were also littered with complaints about the biases of colonial presses. Individuals frequently attacked printers for misprinting, "framing," or omitting public commentary.

13. Charles R. Hildeburn, *Sketches of Printers and Printing in Colonial New York,* 25–26.

14. James Alexander, *A Brief Narrative of the Case and Trial of John Peter Zenger,* 1.

15. Ibid., 2.

16. *New York Weekly Journal,* no. 7, December 17, 1733; cited in Stanley N. Katz's introduction to James Alexander's *A Brief Narrative . . .*

17. James Alexander, *A Brief Narrative . . . ,* 11.

18. *New York Weekly Journal,* no. 18, February 25, 1734; cited in Stanley N. Katz's introduction to James Alexander's *A Brief Narrative . . .*

19. Leonard W. Levy, "Did the Zenger Case Really Matter?" 35–50.
20. James Alexander, *A Brief Narrative . . .* , 26.
21. Ibid., 1.
22. Benedict Anderson, *Imagined Communities,* 9–36.

Three

1. Benjamin Franklin, *The Autobiography,* 180; hereafter cited parenthetically.
2. Benjamin Franklin, "Apology for Printers," 172.
3. See Elizabeth Fox-Genovese, *The Origins of Physiocracy;* and Ronald L. Meek, *The Economics of Physiocracy.* For accounts of eighteenth-century theories of *le doux commerce,* see Albert O. Hirshman, *The Passions and the Interests;* J. G. A. Pocock, "Virtue and Commerce in the Eighteenth Century," 119–134; and *The Machiavellian Moment;* and Joyce Appleby, *Capitalism and a New Social Order.*
4. I am indebted here to Mitchell Breitweiser who points out this juxtaposition in his fine *Cotton Mather and Benjamin Franklin,* 216, 274.
5. Michael Warner, *The Letters of the Republic,* 81–82; Jürgen Habermas, *The Structural Transformation of the Public Sphere.*
6. Georg Lukács, *History and Class Consciousness,* 87. For further discussion of Lukác's concept of reification and its application to the canon of American writing, see chap. 8 in Andrew Arato and Paul Breines's *The Young Lukács;* Carolyn Porter's *Seeing and Being;* and her "Reification in American Literature."
7. Raymond Williams, *Marxism and Literature,* 121–127.
8. See Michael Warner, *The Letters of the Republic,* xiii–xv, 73–117, passim; Robert A. Ferguson, "We Hold These Truths." See also Lewis Simpson's "Printer as a Man of Letters: Franklin and the Symbolism of the Third Realm."
9. Jürgen Habermas, *The Structural Transformation of the Public Sphere,* passim; Michael Warner, *The Letters of the Republic,* passim; Michael Shudson, "Was There Ever a Public Sphere? If So, When? Reflections on the American Case," 143–161.
10. Mitchell Robert Breitweiser, *Cotton Mather and Benjamin Franklin,* 180, 200, 207.
11. Michael T. Gilmore, "Franklin and the Shaping of American Ideology," 108; Myra Jehlen, "'Imitate Jesus and Socrates,'" 504.
12. Perry Miller, "Benjamin Franklin and Jonathan Edwards," in his *Major Writers of America,* vol. 1; David Levin, "*The Autobiography of Benjamin Franklin:* The Puritan Experimenter in Life and Art"; Robert F. Sayre, *The Examined Self.*
13. Max Weber, *The Protestant Ethic and the Spirit of Capitalism.*
14. D. H. Lawrence, *Studies in Classic American Literature,* 18–21; C. B. Macpherson, *The Political Theory of Possessive Individualism,* passim.
15. Michael Warner, "Franklin and the Letters of the Republic," 114.
16. Mitchell Robert Breitweiser, *Cotton Mather and Benjamin Franklin,* 214.
17. See Lewis A. Coser et al., *Books;* Elizabeth L. Eisenstein, *The Printing Press as*

an Agent of Cultural Change. See especially D. F. McKenzie, *Bibliography and the Sociology of Texts;* Walter J. Ong, *Orality and Literacy;* Lucien Febvre and Henri-Jean Martin, *The Coming of the Book,* trans. David Gerard; and Robert Darnton, *The Business of Enlightenment.*

18. See all of chap. 4 in Georg Simmel, *The Philosophy of Money,* trans. Tom Bottomore and David Frisby.

19. Jay Fliegelman, *Prodigals and Pilgrim,* 9–10

20. Ibid., 23.

21. See J. Paul Hunter, *Before Novels,* for a discussion of guide books as a new use for the medium of print.

22. Donald Pease, "The Author," 106.

23. Clyde Duniway, *The Development of Freedom of the Press in Massachusetts;* Leonard W. Levy, *Legacy of Suppression.* Franklin, for instance, errs in claiming that the *New England Courant* was the "second newspaper in America"—itself a telling claim since Cambridge had possessed a printing press for nearly a century—overlooking the fact that the first newspaper in America, Benjamin Harris's *Publick Occurrences,* was banned by the Puritan state after only two issues. As I have suggested, Franklin's Peter Folger was just one of many religious and political dissenters who used the medium of print to circumvent the control of the New England theocracy by having their social criticism printed abroad. See, e.g., Philip F. Gura, *A Glimpse of Sion's Glory.*

24. Annabel M. Patterson, *Censorship and Interpretation.*

25. This relationship is also dramatized in Franklin's recounting of his youthful project to build a wharf out of stones stolen from a nearby house under construction. Franklin terms it rather enthusiastically as "an early projecting of public spirit, tho' not then justly conducted." When reprimanded by his father, Franklin pleads "the usefulness of the work," but is told by Josiah that "nothing was useful which was not honest." Yet the reader is left with the suspicion that Franklin sees instances of social transgression as the necessary preconditions to civic virtue.

26. Benjamin Franklin, "Silence Dogood, No. 1," 5–6.

27. Michael Warner, "Franklin and the Letters of the Republic," 116.

28. For a summary of Franklin's views on economics and his physiocratic theories of value, see William A. Wetzel, *Benjamin Franklin as an Economist.* For a discussion of Franklin's various writings on currency, see Mitchell Robert Breitweiser, *Cotton Mather and Benjamin Franklin.*

29. Georg Simmel, *Philosophy of Money,* passim; see also the introduction to Marc Shell, *The Economy of Literature.*

30. Adam Smith, *The Wealth of Nations,* 10–11.

31. Georg Simmel, *Philosophy of Money,* passim.

32. The charge of plagiarism was a common attack made on Franklin. For a theoretical discussion of how Franklin's method "to submit himself to language—to become, as it were, an instance of a discourse that he encountered ready-made"

may have led him to an unclear usage of sources (see Christopher Looby, "'The Affairs of the Revolution Occasion'd the Interruption': Writing, Revolution, Deferral, and Conciliation in Franklin's *Autobiography*," 78–80).

33. Joseph Dennie, "An Author's Evenings from the Shop of Messrs. Colon and Spondee," 53–54.

34. See Gordon S. Wood, *The Radicalism of the American Revolution,* for a discussion of the creation of the Franklinian image of the self-made man.

35. Dennie, no doubt, was also alluding here to the popular success of Joseph Alleine's *An Alarm to Unconverted Sinners* which, together with a version titled *The Sure Guide to Heaven,* became something of an early American best-seller.

36. I realize that the terminology of the 1790 Federal Copyright Act was taken directly from its English antecedent, the 1709 Statute of Anne. I am not making an exceptionalist claim here; rather, I am just alluding to how the wording of the law reflected widespread cultural definitions of authorship, writers, and texts.

37. William Charvat, *The Profession of Authorship in America.*

Four

1. Washington Irving, *The Sketch Book.*
2. Robert A. Ferguson, *Law and Letters in American Culture,* 150–172.
3. I am delineating this dichotomy between "Lockean" and "utilitarian" conceptions with some exaggeration and generalization. I make this general categorization inductively and descriptively on the basis of a sample of over one hundred documents on "copyright" and "literary property" I culled from sources printed in America between 1790 and 1860. This is a general typology, and I recognize that most accounts conflate various rationales for authorial activity. In referring to Lockean conceptions of authorship, I want to emphasize that intellectuals turned to precedents in "common law" to find evidence to argue against utilitarian conceptions; and in doing so, they blurred the distinction between property as "right" and property as "thing" to support claims for exclusive and perpetual ownership. I do not mean to equate common law with the thinking of Locke, and I certainly do not mean to deny Blackstone's emphasis on "alienability" nor the long tradition of equity in common law. By the same token, I do not mean to collapse the differences between republican and utilitarian thinking, although I would venture to argue that any "republican thinking" on copyright in the years following the Revolution increasingly became more utilitarian over the course of the nineteenth century. I use "utilitarian" here because Irving was writing in 1819 when utilitarian conceptions of authorship had largely displaced any remaining "republican" emphasis. See Meredith McGill's unpublished essay on *Wheaton v. Peters* for what she argues was the persistence of republican ideology into nineteenth-century copyright jurisprudence ("*Wheaton v. Peters* and the Materiality of the Text"). For an attempt at a classification of doctrines across the whole spectrum of continental copyright thinking, see F. J. Kase, *Copyright Thought in Continental Europe.*

4. This association was even encouraged by some republican writers. Poet Joel Barlow, for instance, joined with inventor Robert Fulton in calling for an association to protect property rights for first inventors. See "New-England Association in Favor of Inventors and Discoverers, and Particularly for the Protection of Intellectual Property," 302–306.

5. In his *Second Treatise of Civil Government,* Locke argued famously that
every man has a *property* in his own *person*. This no body has any right to but himself. The *labour* of his body, and the work of his hands, we may say, are properly his. Whatsoever he removes out of the state that nature hath provided, and left it in, he hath mixed his *labor* with, and joyned to it something that is his own, and thereby makes it his *property*.

See John Locke, *Two Treatises of Government,* 305–306. See Anon., "The Rights of Authors," 277–282, for a typical argument over how common law rights to literary property existed prior to the 1790 Federal Copyright statute.

6. I say "altered" common law assumptions, since common law in the eighteenth-century often allowed for alienability, at least before the influence of Locke. Advocates of Lockean rights to literary property, however, turned to *their* version of Blackstone to counter the claims of the utilitarians. See C. B. Macpherson, "The Meaning of Property," 1–13, for an account of how an age-old "idea of common property drops virtually out of sight . . . becoming an individual right unlimited in amount, unconditional on the performance of social functions, and freely transferable, as it remains to the present day."

7. The verdict itself in the *Wheaton v. Peters* case reflected this vacillation. The majority opinion decided that while an author's right could be absolute prior to publication, with such publication an author surrendered such autonomy to the general interests of American society. Yet the dissenting view by Justice Thompson reflected a Lockean conception of authorship:
The great principle on which the author's right rests, is, that it is the fruit or production of his own labour, and which may, by the labour of the faculties of the mind, establish a right of property, as well as by the faculties of the body; and it is difficult to perceive any well-founded objection to such a claim of right.

See *Wheaton v. Peters,* 669–670. Meredith McGill has argued that the *Wheaton v. Peters* case demonstrated the persistence of republican ideology in American copyright thinking. Although I agree with her assessment that the case countered the Lockean idea of the proprietary author, I am more inclined to see the decision, like contemporaneous legal arguments in England, as addressing utilitarian rather than republican concerns.

8. See Bernard Edelman, *Le Droit Saisi par la Photographie* (trans. Elizabeth Kingdom as *Ownership of the Image).* Edelman argues that "photography, a technical innovation developing independently of law, contradict[ed] the existing formulations of property right in representations of things." As Paul Hirst notes in his introduction to *Ownership of the Inage:* "Edelman attempts to use this surprise as a

device to reveal the categories constitutive of property law." That is, he attempts to demonstrate how the law "constitutes the very subject [e.g. the proprietary author] whose existence it refers to, interpellating individuals as subjects with certain attributes through the practice of law." Edelman demonstrates how the law was "surprised" by the advent of the photographer, who seemed to be a mechanical attendant rather than an artistic creator. He notes how at first jurisprudence denigrated this attendant, designating it "soulless labor" and hence not eligible for property rights. As the industry matures, however, Edelman reveals how the law "corrected" its perception and replaced this subject with the "soul of labor." He concludes that in terms of jurisprudence, the "photographer and film-maker must become creators, or the industry will lose the benefit of legal protection" (44).

9. For discussions of these three positions, see essays in *Liberalism and Its Critics,* ed. Michael Sandel.

10. Evidence for such anxiety is sketchy but pervasive among writers in antebellum America. Hawthorne, taking an arbitrary example, notes in the introduction to *A Wonder Book* that although he rendered his classical myths "into very capital reading for children," making the "legends malleable in his intellectual furnace . . . no epoch of time can claim a copyright in [the] immortal fables. They seem never to have been made." Hawthorne concludes by noting that such tales are the "legitimate subjects [not objects] for every age to clothe with its own garniture of manners." For a thorough discussion of antebellum writers' mixed resistance to and complicity with the exploding book trade, see Michael T. Gilmore, *American Romanticism and the Marketplace.*

11. See Granville Sackett, *A Plea for Authors, and the Rights of Literary Property,* for Irving's possible public comments on copyright. See note on problem of attribution below. See also Washington Irving, "To The Editor of the Knickerbocker," 78–79.

12. William Charvat in *The Profession of Authorship in America,* 6.

13. Along these lines, David Saunders makes the persuasive argument that, at the turn of the nineteenth century, even the category of " 'literature' had not yet taken on the aesthetic attributes which we now recognise when distinguishing between 'literary' and 'non-literary' types of writing and reading." He suggests that "in the late eighteenth century, 'literature' still referred to written or printed matter of any kind" (*Authorship and Copyright,* 154).

14. For a thorough treatment of this tradition, see essays by Robert A. Ferguson, David S. Shields, and Michael T. Gilmore in *The Cambridge History of American Literature,* ed. Sacvan Bercovitch.

15. In saying this, I do not mean to suggest that before copyright public writing was not an economic activity; rather, I would argue that in the seventeenth and early eighteenth centuries economic activity was not accorded a separate realm from politics. See, e.g., Eli F. Heckscher, *Mercantilism,* 2–30. Joyce O.

Appleby traces the separation of economics from politics in late seventeenth-century England in her fine *Economic Thought and Ideology in Seventeenth-Century England*.

16. I am talking about an eighteenth-century transformation in the American colonies where the New England theocracy managed to maintain tight political control over a few colonial presses, and where the southern colonies did not get their first independent press until 1726 (after William Nuthead's 1685 government press). The transformation I am alluding to in America began much earlier—and transpired with more unevenness—in England where the political function of the Star Chamber was entwined with the commercial interests of the Stationer's Company (a consortium of booksellers) by the late seventeenth century. See Benjamin Kaplan who claims copyright "had the look of being gradually secreted in the interstices of censorship" *(An Unhurried View of Copyright)*. See also Lyman Ray Patterson, *Copyright in Historical Perspective;* and John Feather, *A History of British Publishing*. See also Martha Woodmansee, *The Author, Art, and the Market;* and Mark Rose, *Authors and Owners*.

17. Louis Dumont, *From Mandeville to Marx,* 36–38. For an account of how Smith worked to justify the then scandalous premise that an autonomous economic system of competitive markets was more efficient and just than one in which the polity policed the markets, even, say, for the laboring poor, see Istvan Hont and Michael Ignatieff, "Needs and Justice in the *Wealth of Nations:* An Introductory Essay."

18. A posteri libel and sedition laws, in contrast, developed alongside copyright, beginning in the seventeenth century and marked by such famous cases as *Rex v. Curll* in 1727. Although such jurisprudence reflected the law's continuing acknowledgment of the *political* nature of public writing, the move from a priori to a posteri modes of regulating authorship really demonstrated how the social *effect* of authorship was rendered a separate issue from the individual *act* of authorship as the latter was increasingly defined in terms of material production. For an account of this transformation in Anglo-American jurisprudence (and focusing on the American scene which he argues was more suppressive than that in England), see Leonard W. Levy, *Legacy of Suppression*.

19. For accounts of the explosion of the book trade in America and the rise of the professional writer, see William Charvat, *Literary Publishing in America;* and *The Profession of Authorship in America;* Charles A. Madison, *Book Publishing in America;* Cathy N. Davidson, *Revolution and the Word;* and Lawrence Buell, *New England Literary Culture*. For accounts of changes in reading habits, see James D. Hart, *The Popular Book;* David D. Hall, *Worlds of Wonder, Days of Judgment;* and essays in Cathy N. Davidson, *Reading in America*. For the classic account of the rise of bourgeois individualism and the origins of the professional writer, see Ian Watt, *The Rise of the Novel*. For two revisions which look at, respectively, the role of genre and domestic writers in producing the conditions of modern bourgeois individualism, see

Michael McKeon, *The Origins of the English Novel;* and Nancy Armstrong, *Desire and Domestic Fiction.*

20. Charles Brockden Brown makes this residual notion of the former clear in an 1803 essay when he claimed:

While the *poor author,* that is to say, the author by trade, is regarded with indifference or contempt, the *author,* that is, the man who devotes to composition the leisure secured to him by hereditary affluence, or by a lucrative position or office, obtains from mankind a higher, and more lasting, and more genuine reverence than any other class of mortals. As there is nothing I should more fervently deprecate than to be enrolled in the former class, so there is nothing to which I more ardently aspire, than to be numbered among the latter.

See Charles Brockden Brown, "Extracts from a Student's Diary: Authorship," 8–9.

21. The Connecticut statue ambiguously mixed Lockean and utilitarian conceptions. While the beginning of the act stated that "it is perfectly agreeable to the principles of natural equity and justice, that every author be secured in receiving the profits that may arise from the sale of his works," the law also maintained that it was "equally necessary for the inhabitants of this state [to] be furnished with useful books, & ec., at reasonable prices . . . A judge, on complaint, shall investigate the matter and may require a sufficient number of the copyrighted articles to be offered for sale at a reasonable price fixed by the court." See reprint of statute in Karl Fenning, "Copyright before the Constitution," 1336.

22. J. G. A. Pocock, *Virtue, Commerce, History.* See also C. B. Macpherson, "The Meaning of Property." It is interesting that Barlow's notion of authorial independence echoes the French legal tradition of *des droits des auteurs* more than the Anglo-American tradition of copyright, that is, the concern over the rights of a protected authorial personality rather than the material domain of property. In *Author and Copyright,* David Saunders accords this difference to two different models of state formation. He argues that

in Britain and the American territories a private, commerce-led expansion was accompanied by a primarily commercial and contract-oriented law; in central Europe (notably in Prussia) expansion was of a more public, state-led character, with codified statute law of central importance. Between the British type of loose commercial and capitalistic network driven by private commercial interests and the Prussian type of unitary network of state agencies—bureaucracy, army, university and government controlled press—lies a mixed mode of commercialism and statism that could be said to characterise the historical development in France.

French Jurist Marcel Plaisant described such personality rights at a 1934 international conference on artistic property, arguing that "above and beyond the pecuniary and patrimonial right . . . the author exercises a lofty sovereignty over his work, such that when it is damaged he is injured. Publication is envisaged as a phenomenon that extends the personality of the author and thus exposes him to further injuries because the surface of his vulnerability has been enlarged" (see Saunders, *Authorship and Copyright,* 31, 75–76). Barlow's intimation did not fade entirely. The idea was to find expression in American jurisprudence in Louis Brandeis and Samuel Warren's famous decree that "the principle which protects personal writings and all other personal productions, not against theft and physical appropriation but publication in any form, is in reality not the principle of private property, but that of inviolate personality" ("The Right to Privacy," 193–220).

23. Charles Jared Ingersoll, *A Discourse Concerning the Influence of America on the Mind.*

24. Immanuel Kant, "An Answer to the Question: 'What is Enlightenment?'" 59.

25. James Fenimore Cooper, for instance, endorsed copyright along similar lines as Barlow; that is, he saw it as a necessary juridical means to authorial control. Writing to the American Copyright Club in 1843, Cooper claimed to be "of the opinion that this country, in common with all other countries, is bound to protect literary property, *on principles connected with common honesty"* (emphasis mine). Cooper, however, declined to join the cause, claiming that he asked "nothing from the American Public, and he owe[d] them nothing." He concludes, "I wish to keep the account square. I am certain the tax gatherers will not overlook me, and this will be sure to keep me up to the discharges of all my duties as a citizen" (see John Kouwenhoven, "Cooper and the American Copyright Club").

26. See Henry Charles Carey, *Letters on International Copyright,* who argued, paraphrasing Justice Joseph Story, that a "great work is . . . but a new combination and arrangement of old materials, in which the skill and judgment of the author in the selection and exposition, and accurate use of those materials, constitute the basis of his reputation, as well as of his copyright." Not surprisingly, these debates were usually inflected with issues of class: the critics of the utilitarian position usually condemning the emergence of a "cheap literature" and calling into question the "agrarianism" implicit in allowing that literary works were the property of all mankind; the assailants of the Lockean position criticizing the elitism of a "high literature" and attacking the monopoly on ideas which perpetual copyright would entail.

27. See Noah Webster, *A Collection of Papers on Political, Literary, and Moral Subjects;* and quote from George Merriam in "Who Owns an Author's Ideas?" 520–522.

28. Thomas Skidmore, *The Rights of Man to Property!*

29. Anon., "Intellectual Economy," 272.

30. George T. Curtis, *Theory of the Law of Copyright.*

31. In this context, Wai Chee Dimock argues that national expansionism struck a writer like "Melville as the ultimate model of authorship," and she goes on to sug-

gest how "Melville's authorial enterprise can be seen . . . as a miniature version of the national enterprise . . . as a miniature version of Manifest Destiny." Dimock argues persuasively how this conception of authorship—and the problems of the antebellum marketplace—were Melville's "straight-jacket" (see *Empire for Liberty: Melville and the Poetics of Individualism*).

32. Anon., "English and American Literature," 207–215.

33. Anon., "International Copyright: Review of Nicklin," 257–270.

34. Anon., "International Copyright," 1–46.

35. Anon., "Literary Property," 294–295.

36. Anon., "International Copyright," 257.

37. Anon., "The Copyright Bill," 523–528.

38. C. B. Macpherson, *The Political Theory of Possessive Individualism*. I realize that Macpherson has come under attack in the last fifteen years or so. Despite the rehabilitation of figures like Mandeville and Locke by scholars like J. A. Gunn and James Dickey (who link Mandeville and Locke to the Jansensits and Socinianism), I think his argument still uniquely explains a mode of thinking in republican and antebellum America. That is, it explains how a figure like Locke was radically appropriated by proponents of liberalism. For Locke's account of a civil society separate from the Church which would regulate the possession of property, see John Locke, *A Letter Concerning Toleration*.

39. Francis Lieber, *On International Copyright*, 1–67.

40. Cornelius Mathews, *The Better Interests of the Country, in Connexion with International Copyright*.

41. Anon., "International Copyright: Review of Nicklin," 257–270.

42. Copyright bibliographer Torvald Solberg attributes the treatise to Granville Sackett alone, but it is attributed to Washington Irving as well in other sources, including the Library of Congress. See Sackett's *A Plea for Authors and the Rights of Literary Property*.

43. Anon., "Cheap Literature: Its Character and Tendencies," 33–39.

44. George Frederick Holmes, "The Present Condition of Letters," 673–678.

45. Anon., "From Our Armchair," 179–180. For more overdetermined arguments of this sort, see Francis Lieber, *Essays on Property and Labor*.

46. David Saunders, *Authorship and Copyright*, 75–121; Carla Hesse, *Publishing and Cultural Politics in Revolutionary Paris, 1789–1810*.

47. Mark Rose, *Authors and Owners*. With historical sensitivity, Martha Woodmansee has traced a parallel development in eighteenth-century Germany, claiming that from the Renaissance to the first half of the eighteenth century two conceptions of the writer obtained in popular thinking. Neither of these two formulations, writer as craftsman and writer as one divinely inspired, held the author *personally* responsible for his creation, since the former was seen as a manipulator of things while the latter one was seen as empowered by God. In the most interesting part of her argument, she traces how copyright, underwritten by the rise of aes-

thetic theory, transformed the writer from a vehicle for preordained "truths" to the creative genius. See her "The Genius and the Copyright," 425–448; and *The Author, Art, and the Market.*

48. Trevor Ross, "Copyright and the Invention of Tradition." See also Meredith L. McGill who argues along similar lines that classic liberal claims in America were countered in the *Wheaton v. Peters* case by notions of an open public print sphere.

49. David Saunders and Ian Hunter, "Lessons from the 'Literatory': How to Historicize Authorship"; Saunders, *Authorship and Copyright.*

50. *Quarterly Review* 8 (September 1812): 93.

51. Anon., "The Want of Money, or The Miseries of Authors," 39.

52. Hannah Arendt, *The Human Condition,* 55–56.

53. *The Key* [Maryland] 37 (1798): 189.

54. *The Pocket Magazine,* &c.[New York], (1796): 199.

55. Anon., "Miseries of Authorship," 33–34.

56. Kenneth Dauber, "Criticism of American Literature," 55.

Five

1. J. Hector St. John de Crèvecoeur, *Letters from an American Farmer and Sketches of Eighteenth-Century America,* ed. Albert E. Stone (New York, 1986), 37. References hereafter cited in text. An earlier—and substantively different—version of this chapter appeared in *Early American Literature* (Fall 1992).

2. Dennis Moore, *More Letters from an American Farmer.*

3. I realize that Raynal's *Histoire Philosophique et Politique des Etablissemens et du Commerce des Europeens dans les Deux Indes* (1770) was the collaborative work of many writers including Diderot. I am following convention by referring to Raynal—as Crèvecoeur does—as principal author. Page references are to English edition of 1783 (see Bibliography).

4. Guillaume Thomas François Raynal, *A Philosophical and Political History of the Settlements and Trade of the Europeans in the East and West Indies.*

5. Robert Darnton, *The Forbidden Best-Sellers of Pre-Revolutionary France.*

6. Bernard Fay, *The Revolutionary Spirit in France and America,* 10.

7. Guillaume Thomas François Raynal, *The Revolution of America.*

8. Raynal does not go so far as to declare faith in egalitarianism. In his invective on the Anabaptists, a religious system he argues was "founded on charity and mildness, yet it produced nothing but violence and iniquity," Raynal proclaims that "the chimerical idea of an equality of stations is the most dangerous one that can be adopted in a civilized society. To preach this system to the people is not to put them in mind of their rights; it is leading them on to assassination and plunder. It is letting domestic animals loose, and transforming them into wild beasts. The rulers of the people must be more enlightened . . . but there is no such thing in nature as a

real equality; it exists only in the system of equity" (see *A Philosophical and Political History . . .* , [7:281–282]).

9. Mary Poovey, "The Social Constitution of 'Class': Toward a History of Classificatory Thinking." Poovey outlines two phases in the history of classifactory thinking, which she terms political and scientific rationality, which together produced the nineteenth-century category of class. She argues that the former, picking up on the vestiges of political reasoning of Hobbes, yielded the analytical tradition of Marx. The latter, founded in the empiricism of Bacon, gave rise to the ideological commentary of Ricardo. Poovey documents how the tension between theory and description in each mode of classifying the world excluded some part of the universe it purported to describe.

10. As evidence of this preoccupation with process, readers of *Letters from an American Farmer* will recall that the organizing trope that James invokes again and again in the narrative is the idea that he follows "the progressive steps" of the Americans such as himself, Andrew the Hebredian, the Cape islanders, and the frontiersmen.

11. See George Lakoff, *Women, Fire, and Dangerous Things,* 77–90. For an argument which ties metonymic reasoning to the nineteenth-century critique of modernism, specifically Marx's reduction of producers, see Wai Chee Dimock, "Class, Gender, and a History of Metonymy."

12. Describing the settlement of South Carolina at the end of Book 18, Raynal blurts out rhetorically, "But without this [slave] labor, these lands, acquired at such a high cost, would remain uncultivated," to which he answers emphatically, "Well then, let them lie fallow, if it means that to make these lands productive, man must be reduced to brutishness, whether he be the man who buys, or he who sells, or he who is sold" (see *A Philosophical and Political History,* 7:297).

13. While not specifically incorporating Raynal, Myra Jehlen offers perhaps the best reading of *Letters* to date by focusing on the deterioration of James's idealized fusion of social and economic spheres. Jehlen gets at Raynal's theories indirectly by seeing Crèvecoeur's farmer as an agrarian caught up in the impending rise of the marketplace. This is one of only several readings I could find that view *Letters* as a fictionalized and theorized economic history of America. Other notable exceptions include Albert Stone's foreward to the 1963 edition of *Letters,* Thomas Philbrick in chap. 3 of his fine *St. John de Crèvecoeur,* and Michael T. Gilmore's preface to the 1971 Everyman's Library edition of *Letters.* See Myra Jehlen, "J. Hector St. John Crèvecoeur: A Monarcho-Anarchist in Revolutionary America," 204–222; Mary Rucker, "Crèvecoeur's Letters and Enlightenment Doctrine," 193–212; and Robert Lawson-Peebles, *Landscape and Written Expression in Revolutionary America,* 100–109; also see James engaged with historical process.

14. Thomas Jefferson's *Notes on the State of Virginia,* manuscripts of which were circulating at the same time Crèvecoeur was apparently composing his *Letters,* takes a similar organizational stance. Intended, like James's letters to Mr. F. B., for an

audience of one, Buffon, Jefferson structured his "notes" according to the queries of a questionnaire circulated by François Marbois. Robert Ferguson argues that this writerly design made it possible for Jefferson to appear self-effacingly in print as "a representative voice" answering questions without design. The structural affinities between *Notes on the State of Virginia* (which despite its panegyric optimism reveals Jefferson's anxieties about corruption within the state and the specter of slavery) and *Letters* are striking, leading one to suspect both authors' conformity to unarticulated conventions of late eighteenth-century print culture (Robert A. Ferguson, *Law and Letters in American Culture,* 34–58).

15. See Robert A. Ferguson, *Law and Letters in American Culture,* 25.

16. Charles Sellers, *The Market Revolution,* 47; Morton J. Horwitz, *The Transformation of American Law, 1780–1860*; William Nelson, *Americanization of the Common Law.*

17. Perry Miller, *The Life of the Mind in America,* 102–104.

18. Evidence of the historical passing of James's agrarian idyll insists its way into his narrative from the second letter where he notes the impending extinction of the carrier pigeon and the wasteful extermination of quail. Regarding the difference between what James *says* and what he *observes,* Nathaniel Philbrick has recently argued that on Nantucket James the farmer "sounds like Gulliver describing the Houyhnhnms: he is unwilling to draw appropriate conclusions from the evidence arrayed before him." This strikes me as a persuasive way of looking at James's narrative stance in the Nantucket and Martha's Vineyard letters. Less convincing is his division of the narrator into James and "the Farmer," two voices which compete, respectively, for an emotional and a predetermined theoretical understanding of America. While this antithesis is compelling, I do not see a need to solidify James's ambiguous voice into two discrete narrative identities. See Nathaniel Philbrick, "The Nantucket Sequence in Crèvecoeur's *Letters from an American Farmer,*" 414–432.

19. Although I think Robert Winston is on the right track when he develops Albert Stone's argument that *Letters* is a "prototypical romance" and Harry Henderson's assertion that it is "an epistolary romance of ideas," I would hesitate, for obvious reasons, to label Crèvecoeur's work, as both critics do, a "romance." Lennard Davis outlines a useful distinction between the romance and the novel which makes my quibble over this point clear. He notes that whereas the romance is set in a distant, idealized past, the novel is in a more recent, less heroic setting; whereas the romance is based on the epic, the novel is modeled on history and journalism; whereas the romance is set abroad, the novel tends to be a national literature; whereas romances value the preservation of virtue, novels tend to focus on the forbidden; whereas romances tend to make it clear they are mixing fact and fiction, novels tend to deny they are fictional; and while novels of the eighteenth century are composed almost without exception in the first person, romances are almost *never* written in the first person. See Winston, "Strange Order of Things!:

The Journey to Chaos in *Letters from an American Farmer,*" Robert Stone's introduction to *Letters from an American Farmer;* Harry Henderson, *Versions of the Past,* passim; and Leonard J. Davis, *Factual Fictions,* 40.

20. Gay Wilson Allen and Roger Asselineau, *St. John de Crèvecoeur,* 29.

21. Gary B. Nash, for instance, notes how social historians have contributed to the myth of a classless pre-Revolutionary American society by extracting evidence from the idealistic "What Is an American" chapter in Crèvecoeur's *Letters.* Failing to read this early chapter as conditional in light of James's experience in later sections of *Letters,* many social historians have taken *Letters* as documentary evidence. See *Class and Society in Early America,* 21–50.

22. Michael Warner, *The Letters of the Republic,* xi.

23. Going so far as to name his first daughter "America-Frances," Crèvecoeur was preoccupied with "hyphenated" identities. Born the son of a landed gentleman in Normandy and schooled as a Jesuit, Crèveocoeur immigrated to Salisbury, England, before joining the French colonial army in 1757 to serve as a cartographer in the final days of the French and Indian Wars. After receiving a commendation for his part in an assault on Col. George Monro's Fort William Henry, Crèvecoeur landed in New York, commencing a series of travels and becoming an adopted member of the Oneidas in Vermont. Returning to New Jersey, Crèveocoeur married the daughter of a prominent New York Tory (and a Protestant), evoking suspicion from both Loyalists and Patriots in the years leading up to the Revolution.

24. Quoted in Everyman's Library edition of *Letters.* This reading has become a cliché for *Letters,* but a persistent one. David Brion Davis's Pulitzer Prize–winning *The Problem of Slavery in Western Culture,* for instance, a book that discusses Raynal at some length, argues that in *Letters* "we see perhaps the clearest picture of the American Idyll, a skillfully weaving together of primitivist, pastoral, and democratic themes, the portrayal of a land in which individual opportunity and social progress are somehow merged with the simple, self-denying virtues of Seneca and Vergil" (7). For an earlier essay which links Crèvecouer with Rousseau and contrasts him with a cynical Thoreau, see John Brooks Moore, "Crèvecoeur and Thoreau," 309–332. I see less of a contrast between Crèvecoeur and Thoreau; both *Letters* and *Walden* seem to be texts whose myths of historical withdrawal are defeated by market forces.

25. David Eisermann, *Crèvecoeur, oder, Die Erfindung Amerikas,* 188.

26. Stanley Kunitz and Howard Haycraft, *American Authors 1600–1900,* 193.

27. Everett Emerson, "Hector St. John de Crèvecoeur and the Promise of America," 46, 47.

28. Gay Wilson Allen and Roger Asselineau, *St. John de Crèvecoeur,* 96; Everett Emerson, "Hector St. John de Crévecoeur and the Promise of America," 45–55.

29. Everett Emerson, "Hector St. John de Crèvecoeur and the Promise of America," 48.

30. Ibid.

31. Marcus Cunliffe, "Crèvecoeur Revisited," 139.

Six

1. See Emory Elliott, *Revolutionary Writers,* 184–217; Joseph J. Ellis, *After the Revolution.* A version of this chapter appeared as an essay titled "Brackenridge and the Resistance to Textual Authority," *American Literature* (June 1995).

2. Hugh Henry Brackenridge, *Modern Chivalry,* 406. Subsequent references cited parenthetically. While I have some quibbles with Newlin's editing of the text, especially with his inclusion of vol. 4 of the 1815 Johnson and Warner edition under "Part 2," it is far and away the best reprint.

3. The bibliographic history of *Modern Chivalry* is, as I hope this essay will make apparent, a labyrinth, and it demonstrates how open Brackenridge's text is to reformation by readers, editors, critics, and bibliographers. If we follow Newlin's lead and accept the amended fourth volume of Johnson and Warner's 1815 revised four-volume edition of all six volumes of Parts 1 and 2 as a discrete volume, then *Modern Chivalry* consists of at least seven volumes written over a period of twenty-three years and published by four publishers in three locations. But even this compilation understates the shapelessness of the "work," if we can call it such, since Patterson and Lambdin's 1819 abridged two-volume edition of the whole was advertised as containing the last corrections and additions of the author. Moreover, these editions constitute only the initial appearances of work on *Modern Chivalry* by Brackenridge. There were, in addition to the seven first-edition volumes, seven additional volumes of various compilations of *Modern Chivalry* in concurrent circulation, often under different titles, published in at least three additional locations.

4. Michael Warner, *The Letters of the Republic,* 97–117; Robert A. Ferguson, "We Hold These Truths," 1–28. Warner defines "republican print ideology" as a set of beliefs that offered writing as a neutral medium of pure socialization because it was "freed from the localization of the personal, the body, the corruptible" (87).

5. Frederick Jameson, *Marxism and Form,* 23; Max Horkheimer and Theodore Adorno, *Dialectic of Enlightenment;* Theodor Adorno, *The Culture Industry.*

6. Walter Benjamin shared Adorno's fear that the explosion of the print sphere and the popularizing of a free press worked to homologize author and society. Benjamin noted that "as writing gains in breadth what it loses in depth, the conventional distinction between author and public, which is upheld by the bourgeois press, begins to disappear." See "The Author as Producer."

7. Alexis de Tocqueville, *Democracy in America,* 399–400, 644–645, 656, 667.

8. Tocqueville even evaluated the effects of hegemony on the writer in America, claiming that "the majority has enclosed thought within a formidable fence. The writer is free inside that area, but woe to the man who goes beyond it. Not that

he stands in fear of an *auto-da-fé*, but he must face all kinds of unpleasantness and everyday persecution" (255). Criticism of the influence of public opinion on writers goes back to Shaftsbury who claimed:

Our modern authors are turned and modelled . . . by the public relish and current humour of the times. They regulate themselves by the irregular fancy of the world . . . in order to accommodate themselves to the genius of the age. In our days the audience makes the poet, and the bookseller the author, with what profit to the public, or what prospect of lasting fame and honour to the writer, let any one who has judgement imagine.

See Anthony Ashley Cooper, Earl of Shaftsbury, *"Soliloquy* or Advice to an Author,"* 1:172–173.

9. Fisher Ames, "Hercules."

10. *The Worcester Magazine* (1787): 253; *New Haven Gazette and Connecticut Magazine* 16 (1787): 210.

11. An anonymous writer in a 1788 issue of *American Museum or Universal Magazine,* for instance, responded to Francis Hopkinson's famous "Art of the Paper War" with an ironic discussion on how to deceive in print and suggested how the power of typography had the potential to alter public sentiments; in 1789 Benjamin Rush suggested a precursor to Gresham's Law by explaining how the free press could amplify the vice circulating in the public realm and ultimately suppress virtuous individuals; and by 1791 the *Universal Asylum and Columbian Magazine* was running a long series on writing in which the author claimed the art of letters had "to the shame of literary genius, degenerated from its first principles" and asserted that printing had "added no improvement to orthography, but rather served to confirm its defects." See Anon., "Directions to Conduct a Newspaper Dispute," 271; Benjamin Rush, "Directions for Conducting a Newspaper," 488; Anon., "Elements of Orthography," 33.

12. William Dunlap, *The Life of Charles Brockden Brown,* 1:17.

13. Samuel Miller, cited in Warner, *The Letters of the Republic,* 34.

14. *The United States Magazine* (1779): 1.

15. Ibid., 483–484.

16. See Michael T. Gilmore "Eighteenth-Century Oppositional Ideology and Hugh Henry Brackenridge's *Modern Chivalry,"* 181–192.

17. Emory Elliott, *Revolutionary Writers,* 188–189.

18. I am speaking in general. As scholars like David Hall and Roger Thompson have pointed out, the reading habits of the colonists, even the stereotypically monotextual Puritans, were far more diverse than we have thought. Nevertheless, my assumptions are in line with Rolf Engelsing's theoretical work on the transcultural move from intensive to extensive reading habits. For a study which applies Engelsing's theories to colonial America, see David D. Hall, *Worlds of Wonder, Days of Judgment.*

19. Brackenridge's attempts to demystify the sacralizing function of "republican print ideology" found correlatives in the popular press. In the April 1796 edi-

tion of the *Massachusetts Magazine* (221), an essay titled "Humorous Apology for Authors" suggested how writers toiled "in the field of fame, merely to reap a harvest of chaff." The writer asserted that in modern times "our authors write with less labor, our critics review with less care" and that because "traders will cry up the commodity they deal in . . . [a] great respect is paid to an author by those who cannot read him." The "General Observer" in the March 1791 *Massachusetts Magazine* (156) went right to the core of "republican print ideology" by questioning the fairness of anonymous articles. Addressing the licentiousness of the free press, the writer asked, "[O]ught a man's private character be called into question, treated with asperity, wounded by sarcasms, and blackened by infamous aspersions in a publick paper, unless the writer affixes his name? Do not publications of this kind marr the happiness of society . . . Ought not writings of this complexion to be precluded from the press, at least, till the writer is willing to expose his name?"

20. Emory Elliott, *Revolutionary Writers,* 184.

21. Brackenridge makes a similar effort to expose the artificiality of apparently mimetic texts in the first volume of Part 2. Here Farrago gives Teague a lesson on the conceits of omniscient narration, the designs of literary form, and the instability of narrative truth, even asserting that in writing Teague "need not stick pertinaciously to the truth; for travellers have a license to deviate; and they are not considered as on oath, or upon honour in giving their accounts; embellishment is allowable" *(Modern Chivalry,* 354).

22. Brackenridge's narrator makes this point clear in the chapter immediately following where, after giving brief histories of the doctrines of innate depravity, contrition, and salvation for a variety of sects, he exaggerates the problem of textual hermeneutics in a secular print culture. Noting that if he should agree with M'Donald in going so far as to argue that there is no hell at all, then "the thing . . . might go to the other extreme, and be all hell; so that none should be saved; and instead of universal salvation, we should then have the doctrine of the damnation of the whole" (122).

23. While, as Sargent Bush has argued, the review from the fictional *Young's Magazine* was occasioned by an actual review in William Young's 1792 *Universal Asylum and Columbian Magazine,* Brackenridge's adaptation is substantively different. See Sargent Bush. "Modern Chivalry and 'Young's Magazine,'" 292–299.

24. Anon., "On the Practice of Reading Novels and Romances," 146.

25. See Lennard J. Davis, *Factual Fictions.*

26. For a discussion of the antinovel movement in America, see G. Harrison Orians, "Censure of Fiction in American Romances and Magazines, 1789–1810," 195–224; and Cathy N. Davidson, *Revolution and the Word, 38*–54. Making a foray into the psychodynamics of reader response, Brackenridge suggests that since "the greater part of our romances and comedies . . . are calculated to depreciate the respect which a young lady ought to have for the opinion of aged and grave persons," defeating the art of Teagueomania required subtle knowledge of its workings (242). Because "the appearance of security on the part of the lover, gives the lady

to suppose that he is conscious of advantages,"Brackenridge's reasoning goes, "she makes it an object to inspire his attachment, and the very exercise of her passions kindles a flame" (241). Because Teague "has no sentiments of his own and therefore he approves all the reason and laughs at all the wit of the lady,"he obtains her affection by putting her in love with herself" (241). Thus, like the text which presents itself confidently in the public realm as being, mysteriously, all style and no content, and which nevertheless receives critical pronouncements, Teague solicits desire by creating a sense of sensational curiosity in his audience; like a text which caters only to the desires of public opinion, Teague tricks his victims into thinking they are in love with him by putting them in love with themselves.

27. Elliott argues that Brackenridge, "like other writers of his generation . . . came increasingly to realize that the only possibility the writer had of altering attitudes and beliefs of readers was to confront established ideas with direct, overt statements." In contrast, I see a writer who had already given up on pure didacticism because a post-Revolutionary readership found it paternalistic, elitist, and unengaging. Thus Brackenridge's failure to find a way to combine the intellectual, political, and moral strengths of *belles lettres* with the wide reach of popular fiction marks an even graver set of circumstances: it suggests a potential impotence of all printed commentary in a democratic print culture. See Emory Eliot, *Revolutionary Writers,* 202–217.

28. Given Brackenridge's sensitivity to textuality in *Modern Chivalry,* Cary and Hart's "explanatory" footnotes are fascinating because they suggest the extent to which different generations reinvent texts to suit their own exigencies. They also suggest the apparent need for publishers to establish interpretive frames or parallel texts to control their consumers' reading experiences. Most of these commentaries work to valorize the author and to dress up some of his more unsettling commentary, as does one of the footnotes on the first page of chap. 2 (Part 1, vol. 1) which explains Brackenridge's antidemocratic admonishment "let the cobbler stick to his last." The lengthy rationalization claims that although Brackenridge thought that "an ignorant people must need be led by the demagogue . . . he was an enemy to all hereditary privileged orders."

29. Here I disagree with Joseph Ellis, who suggests the volumes sold well. None of the printers of the first volumes apparently published second editions, and while other early American writers were receiving some notice in the magazines, the original six volumes of *Modern Chivalry* appear to have been reviewed only in the *Universal Asylum and Columbian Magazine* (February and August 1792) and the *Massachusetts Asylum* (September and October 1808).

Seven

1. Anon, "Of the Duty of Authors," 131.
2. See, for instance, Cathy N. Davidson's account of Susanna Rowson's struggle

to earn a living from writing in "Ideology and Genre: The Rise of the Novel in America," 299–301.

3. Nancy Armstrong, *Desire and Domestic Fiction*, 3, 5, 18.

4. See Charles Taylor, *Sources of the Self*, for a discussion of the new valuation of the particulars of ordinary experience following the Renaissance.

5. Steven Watts, *The Romance of Real Life*.

6. Ian Watt, *The Rise of the Novel*.

7. Michael McKeon, *The Origins of the English Novel 1600–1740*, 1–21.

8. Raymond Williams, *The Sociology of Culture*, 44–51.

9. Too often, I think, we project modern conceptions of polarized and antagonistic class relationships back into eighteenth-century America. Instead of using history as a site to wage modern battles of interest politics, raising heroes and demonizing tyrants among the cast of historical agents, we should probably be asking more questions about the structural, socioeconomic vicissitudes which compromised the activities of even the best-intentioned. In accepting the liberal platitudes of unfettered free agency, too often we forget that the historical actors we often chastise were inscribed within social structures which prevented them from making their world into something we, as twentieth-century critics, arrogantly presume, in hindsight, to be so obviously right. And we do this at the same time that we ignore—in our misguided belief that what we do as historians is translatable onto the sociopolitical register—the problems of our own age. By the by, Herbert Marcuse, in his discussion of the aesthetic realm in his essay "On the Affirmative Concept of Culture," makes a similar observation: "[T]he task of criticism must be not so much to search for the particular interest-groups to which cultural phenomena have to be assigned, but rather to decipher the general tendencies which are expressed in these phenomena and through which powerful interests realize themselves. Cultural criticism must become social physiognomy" (see Marcuse's *Negations*).

10. Cathy N. Davidson, *Revolution and the Word*, 41–42.

11. Lawrence Buell, *New England Literary Culture*, 58.

12. Cathy N. Davidson, "Ideology and Genre: The Rise of the Novel in America," 41.

13. For a critique of the way in which modern biases tend to link conceptions of an "elite" with oligarchy in a reductive manner, see Hannah Arendt, "The Revolutionary Tradition and Its Lost Treasure," in her *On Revolution*.

14. For caveats to this claim, see David D. Hall, *Worlds of Wonder*.

15. Charles Brockton Brown, "On American Literature," 338.

16. Cathy N. Davidson, *Revolution and the Word*, 66.

17. Michael T. Gilmore, "The Novel," 625.

18. Caroll Smith-Rosenberg, "Domesticating 'Virtue': Coquettes and Revolutionaries in Young America."

19. Michael Warner, *The Letters of the Republic*, 151–176.

20. Steven Watts, *The Romance of Real Life,* 16.

21. Anonymous essay in the *British Critick* (June 1818).

22. See Hannah Arendt for a discussion of freedom in both the political and the economic senses: *On Revolution;* and *The Human Condition.*

23. Anon., "Review of *Self-Control: A Novel,*" 191–192.

24. Cathy N. Davidson, for instance, argues along such lines, claiming that a reader's personal dialogue with a text "can be liberating for the individual reader in ways that are threatening to those who perceive themselves as the arbitrars (or former arbitrars) of cultural work" (see "Ideology and Genre: The Rise of the Novel in America," 303).

25. J. G. A. Pocock, *Virtue, Commerce, History.*

26. J. Horatio Nichols, *The New England Coquette.* Dated Pamphlets, AAS. The existence of this adaptation, coming on the heels of the popularity of Foster's novel, suggests the cultural power of the image of the internally vexed republican daughter.

27. I realize that there may be generic reasons why Nichol's play could articulate the political implications of Foster's novel overtly. In his work on early American drama, Michael T. Gilmore argues that "American drama was the most republican and propagandistic of the literary genres . . . The drama of the early Republic was intimately tied to the civic sphere . . . The most 'residual' of the arts, the theater was the closest to oratory and the world of men; it lagged behind the novel's identification with print and its receptivity to feminization" (see "Drama," 573).

28. See also commentary on marginalia in Cathy N. Davidson's *Revolution and the Word.*

29. We could go so far as to argue that this pedagogical strategy was to linger on in American letters well into the nineteenth century, in both canonical and noncanonical contexts: both in the oft-criticized resemblance of texts like the *Scarlet Letter* and *Huckleberry Finn* to children's literature (and the prevalence of writers who supplemented their major prose fiction with popular children's collections, like Hawthorne did with *The Wonder Book* and *The Tanglewood Tales*); and in what Jane Tompkins and Gillian Brown have argued was the subtle "cultural work" in the texts of "domestic individualism." This is not to say that the didacticism in American prose fiction did not find its origins in the eighteenth-century tradition of popular guidebook writing, a connection illuminated by such scholars as J. Paul Hunter and Jay Fliegelman. Rather, I want to suggest that this pedagogical tradition was itself part of a larger transformation in the conditions of authorship; that rise of the novel in America reflected, at least in part, a shift in the role of authors from one of political participation and critique to one of mass education. See Jane Tompkins, *Sensational Designs;* Gillian Brown, *Domestic Individualism;* J. Paul Hunter, *Before Novels;* Jay Fliegelman, *Prodigals and Pilgrims.* For an account of how American individualism was built on a Puritan tradition of "leaving home," for-

saking the guidance of parents to achieve conversion and to establish an individual relation to God, see Robert N. Bellah et al., *Habits of the Heart.*

30. For account of the homogeneity attendant to commodity production, see chaps. 1–5 and 7 of Isaak I. Rubin, *Essays on Marx's Theory of Value;* Max Horkheimer and Theodor Adorno, "The Culture Industry: Enlightenment as Mass Delusion," in their *Dialectic of Enlightenment;* and especially Georg Simmel, *The Philosophy of Money,* throughout, but particularly the chapter titled "Exchange as a Means of Overcoming the Purely Subjective Value of an Object."

31. For a provocative study of the function of obscurity in Early Modern literature, see Allon White, *The Uses of Obscurity.*

32. Anon., "On Modern Novels, and Their Effects," 663. Along these same lines, another anonymous essayist, in a piece titled "On the Moral Tendency of Novel Reading," wrote in 1823 that "there seems in novel reading to be an unaccountable fascination. A person once habituated in it, becomes abstracted from every other object; he can attend to nothing else; all his senses are absorbed in his favorite amusement."

33. Michael T. Gilmore, "The Novel," 633.

34. Anon., "Anatomical Description of the Heart of a Coquette," 265.

35. Anon., "A Coquette's Account of Herself," 109.

36. David Hume, "On the Independency of Parliament." I recognize a possible qualification to this characterization in what political economists and philosophers have called the "Adam Smith problem." This is the problematic of trying to reconcile the moral claims of a work like *The Theory of Moral Sentiments* with the economic paradigm of *The Wealth of Nations.* I am focusing, however, on the subsequent reception of figures like Smith, not their intentions. For an attempt to reconcile the "Adam Smith problem," see Istvan Hont and Michael Ignatieff, "Needs and Justice in the Wealth of Nations."

37. Alexander Hamilton, "Letters from Phocion," no. I, cited in Albert O. Hirschman, "Interests," 160.

38. I realize that I am here arguing against feminist readings of this passage. But I have a hard time reconciling a feminist interpretation of "marriage is the tomb of friendship" with Eliza's subsequent actions in the novel. See, for instance, Cathy N. Davidson's meticulous reading in *Revolution and the Word* where she ponders whether "marriage to a Boyer [is] the best that an intelligent, well-educated woman can do," and wonders if Eliza's death conveys "the conservative moral that many critics of the time demanded," whether "the circumstances of that death seem designed to tease the reader into thought" (147–148.

39. Carole Pateman, *The Sexual Contract.* Although I do not wholly agree with the substance of Pateman's overall argument, I admire her juxtaposition of the changes in marriage to American and British political thought.

40. My comments here on value, perhaps the most controversial concept in traditional economic theory, are unavoidably reductive. For a broader understanding,

see Ian Steedman et al., *The Value Controversy;* and Isaak I. Rubin, *Essays on Marx's Theory of Value.*

41. See J. E. Crowley, *This Sheba, Self,* 101–116, for an account of the distrust of economic man in eighteenth-century America.

42. Georg Simmel, "Die Koketterie," 142–145.

43. Speculating how, under coverture, women found few occasions on which they could decide on the fundamental questions of life, most notably in choosing a partner, Simmel notes that in flirtation "there is a sense in which [the coquette] chronically takes on this decision, even if only in a symbolic and approximate fashion. Suppose she creates the impression that consent and refusal, inclination and aversion, either dominate one another by turns or have the same force. In that case, she withdraws herself from both and manipulates each as an instrument, behind which her own unbiased personality stands in complete freedom" (see ibid., 141).

44. N. N. Feltes, *Modes of Production of Victorian Novels.* See also his *Literary Capital and the Late Victorian Novel.*

45. See Cathy N. Davidson, *Revolution and the Word;* and G. Harrison Orians, "Censure of Fiction in American Romances and Magazines, 1789–1810." My disagreement about most scholarly characterizations of the late eighteenth-century antinovel movement has to do with their assumptions about the ideological motivations behind the rhetoric.

46. William Charvat, *The Origins of American Critical Thought, 1810–1835.*

Afterword

1. Michael T. Gilmore, "The Artist and the Marketplace in *The House of the Seven Gables,*" 172–189. See also Brook Thomas, "*The House of the Seven Gables:* Reading the Romance of America," 195–211; and Nina Baym, *The Shape of Hawthorne's Career.*

2. See prefaces. Nathaniel Hawthorne, *The House of the Seven Gables.* Page references will be cited in text.

3. Holgrave's statement clearly parallels one of the tenets of the country tradition in Anglo-American politics which stressed the importance of active civic renewal. As J. G. A. Pocock has argued, this regenerative tradition maintained that "the people, being propertied and independent, were by definition virtuous, but that their representatives were constantly exposed to the temptations of power and corruption; it was therefore necessary that the representation should return regularly to the represented, to have virtue renewed" (see J. G. A. Pocock, *The Machiavellian Moment;* and Peter Zagorin, *The Court and the Country*).

4. Surprisingly, I could find no reference to this connection in the scholarship on Hawthorne. Michael Colacurcio's *The Province of Piety,* which looks specifically at how "Hawthorne carried on a life-long dialectic with the historical 'thesis' of American Puritanism" in the early tales, does not mention Maule. And the con-

nection is not made in Kenneth Harris's "Judge Pyncheon's Brotherhood" which examines Puritan writers and conceptions of Puritan authority. Amy Shrager Lang ties Hawthorne to an American tradition of dissent in her *Prophetic Woman* but focuses almost exclusively on the relationship between gender and radical antinomianism.

5. In *An Abstract of a Letter to Cotton Mather,* Maule revealed what may have been the secret to such success as a merchant, asserting that while Puritans believed in the desirability of making interest on their money, he refused to engage in usury, asserting that, although it was lawful, he regarded it as "not expedient for him to do." See Maule's account of his struggle in Salem in *New England Pe[r]secutors Mauled with Their Own Weapons.* For an account of Maule's writings, see Matt Bushnell Jones, "Thomas Maule, the Salem Quaker and Free Speech in Massachusetts Bay."

6. See Matt Bushnell Jones's account of the Essex County records.

7. Quoted in Philip F. Gura, *A Glimpse of Sion's Glory.*

8. See Joseph B. Felt, *The Annals of Salem,* 182–. See also accounts of Pychon in Clyde Duniway, *The Development of Freedom of the Press in Massachusetts,* 32–33; Leonard W. Levy, *Legacy of Suppression,* 31; and Philip F. Gura, *A Glimpse of Sion's Glory,* 304–322.

9. Along these lines, although in a slightly different context, Donald Pease has noted how what he calls "Hawthorne's Discovery of a Pre-Revolutionary Past" allowed him to counter the loss of a civic life, engendering "A Romance with a Public Will" (see *Visionary Compacts,* 49–107).

10. Brook Thomas, *The House of the Seven Gables,* 203.

11. Nathaniel Hawthorne, *Mosses from the Old Manse,* 26.

Adams, Percy G. *Crèvecoeur's Eighteenth-Century Travels in Pennsylvania and New York*. Louisville, 1961.

Adorno, Theodor W. *The Culture Industry: Selected Essays on Mass Culture*. London, 1991.

Agnew, Jean Christophe. *World's Apart: The Market and Theater in Anglo-American Thought*. New Haven, 1986.

Alexander, James. *A Brief Narrative of the Case and Trial of John Peter Zenger*. Edited by Stanley N. Katz. Cambridge, MA, 1972.

Alleine, Joseph. *An Alarm to Unconverted Sinners*. Boston, 1739 [London, 1671].

———. *The Sure Guide to Heaven*. London, 1688.

Allen, David Grayson. *In English Ways: The Movement of Societies and the Transferral of English Law and Custom to Massachusetts Bay in the Seventeenth Century*. Chapel Hill, 1981.

Allen, Gay Wilson, and Roger Asselineau. *St. John de Crèvecoeur*. New York, 1987.

Altick, Richard D. *The English Common Reader: A Social History of the Mass Reading Public, 1800–1900*. New York, 1957.

Ames, Fisher. "Hercules." *The Palladium* (October 1801).

Anderson, Benedict. *Imagined Communities: Reflection on the Origin and Spread of Nationalism*. London, 1991.

Anderson, David A. "The Origins of the Press Clause." *UCLA Law Review* 30 (1983).

Anon. *British Critick* (1818).

———. *The Key* [Maryland] (1798).

———. *New Haven Gazette and Connecticut Magazine* (1787).

———. *The Pocket Magazine, &c.* [New York] (1796).

———. *The Quarterly Review* 8 (1812).

———. *The United States Magazine* (1779).

———. *The Worcester Magazine* (1787).

———. "Anatomical Description of the Heart of a Coquette." *Ladies Weekly Miscellany* 6 (1808).

———. "Cheap Literature: Its Character and Tendencies." *Southern Literary Messenger* 10 (1844).

———. "The Copyright Bill." *Pamphleteer* 18 (1822).

———. "A Coquette's Account of Herself." *Weekly Visitor or Ladies Miscellany* 1 (1803).

———. "Directions to Conduct a Newspaper Dispute." *American Museum or University Magazine* (1788).

———. "Elements of Orthography." *Universal Asylum and Columbian Magazine* (1791).

———. "English and American Literature." *United States Magazine and Democratic Review* 2 (1853).

———. "From Our Armchair." *Southern Literary Journal* 1 (1837).

———. "General Observer." *Massachusetts Magazine* (1791).

———. "Intellectual Economy." *Atlantic Monthly* 1 (1825).

———. "International Copyright." *North American Review* 55 (1839).

———. "International Copyright." *Southern Quarterly Review* 4 (1843).

———. "International Copyright: Review of Nicklin." *North American Review* 48 (1832).

———. "Literary Property." *Democratic Review* (1838).

———. "Miseries of Authorship." *The Parterre* [Philadelphia] (1816).

———. "Of the Duties of Authors." *New England Magazine* [Boston] (1758).

———. "On Modern Novels, and Their Effects." *Massachusetts Magazine* 3 (1791).

———. "On the Moral Tendency of Novel Reading." *The Minerva* 28 (1823).

———. "On the Practice of Reading Novels and Romances." *United States Magazine* (1794).

———. "Review of Self Control: A Novel." *General Repository and Review* 1 (1812).

———. "The Rights of Authors." *Hesperian* 3 (1839).

———. "The Want of Money, or the Miseries of Authors." *The Minerva* 28 (1823).

Appadurai, Arjun. *The Social Life of Things: Commodities in Cultural Perspective.* New York, 1986.

Appleby, Joyce. *Capitalism and a New Social Order: The Republican Vision of the 1790s.* New York, 1984.

———. *Economic Thought and Ideology in Seventeenth-Century England.* Princeton, 1978.

———. *Liberalism and Republicanism in the Historical Imagination.* Cambridge, MA, 1992.

———. "Republicanism and Ideology." *American Quarterly* 37 (1985).

———. "Republicanism in Old and New Contexts." *William and Mary Quarterly* 43 (1986).

Arato, Andrew, and Paul Breines. *The Young Lukács and the Origins of Western Marxism.* New York, 1979.

Arendt, Hannah. *The Human Condition.* Chicago, 1958.

———. *On Revolution.* New York, 1981.

Armstrong, Nancy. *Desire and Domestic Fiction*. New York, 1987.

Auerbach, Eric. *Mimesis*. Princeton, 1974.

Ayscough, Samuel. *Remarks on the Letters from an American Farmer; or a Detection of the Errors of Mr. Hector St. John; Pointing to the Pernicious Tendency of These Letters to Great Britain*. London, 1783.

Bailyn, Bernard. *Ideological Origins of the American Revolution*. Cambridge, MA, 1967.

Barbour, Brian M. *Benjamin Franklin: A Collection of Critical Essays*. Englewood Cliffs, NJ, 1979.

Barlow, Joel, and Robert Fulton. "New-England Association in Favor of Inventors and Discoverers, and Particularly for the Protection of Intellectual Property." *Medical Repository* 2 (1808).

Barnes, James J. *Authors, Publishers, and Politicians: The Quest for an Anglo-American Copyright Agreement 1815–1854*. Columbus, OH, 1974.

Barthes, Roland. *Mythologies*. New York, 1972.

Baym, Nina. *Novels, Readers, Reviewers*. New York, 1984.

———. *The Shape of Hawthorne's Career*. Ithaca, NY, 1976.

Bell, Michael Davitt. *The Development of American Romance: The Sacrifice of Relation*. Chicago, 1980.

Bellah, Robert N., et al. *Habits of the Heart: Individualism and Commitment in American Life*. Berkeley, 1985.

Benjamin, Walter. "The Author as Producer." In *Reflections: Essays, Aphorisms, Autobiographical Writings*. New York, 1978.

———. *Illuminations*. New York, 1971.

Bercovitch, Sacvan. *The American Jeremiad*. Madison, WI, 1978.

———, ed. *Cambridge History of American Literature*. New York, 1994.

———. *The Puritan Origins of the American Self*. New Haven, 1978.

———. *Typology and Early American Literature*. Amherst, 1972.

Bercovitch, Sacvan, and Myra Jehlen, eds. *Ideology and Classic American Literature*. New York, 1986.

Berlin, Isaiah. "Two Concepts of Liberty." In *Four Essays on Liberty*. New York, 1969.

Bledstein, Burton. *The Culture of Professionalism*. New York, 1976.

Blumin, Stuart M. *The Emergence of the Middle Class: Social Experience in the American City, 1760–1900*. New York, 1989.

Boorstin, Daniel. *The Americans: The Colonial Experience*. New York, 1968.

Bourdieu, Pierre. *Distinction: A Social Critique of the Judgement of Taste*. Cambridge, MA, 1984.

Bowker, Richard Rogers. *Copyright: Its History and Its Law*. Boston, 1912.

Brackenridge, Hugh Henry. *Modern Chivalry*. Edited by Claude M. Newlin. New York, 1937.

Brandeis, Louis, and Samuel Warren. "The Right to Privacy." *Harvard Law Review* 4 (1890).

Braudel, Fernand. *Capitalism and Material Life, 1400–1800.* New York, 1975.

Breen, T. H. *Character of the Good Ruler: A Study of Puritan Political Ideas in New England, 1630–1730.* New Haven, 1970.

Breitweiser, Mitchell Robert. *Cotton Mather and Benjamin Franklin.* New York, 1984.

Brigham, Clarence. *History and Bibliography of American Newspapers:* 1690–1820. Worcester, MA, 1947.

Brooke, Robert Greville. *The Nature of Truth.* London, 1640.

Brown, Charles Brockden. "Extracts from a Student's Diary: Authorship." *Library Magazine and American Register* 1 (1803).

———. "On American Literature." *Monthly Magazine and American Review* 1 (1799).

Brown, Gillian. *Domestic Individualism.* Berkeley, 1990.

Brown, Richard. *Knowledge is Power: The Diffusion of Information in Early America, 1700–1865.* New York, 1989.

Brown, Richard D. *Modernization: The Transformation of American Life, 1600–1865.* New York, 1976.

Buell, Lawrence. *New England Literary Culture: From Revolution through Renaissance.* New York, 1986.

Bugbee, Bruce W. *The Genesis of American Patent and Copyright Law.* Washington, D.C., 1967.

Bush, Sargent. "Modern Chivalry and 'Young's Magazine.'" *American Literature* 44 (1972).

Calhoun, Craig. *Habermas and the Public Sphere.* Cambridge, MA, 1992.

Campbell, Colin. *The Romantic Ethic and the Spirit of Modern Consumerism.* Oxford, 1987.

Carey, Henry Charles. *Letters on International Copyright.* New York, 1868.

Chafee, Zechariah. *Free Speech in the United States.* Cambridge, MA, 1948.

Chartier, Roger. *The Cultural Uses of Print in Early Modern France.* Princeton, 1987.

———. *The Culture of Print: Power and the Uses of Print in Early Modern Europe.* Princeton, 1989.

Charvat, William. *Literary Publishing in America, 1790–1850.* Philadelphia, 1959.

———. *The Origins Of American Critical Thought, 1810–1835.* New York, 1968.

———. *The Profession of Authorship in America.* Edited by Matthew J. Bruccoli. Columbus, OH, 1968.

Child, John. *New England's Jonas Cast Up in London.* London, 1647.

Clarke, John. *Ill Newes from New England.* London, 1652.

Clarke, Mary Patterson. *Parliamentary Privilege in the American Colonies.* New Haven, 1943.

Cmiel, Kenneth. *Democratic Eloquence: The Fight over Popular Speech in America.* New York, 1990.

Cobbett, Thomas. *The Civil Magistrates Power in Matters of Religion Modestly Debated.* London, 1653.

Colacurcio, Michael J. *The Province of Piety: Moral History in Hawthorne's Early Tales.* Cambridge, MA, 1984.

Colbourn, H. Trevor. *The Lamp of Experience: Whig History and the Intellectual Origins of the American Revolution.* Chapel Hill, 1965.

Conn, Peter. *Literature in America.* New York, 1989.

Cook, Elizabeth Christine. *Literary Influences in Colonial Newspapers.* New York, 1912.

Cook, Roger F. *Demise of the Author.* London, 1993.

Coser, Lewis A., Charles Kadushin, and Walter W. Powell. *Books: The Culture and Commerce of Publishing.* New York, 1982.

Crèvecoeur, J. Hector St. John de. *Letters from an American Farmer and Sketches of Eighteenth-Century America.* Edited by Albert Stone. New York, 1986.

———. *Sketches of Eighteenth Century America.* Edited by Henri L. Bourdin, Ralph Gabriel, and Stanley T. Williams. New Haven, 1925.

Crowley, J. E. *This Sheba, Self: The Conceptualization of Economic Life in Eighteenth-Century America.* Baltimore, 1974.

Cunliffe, Marcus. "Crèvecoeur Revisited." *Journal of American Studies* 9 (1975).

Curtis, George T. *Theory of the Law of Copyright.* Boston, 1847.

Darnton, Robert. *The Business of Enlightenment: A Publishing History of the Encyclopédie, 1775–1800.* Cambridge, MA, 1979.

———. *The Forbidden Best-Sellers of Pre-Revolutionary France.* New York, 1995.

———. "Reading, Writing, and Publishing in Eighteenth-Century France: A Case Study in the Sociology of Literature." *Daedalus* 100 (1971).

Dauber, Kenneth. "Criticism of American Literature." *Diacritics* 7 (1977).

———. *The Idea of Authorship in America.* Madison, WI, 1990.

Davidson, Cathy N. "Ideology and Genre: The Rise of the Novel in America." *Proceedings of the American Antiquarian Society* 96 (1986).

———. *Reading in America.* Baltimore, 1989.

———. *Revolution and the Word: The Rise of the Novel in America.* New York, 1986.

Davis, David Brion. *The Problem of Slavery in Western Culture.* Ithaca, NY, 1966.

Davis, Lennard J. *Factual Fictions: The Origins of the English Novel.* New York, 1983.

Dell, William. *The Tryall of Spirits.* London, 1653.

Dennie, Joseph. "An Author's Evenings from the Shop of Messrs.

Colon and Spondee." *Port-Folio* 1 (1801).

Denning, Michael. *Mechanic Accents.* New York, 1987.

Derrida, Jacques. *Otobiographies.* Paris, 1984.

Diggins, John P. *The Lost Soul of American Politics: Virtue, Self-Interest, and the Foundations of Liberalism.* Chicago, 1984.

Dimock, Wai Chee. "Class, Gender, and a History of Metonymy." In *Rethinking Class: Liter-*

ary Studies and Social Formations. Edited by Wai Chee Dimock and Michael T. Gilmore. New York, 1994.

———. *Empire for Liberty: Melville and the Poetics of Individualism.* Princeton, 1989.

Dimock, Wai Chee, and Michael T. Gilmore, eds. *Rethinking Class: Literary Studies and Social Formations.* New York, 1994.

Dorfman, Joseph. *The Economic Mind in American Civilization.* New York, 1946.

Dumont, Louis. *From Mandeville to Marx: The Genesis and Triumph of Economic Ideology.* Chicago, 1977.

Duniway, Clyde. *The Development of Freedom of the Press in Massachusetts.* Cambridge, MA, 1906.

Dunlap, William. *The Life of Charles Brockden Brown.* Philadelphia, 1815.

Edelman, Bernard. *Ownership of the Image: Elements for a Marxist Theory of Law.* Translated by Elizabeth Kingdom. Introduction by Paul Hirst. London, 1979.

Eisenstein, Elizabeth L. *The Printing Press as an Agent of Cultural Change.* New York, 1979.

Eisermann, David. *Crèvecoeur, oder, Die Erfindung Amerikas: en literarischer Gründervater der Vereinigten Staaten.* Rheinbach-Merzbach, 1985.

Elliot, Emory. *Revolutionary Writers: Literature and Authority in the New Republic.* New York, 1986.

Ellis, Joseph J. *After the Revolution.* New York, 1979.

Emerson, Everett. "Hector St. John de Crèvecoeur and the Promise of America." In *Forms and Functions of History in American Literature.* Edited by Winfried Fluck. Berlin, 1981.

Englessing, Rolf. *Der Bürger als Leser. Lesergeschichte in Deutschland 1500–1800.* Stuttgart, 1974.

———. "Die Perioden der Lesergechichte in der Neuzeit. Das statistische Ausmass und die soziokulturelle Bedeutung der Lektüre." *Archive füe Geschichte des Buchswesens* 10 (1969).

Fay, Bernard. *The Revolutionary Spirit in France and America.* New York, 1927.

Feather, John. *A History of British Publishing.* London, 1988.

Febvre, Lucien, and Henri-Jean Martin. *The Coming of the Book: The Impact of Printing, 1450–1800.* Translated by David Gerard. London, 1976.

Felt, Joseph B. *The Annals of Salem.* Salem, 1827.

Feltes, N. N. *Literary Capital and the Late Victorian Novel.* Madison, WI, 1993.

———. *Modes of Production of Victorian Novels.* Chicago, 1986.

Fenning, Karl. "Copyright before the Constitution." *Publishers Weekly* 114 (1928).

Ferguson, Robert A. *Law and Letters in American Culture.* Cambridge, MA, 1984.

———. "We Hold These Truths." In *Reconstructing American Literary History.* Edited by Sacvan Bercovitch. Cambridge, MA, 1986.

Fish, Stanley. "Critical Self-Consciousness, or Can We Know What We're Doing." In *Doing What Comes Naturally.* Durham, 1989.

Fliegelman, Jay. *Prodigals and Pilgrims: The American Revolution against Patriarchal Authority, 1750–1800.* New York, 1982.

Foster, Hannah. *The Coquette.* Edited by Cathy N. Davidson. New York, 1986.

Foucault, Michel. "What Is an Author?" *Language, Counter-Memory, Practice: Selected Essays and Interviews.* Ithaca, NY, 1977.

Fox-Genovese, Elizabeth. *The Origins of Physiocracy.* Ithaca, NY, 1976.

Franklin, Benjamin. "Apology for Printers." In *Writings.* Edited by Leo Lemay. New York, 1987.

———. *The Autobiography.* Edited by Leonard Labaree. New Haven, 1964.

———. "Silence Dogood, no. l." In *Writings.* Edited by Leo Lemay. New York, 1987.

Friedman, Lawrence M. *A History of American Law.* New York, 1985.

Furtwangler, Albert. *The Authority of Publius: A Reading of the Federalist Papers.* Ithaca, NY, 1984.

Gilmore, Michael T. *American Romanticism and the Marketplace.* Chicago, 1985.

———. "The Artist and the Marketplace in *The House of the Seven Gables.*" *ELH* 48 (1981).

———. "Drama." In *The Cambridge History of American Literature.* Edited by Sacvan Bercovitch. New York, 1994.

———. "Eighteenth-Century Oppositional Ideology and Hugh Henry Brackenridge's *Modern Chivalry.*" *Early American Literature* 13 (1978).

———. "Franklin and the Shaping of American Ideology." In *Benjamin Franklin: A Collection of Critical Essays.* Edited by Brian M. Barbour. Englewood Cliffs, NJ, 1979.

———. *The Middle Way: Puritanism and Ideology in American Romantic Fiction.* New Brunswick, 1977.

———. "The Novel." In *The Cambridge History of American Literature.* Edited by Sacvan Bercovitch. New York, 1994.

Gilmore, William. *Reading Becomes a Necessity of Life: Material and Cultural Life in Rural New England, 1780–1835.* Knoxville, 1989.

Gilreath, James. *Federal Copyright Records 1790–1800.* Washington, D.C., 1987.

Goff, Frederick Richmond. "The First Decade of the Federal Act for Copyright, 1790–1800." *Essays Honoring Lawrence C. Wroth.* Portland, ME, 1646.

Goldberg, Jonathan. *Writing Matter.* Stanford, 1990.

Goldman, Lucien. *Towards a Sociology of the Novel.* London, 1975.

Gorton, Samuel. *Simplicities Defense against Seven-Headed Policy.* London, 1646.

Gouldner, Alvin. *Dialectic of Ideology and Technology.* New York, 1982.

Greenblatt, Stephen. "The Word of God in the Age of Mechanical Reproduction." In *Renaissance Self-Fashioning.* Chicago, 1980.

Gura, Philip F. *A Glimpse of Sion's Glory: Puritan Radicalism in New England, 1620–1660.* Middletown, CT, 1984.

————. *The Wisdom of Words: Language, Theology, and Literature*. Middletown, CT, 1981.

Habermas, Jürgen. *Communication and the Evolution of Society*. London, 1979.

————. *Knowledge and Human Interests*. Boston, 1971.

————. *The Philosophical Discourse of Modernity*. Cambridge, MA, 1987.

————. "The Public Sphere: An Encyclopedia Article." *New German Critique* 3 (1974).

————. *The Structural Transformation of the Public Sphere: An Inquiry into a Category of Bourgeois Society*. Translated by Thomas Burger. Cambridge, MA, 1991 [1989].

————. *The Theory of Communicative Action*, vol. 1: *Reason and the Rationalization of Society*. Boston, 1984.

Hall, Basil. "Puritanism: The Problem of Definition." *Studies in Church History* 2 (1965).

Hall, David D. *Worlds of Wonder, Days of Judgment: Popular Religious Belief in Early New England*. Cambridge, MA, 1989.

Hanson, L. W. *Government and the Press, 1595–1673*. London, 1936.

Haraszti, Miklós. *The Velvet Prison: Artists under State Socialism*. New York, 1987.

Harris, Kenneth. "Judge Pyncheon's Brotherhood." *Nineteenth Century Literature* 39 (1984).

Hart, James D. *The Popular Book: A History of America's Literary Taste*. New York, 1950.

Hartz, Louis. *The Liberal Tradition in America*. New York, 1955.

Hawthorne, Nathaniel. *The House of the Seven Gables*. Edited by William Charvat. Columbus, OH, 1965.

————. *Mosses from the Old Manse*. Edited by William Charvat. Columbus, OH, 1965.

————. *Tanglewood Tales*. Edited by Fredson Bowers. Columbus, OH, 1972.

————. *A Wonder Book*. Edited by Fredson Bowers. Columbus, OH, 1972.

Heckscher, Eli F. *Mercantilism*. 2 vols. New York, 1935.

Henderson, Harry B. *Versions of the Past: The Historical Imagination in American Fiction*. New York, 1974.

Hesse, Carla. "Enlightenment Epistemology and the Laws of Authorship in Revolutionary France, 1777–1793." *Representations* 30 (1990).

————. *Publishing and Cultural Politics in Revolutionary Paris, 1789–1810*. Berkeley, 1991.

Hildeburn, Charles R. *Sketches of Printers and Printing in Colonial New York*. New York, 1895.

Hill, Christopher. *Intellectual Origins of the English Revolution*. Oxford, 1965.

————. *Puritanism and Revolution*. Oxford, 1958.

————. *Society and Puritanism*. New York, 1964.

————. *The World Turned Upside Down: Radical Ideas during the English Revolution*. New York, 1972.

Hirschman, Albert O. "Interests." In *The Invisible Hand*. Edited by John Eatwell et al. New York, 1989.

————. *The Passions and the Interests: Political Arguments for Capitalism before Its Triumph*. Princeton, 1977.

Hobbes, Thomas. *Leviathan*. Buffalo, NY, 1988.

Hobsbawm, E. J. *Nations and Nationalism since 1780: Programme, Myth, Reality*. New York, 1990.

Hoggart, Richard. *The Uses of Literacy: Changing Patterns in English Mass Culture*. Fair Lawn, NJ, 1957.

Holmes, George Frederick. "The Present Condition of Letters." *Southern Literary Messenger* 10 (1844).

Hont, Istvan, and Michael Ignatieff. "Needs and Justice in the *Wealth of Nations*: An Introductory Essay." In *Wealth and Virtue: The Shaping of Political Economy in the Scottish Enlightenment*. New York, 1983.

Horkheimer, Max, and Theodor W. Adorno. *Dialectic of Enlightenment*. New York, 1991.

Horwitz, Howard. *By the Law of Nature: Form and Value in Nineteenth-Century America*. New York, 1991.

Horwitz, Morton J. *The Transformation of American Law, 1780–1860*. Cambridge, MA, 1977.

Hume, David. "On the Independency of Parliament." In *Essays, Literary, Moral, and Political*. London, 1898.

Hunter, J. Paul. *Before Novels*. New York, 1990.

Ingber, J. "The Marketplace of Ideas: A Legitimizing Myth." *Duke University Law Journal* 1 (1984).

Ingersoll, Charles Jared. *A Discourse Concerning the Influence of America on the Mind*. Philadelphia, 1823.

Irving, Washington. *The Sketch Book*. New York, 1961.

———. "To the Editor of the Knickerbocker." *Knickerbocker* 15 (1840).

Iser, Wolfgang. *The Implied Reader*. Baltimore, 1974.

Jameson, Frederic. *Marxism and Form*. Princeton, 1971.

———. *The Political Unconscious: Narrative as Socially Symbolic Act*. Ithaca, NY, 1981.

Jaszi, Peter, and Martha Woodmansee. "Intellectual Property and the Construction of Authorship." *Cardozo Arts and Entertainment Journal* 10 (1992).

———. "Toward a Theory of Copyright: The Metamorphoses of Authorship." *Duke University Law Journal* (1991).

Jauss, Hans Robert. *Towards an Aesthetics of Reception*. Minneapolis, 1982.

Jefferson, Thomas. *Notes on the State of Virginia*. Edited by William Peden. New York, 1982.

Jehlen, Myra. *American Incarnation: The Individual, the Nation, and the Continent*. New York, 1986.

———. "'Imitate Jesus and Socrates': The Making of a Good American." *South Atlantic Quarterly* 89 (1990).

———. "J. Hector St. John Crèvecoeur: A Monarcho-Anarchist in Revolutionary America." *American Quarterly* 31 (1979).

Jones, Matt Bushnell. "Thomas Maule, the Salem Quaker and Free Speech in Massachusetts Bay." *Essex Institute Historical Collections* 72 (1936).

Joyce, William, et al. *Printing and Society in Early America*. Worchester, MA, 1983.

Kant, Immanuel. "An Answer to the Question: 'What is Enlightenment?' In *Kant: Political Writings*. 2d ed. Translated by H. B. Nisbet. Edited by Hans Reiss. Cambridge, MA, 1991.

———. *Critique of Pure Reason*. New York, 1956.

Kaplan, Benjamin. *An Unhurried View of Copyright*. New York, 1967.

Kase, F. J. *Copyright Thought in Continental Europe: Its Development, Legal Theories, and Philosophy. A Selected and Annotated Bibliography*. South Hackensack, NJ, 1967.

Keith, George. *An Appeal from the Twenty Eight Judges*. Philadelphia, 1692.

———. *New England's Spirit of Persecution Transmitted to Pennsylvania*. New York, 1695.

Kelley, Mary. *Private Woman, Public Stage*. New York, 1984.

Kerber, Linda K. *Women of the Republic: Intellect and Ideology in Revolutionary America*. Chapel Hill, 1980.

Klíma, Ivan. "An Upheaval for Czech Readers." *New York Review of Books* 41, October 20, 1994.

Kouwenhoven, John. "Cooper and the American Copyright Club." *American Literature* 13 (1941).

Kramnick, Isaac. *Republicanism and Bourgeois Radicalism: Political Ideology in Late Eighteenth Century England and America*. Ithaca, NY, 1992.

Kunitz, Stanley, and Howard Haycraft. *American Authors 1600–1900*. New York, 1938.

Laclau, Ernesto, and Chantal Mouffe. *Hegemony and Socialist Strategy*. London, 1985.

Lakoff, George. *Women, Fire, and Dangerous Things: What Categories Reveal about the Mind*. Chicago, 1987.

Lang, Amy Shrager. *Prophetic Woman*. Berkeley, 1987.

Lawrence, D. H. *Studies in Classic American Literature*. New York, 1923.

Lawson-Peebles, Robert. *Landscape and Written Expression in Revolutionary America: The World Turned Upside Down*. New York, 1988.

Lehmann-Haupt, Hellmut. *The Book in America*. New York, 1951.

Lennox, Charlotte. *The Female Quixote*. Edited by Sandra Shulman. London, 1986.

Levin, David. *"The Autobiography of Benjamin Franklin:* The Puritan Experimenter in Life and Art." *Yale Review* 53 (1964).

Levy, Leonard W. "Did the Zenger Case Really Matter?" *William and Mary Quarterly* 17 (1960).

———. *Emergence of a Free Press*. New York, 1985.

———. *Freedom of the Press from Zenger to Jefferson*. Indianapolis, 1966.

———. *Legacy of Suppression: Freedom of Speech and Press in Early American History*. Cambridge, MA, 1960.

Lieber, Francis. *Essays on Property and Labor*. New York, 1841.

———. *On International Copyright*. New York, 1840.

Locke, John. *A Letter Concerning Toleration*. Edited by John Horton and Susan Mendus. New York, 1991.

————. *Two Treatises of Government: A Critical Edition.* Edited by Peter Laslett. Cambridge, 1960.

————. *The Works of . . .* London, 1812.

Long, Pamela O. "Invention, Authorship, 'Intellectual Property,' and the Origin of Patents: Notes Towards a Conceptual History." *Technology and Culture* 32 (1991).

Looby, Christopher. "'The Affairs of the Revolution Occasion'd the Interruption': Writing, Revolution, Deferral, and Conciliation in Franklin's *Autobiography.*" *American Quarterly* 38 (1986).

Lowndes, James. *An Historical Sketch of the Law of Copyright.* London, 1840.

Luhmann, Niklas. *Love as Passion: The Codification of Intimacy.* Cambridge, MA, 1986.

Lukács, Georg. *History and Class Consciousness.* Cambridge, MA, 1968.

————. *Studies in European Realism.* London, 1950.

————. *The Theory of the Novel: A Historico-Philosophical Essay on the Forms of Great Epic Literature.* Cambridge, 1989.

McCusker, John J. *Money and Exchange in Europe and America, 1600–1775.* Chapel Hill, 1978.

McGann, Jerome. *The Textual Condition.* Princeton, 1991.

McGill, Meredith L. *"Wheater v. Peters* and the Materiality of the Text." Unpublished essay. Presented before the American Antiquarian Society, 1993.

MacIntyre, Alasdair. *After Virtue.* Notre Dame, 1984.

McKenzie, D. F. *Bibliography and the Sociology of Texts.* London 1986.

McKeon, Michael. *The Origins of the English Novel, 1600–1740.* Baltimore, 1987.

McLuhan, Marshall. *Gutenberg Galaxy.* New York, 1962.

Macpherson, C. B. "The Meaning of Property." In *Property: Mainstream and Critical Positions.* Toronto, 1978.

————. *The Political Theory of Possessive Individualism.* Oxford, 1962.

Madison, Charles A. *Book Publishing in America.* New York, 1966.

Marcuse, Herbert. *Negations: Essays in Critical Theory.* New York, 1968.

Martin, Terence. *The Instructed Vision: Scottish Common Sense Philosophy and the Origins of American Fiction.* Bloomington, 1961.

Mathews, Cornelius. *The Better Interests of the Country, in Connexion with International Copyright.* New York, 1843.

Maule, Thomas. *An Abstract of a Letter to Cotton Mather of Boston in New England.* New York, 1701.

————. *New England Pe[r]secutors Mauled with Their Own Weapons.* New York, 1697.

————. *Truth Held Forth and Maintained.* New York, 1695.

May, Henry F. *Enlightenment in America.* New York, 1976.

Meek, Ronald L. *The Economics of Physiocracy.* Cambridge, MA, 1963.

Merriam, George. "Who Owns an Author's Ideas?" *The Nation,* June 27, 1867.

Mill, John Stuart. *Collected Works*. London, 1984.

Miller, Perry. *The Life of the Mind in America*. New York, 1968.

———. *Major Writers of America*. New York, 1962.

———. *The Puritans*. New York, 1963.

———. "The Puritan State and Puritan Society." *Errand into the Wilderness*. Cambridge, MA, 1956.

Milton, John. *The Prose of John Milton*. Edited by J. Max Patrick. New York, 1968.

Mitchell, Julia Post. *St. John de Crèvecoeur*. New York, 1916.

Moore, Dennis. *More Letters from an American Farmer*. Athens, GA, 1995.

Moore, John Brooks. "Crèvecoeur and Thoreau." In *Papers of the Michigan Academy of Science, Arts, and Letters* 5 (1925).

Morgan, Edward S. *Visible Saints: The History of a Puritan Idea*. New York, 1963.

Murray, Judith Sargent. *The Gleaner*. Edited by Nina Baym. Schenectady, 1992.

Nash, Gary B. *Class and Society in Early America*. Englewood, NJ, 1970.

———. *The Urban Crucible: Social Change, Political Consciousness, and the Origins of the American Revolution*. Cambridge, MA, 1979.

Nedelsky, Jennifer. *Private Property and the Limits of American Constitutionalism*. Chicago, 1990.

Nelson, William. *Americanization of the Common Law: The Impact of Legal Change on Massachusetts Society, 1760–1830*. Cambridge, MA, 1975.

Nichols, T. Horatio. *The New England Coquette: From the History of the Celebrated Eliza Wharton. A Tragic Drama in Three Acts*. Salem, 1803.

Ong, Walter J. *Orality and Literacy: Technologizing the Word*. London, 1982.

Orians, G. Harrison. "Censure of Fiction in American Romances and Magazines 1789–1810." *PMLA* 52 (1937).

Pangle, Thomas. *The Moral Vision of American Founders and the Philosophy of Locke*. Chicago, 1988.

Parrington, Vernon Louis. *Main Currents in American Thought*. New York, 1927.

Pateman, Carole. *The Sexual Contract*. Stanford, 1988.

Patterson, Annabel M. *Censorship and Interpretation: The Conditions of Writing and Reading in Early Modern England*. Madison, WI, 1984.

Patterson, Lyman Ray. *Copyright in Historical Perspective*. Nashville, 1968.

Pease, Donald. "The Author." In *Critical Terms for Literary Study*. Edited by Frank Lentricchia and Thomas McLaughlin. Chicago, 1990.

———. *Visionary Compacts*. Madison, WI, 1987.

Philbrick, Nathaniel. "The Nantucket Sequence in Crèvecoeur's *Letters from an American Farmer.*" *New England Quarterly* 64 (1991).

Philbrick, Thomas. *St. John de Crèvecoeur*. New York, 1970.

Pocock, J. G. A. *The Machiavellian Moment: Florentine Political Thought and the Atlantic Republican Tradition.* Princeton, 1975.

———. "Virtue and Commerce in the Eighteenth Century." *Journal of Interdisciplinary History* 3 (1972).

———. *Virtue, Commerce, History: Essays on Political Thought and History.* New York, 1985.

Polanyi, Karl. *The Great Transformation.* New York, 1944.

Poovey, Mary. "The Social Constitution of 'Class': Toward a History of Classificatory Thinking." In *Rethinking Class: Literary Studies and Social Formations.* Edited by Wai Chee Dimock and Michael T. Gilmore. New York, 1994.

Porter, Carolyn. "Reification in American Literature." In Sacvan Bercovitch and Myra Jehlen, eds., *Ideology and Classic American Literature.* New York, 1986.

———. *Seeing and Being: The Plight of the Participant Observer in Emerson, James, Adams, Faulkner.* Middletown, CT, 1981.

Pynchon, William. *Meritorious Price of our Redemption.* London, 1650.

Rabban, David M. "The Ahistorical Historian: Leonard Levy on Freedom of Expression in Early American History." *Stanford Law Review* 37 (1985).

Railton, Stephen. *Authorship and Audience: Literary Performance in the American Renaissance.* Princeton, 1991.

Raynal, Guillaume Thomas François. *A Philosophical and Political History of the Settlements and Trade of the Europeans in the East and West Indies.* London, 1783.

———. *The Revolution of America.* London, 1781.

Rice, Howard C. *Le Cultivateur Américain: Etude sur l'Oeuvre de Saint John de Crèvecoeur.* Paris, 1932.

Robbins, Caroline. *The Eighteenth-Century Commonwealthman.* Cambridge, MA, 1959.

Roberts, Matt. *Copyright: A Selected Bibliography of Periodical Literature Relating to Literary Property in the United States.* Metuchen, NJ, 1971.

Rose, Mark. "The Author as Proprietor: Donaldson vs. Becket and the Genealogy of Modern Authorship." *Representations* 23 (1988).

———. *Authors and Owners: The Invention of Copyright.* Cambridge, MA, 1993.

Ross, Trevor. "Copyright and the Invention of Tradition." *Eighteenth-Century Studies* 26 (1992).

Rossiter, Clinton. *Seedtime of the Republic.* New York, 1953.

Rowson, Susanna. *Charlotte Temple.* Edited by Cathy N. Davidson. New York, 1986.

Rubin, Isaak I. *Essays on Marx's Theory of Value.* Montreal, 1973.

Rucker, Mary. "Crèvecoeur's Letters and Enlightenment Doctrine." *Early American Literature* 13 (1978).

Rush, Benjamin. "Directions for Conducting a Newspaper." *American Museum or Universal Asylum* (1789).

Sackett, Granville. *A Plea for Authors, and the Rights of Literary Property.* New York, 1838.

Sandel, Michael, ed. *Liberalism and Its Critics.* New York, 1984.

———. *Liberalism and the Limits of Justice.* New York, 1982.

Saunders, David. *Authorship and Copyright.* New York, 1992.

Saunders, David, and Ian Hunter. "Lessons from the Literary: How to Historicize Authorship." *Critical Inquiry* 17 (1991).

Sayre, Robert F. *The Examined Self.* Princeton, 1964.

Schlesinger, Arthur M. *Prelude to Independence.* New York, 1958.

Sellers, Charles. *The Market Revolution.* New York, 1991.

Sennett, Richard. *The Fall of Public Man.* New York, 1978.

Shaftesbury [Cooper, Anthony Ashley, Earl of]. *"Soliloquy* or Advice to an Author." In *Characteristics of Men, Manners, Opinions, Times.* 2 vols. Edited by John M. Robertson. Indianapolis, 1964.

Shalhope, Robert. "Toward a Republican Synthesis: The Emergence of an Understanding of Republicanism in Early American Historiography." *William and Mary Quarterly* 29 (1972).

Shell, Marc. *The Economy of Literature.* Baltimore, 1978.

———. *Money, Language, and Thought.* Berkeley, 1982.

Shudson, Michael. "Was There Ever a Public Sphere? If So, When? Reflections on the American Case." In Craig Calhoun, ed., *Habermas and the Public Sphere.* Cambridge, MA, 1992.

Siebert, F. S. *Freedom of the Press in England, 1476–1776.* Urbana, 1952.

Siegal, Jules Paul. "Puritan Light Reading." *New England Quarterly* 37 (1964).

Simmel, Georg. "Die Koketterie." *Georg Simmel: On Women, Sexuality, and Love.* Edited by Guy Oaks. New Haven, 1984.

———. *The Philosophy of Money.* Translated by Tom Bottomore and David Frisby. New York, 1990.

Simpson, Lewis. *Men of Letters in Colonial Maryland.* Baton Rouge, 1978.

———. "Printer as a Man of Letters: Franklin and the Symbolism of the Third Realm." In *Benjamin Franklin: A Collection of Critical Essays.* Edited by Brian M. Barbour. Englewood Cliffs, NJ, 1979.

Skidmore, Thomas. *The Rights of Man to Property!* New York, 1829.

Skinner, Quentin. "The Republican Ideal of Political Liberty." *Machiavelli and Republicanism.* Edited by Gisela Block, Quentin Skinner, and Maurizio Viroli. New York, 1990.

Smith, Adam. *The Wealth of Nations.* New York, 1991.

Smith, Henry Nash. *Democracy and the Novel: Popular Resistance to Classic American Writers.* New York, 1964.

Smith, James Morton. *Freedom's Fetters: The Alien and Sedition Laws and American Civil Liberties.* Ithaca, NY, 1956.

Smith, Jeffery Alan. *Printers and Press Freedom: The Ideology of Early American Journalism.* New York, 1988.

Smith-Rosenberg, Caroll. "Domesticating 'Virtue': Coquettes and Revolutionaries in Young America." *Literature and the Body.* Edited by Elaine Scarry. Baltimore, 1988.

Solberg, Thorvald. *Copyright in Congress 1789–1904.* Washington, D.C., 1905.

Sombert, Werner. *Luxury and Capitalism.* Ann Arbor, 1967.

Spiller, Robert E., Willard Thorp, Thomas Johnson, and Henry Canby. *Literary History of the United States.* New York, 1948.

Spofford, Ainsworth R. *The Copyright System of the United States / Celebration of the Beginning.* Washington, D.C., 1892.

Stallybrass, Peter, and Allon White. *The Politics and Poetics of Transgression.* Ithaca, NY, 1986.

Steedman, Ian, et al. *The Value Controversy.* London, 1981.

Stewart, Susan. *Crimes of Writing: Problems in the Containment of Representation.* New York, 1991.

Strauss, Leo. *Persecution and the Art of Writing.* Westport, CT, 1952.

———. *The Rebirth of Classical Political Rationalism.* Edited by Thomas Pangle. Chicago, 1989.

Tawney, R. H. *The Acquisitive Society.* London, 1921.

Taylor, Charles. *Sources of the Self: The Making of the Modern Identity.* Cambridge, MA, 1989.

Taylor, John. *An Inquiry into the Principles and Policy of the Government of the United States.* Fredericksburg, VA, 1814.

Tenney, Tabitha. *Female Quixotism.* Edited by Cathy N. Davidson. New York, 1992.

Thomas, Brook. *"The House of the Seven Gables:* Reading the Romance of America." *PMLA* 97 (1982).

Thomas, Donald. *A Long Time Burning: The History of Literary Censorship in England.* London, 1969.

Thomas, Isaiah. *The History of Printing in America.* Worchester, MA, 1810.

Thompson, Roger. "Prurience and the Puritans: Aspects of the Restoration Book Trade." *Contrast and Connection.* Edited by H. C. Allen and Roger Thompson. London, 1976.

Tocqueville, Alexis de. *Democracy in America.* Translated by G. Lawrence. New York, 1969.

Todd, Margo. *Christian Humanism and the Puritan Social Order.* New York, 1987.

Tompkins, Jane. *Sensational Designs.* New York, 1985.

VandenBossche, Chris. "The 1842 Copyright Bill and the Constitution of Authorhood." Unpublished conference paper. Society for the History of Authorship, Reading, and Publishing. 1993.

Van Doren, Carl. *Benjamin Franklin.* New York, 1938.

Walzer, Michael. *The Revolution of the Saints: A Study in the Origins of Radical Politics.* Cambridge, MA, 1965.

Ward, Nathaniel. *The Simple Cobbler of Aggawam.* London. 1647.

Warner, Michael. "Franklin and the Letters of the Republic." *Representations* (1986).

———. *The Letters of the Republic: Publication and the Public Sphere in Eighteenth-Century America.* Cambridge, MA, 1990.

Washburn, Peter T. *The Law of Copyright. Laws of the United States, Now in Force, Relating to Copyrights; with Notes and References to Adjudged Cases.* 1847.

Watt, Ian. *The Rise of the Novel.* Berkeley, 1957.

Watts, Steven. *The Republic Reborn.* Baltimore, 1987.

———. *The Romance of Real Life: Charles Brockden Brown and the Origins of American Culture.* Baltimore, 1994.

Weber, Max. *The Protestant Ethic and the Spirit of Capitalism.* New York, 1958.

Webster, Noah. *A Collection of Papers on Political, Literary, and Moral Subjects.* New York, 1843.

Wetzel, William A. *Benjamin Franklin as an Economist.* Baltimore, 1895.

White, Allon. *The Uses of Obscurity.* London, 1981.

Williams, Raymond. *Marxism and Literature.* New York, 1977.

Williams, Roger. *The Bloudy Tenent of Persecution.* London, 1644.

———. *The Bloudy Tenent Yet More Bloudy.* London, 1652.

Wilson, R. Jackson. *Figures of Speech: American Writers and the Literary Marketplace, from Benjamin Franklin to Emily Dickinson.* New York, 1989.

Winslow, Edward. *The Dangers of Tolerating Levellers in a Civill State.* London, 1649.

———. *Hypocrisy Unmasked.* London, 1646.

———. *New England's Salamander Discovered by an Irreligious and Scornfull Pamphlet, Called New England's Jonas Cast Up at London.* London, 1647.

Winston, Robert P. "Strange Order of Things!: The Journey to Chaos in *Letters From an American Farmer.*" *Early American Literature* 19 (1985).

Wood, Gordon S. *The Creation of the American Republic, 1776–1787.* New York, 1972.

———. "The Democratization of Mind in the American Revolution." *The Moral Foundations of the American Republic.* Edited by Robert H. Horwitz. Charlottesville, 1979.

———. *The Radicalism of the American Revolution.* New York, 1993.

Woodmansee, Martha. *The Author, Art, and the Market.* New York, 1994.

———. "The Genius and the Copyright: Economic and Legal Conditions of the Emergence of the 'Author.'" *Eighteenth-Century Studies* 17 (1984).

Zagorin, Peter. *The Court and the Country: The Beginning of the English Revolution.* New York, 1970.

Ziff, Larzer. "Upon What Pretext? The Book and Literary History." *Proceedings of the American Antiquarian Society* 95 (1985).

———. *Writing in the New Nation: Prose, Print, and Politics.* New Haven, 1991.